FreeHand® 8

An Introduction to Digital Illustration

PRENTICE HALL
Upper Saddle River, NJ 07458

Library of Congress Cataloging-in-Publication Data

FreeHand 8.0: an introduction to digital illustration
      p.   cm. -- (Against the clock)
  ISBN 0-13-921479-8
  1.Computer graphics. 2. FreeHand (Computer File). I. Series.
T385.F6917 1998
006.6' 869 -- dc21
                                  98-29399
                                      CIP

Acquisitions Editor: *Elizabeth Sugg*
Developmental Editor: *Judy Casillo*
Supervising Manager: *Mary Carnis*
Production Editor: *Denise Brown*
Director of Manufacturing & Production: *Bruce Johnson*
Manufacturing Buyer: *Ed O'Dougherty*
Editorial Assistant: *Leanne Nieglos*

Creative Director: *Marianne Frasco*
Marketing Manager: *Danny Hoyt*
Sales Director: *Karen Austin*
Formatting/page make-up: *Against The Clock, Inc.*
Printer/Binder: *Banta/Harrisonburg*
Cover Design: *Joe Sengotta*
Icon Design: *James Braun*

©1998 by Prentice Hall, Inc.
Simon & Schuster/A Viacom Company
Upper Saddle River, New Jersey 07458

All rights reserved. No part of this book may be
reproduced, in any form or by any means,
without permission in writing from the publisher.

The fonts utilized in this training course are the property of Against The Clock, Inc., and are supplied to the legitimate buyers of the Against The Clock training materials solely for use with the exercises and projects provided in the body of the materials. They may not be used for any other purpose, and under no circumstances can they be transferred to another individual, nor copied, nor distributed by any means whatsoever.

A portion of the images supplied in this book are Copyright © PhotoDisc, Inc., 201 Fourth Ave. Seattle, WA 98121. These images are the sole property of PhotoDisc and are used by Against The Clock with the permission of the owners. They may not be distributed, copied, transferred, or reproduced by any means whatsoever other than for the completion of the exercises and projects contained in this Against The Clock training material.

Against The Clock and the Against The Clock logo are trademarks of Against The Clock, Inc., registered in the United States and elsewhere. References to, and instructional materials provided for, any particular application program, operating system, hardware platform or other commercially available product or products does not represent an endorsement of such product or products by Against The Clock, Inc. or Prentice Hall, Inc.

Adobe, Acrobat, Adobe Illustrator, PageMaker, Photoshop, Adobe Type Manager, and PostScript are trademarks of Adobe Systems Incorporated. Macromedia FreeHand is a registered trademark of Macromedia. QuarkXPress is a registered trademark of Quark, Inc. TrapWise and PressWise are registered trademarks of Luminous Corporation. Microsoft, MS-DOS, Windows, and Windows NT are either registered trademarks or trademarks of Microsoft Corporation.

Other products and company names mentioned herein may be the trademarks of their respective owners.

Printed in the United States of America

10 9 8 7 6 5 4 3 2 1

ISBN 0-13-921479-8

Prentice Hall International (UK) Limited, London
Prentice Hall of Australia Pty. Limited, Sydney
Prentice Hall Canada Inc., Toronto
Prentice Hall Hispanoamericana, S.A., Mexico
Prentice Hall of India Private Limited, New Delhi
Prentice Hall of Japan, Inc., Tokyo
Simon & Schuster Asia Pte. Ltd., Singapore
Editora Prentice Hall do Brasil, Ltda., Rio de Janeiro

Contents

Getting Started — 1
- Platform — 1
- Naming Conventions — 1
- Key Commands — 1
- The CD-ROM and Initial Setup Considerations — 2

1. An Introduction — 5
- Digital Graphic Images — 7
- Step by Step — 8
- Some Basic Assumptions — 8
- Other Stuff — 8

2. FreeHand Workflow and Wizards — 9
- The FreeHand Environment — 11
- Saving a Document — 12
- Opening a Document — 14
- Document Inspector — 20
- FreeHand Defaults — 23
- The Status Bar (Windows) — 26
- The Welcome Wizard — 27
- FreeHand Help — 28
- Choose A Wizard — 29

3. The FreeHand Working Environment — 33
- The Toolbox — 35
- The Toolbars — 36
- Flexibility of Toolbars — 37
- Customizing the Toolbars — 43
- Panels — 47
- Inspectors — 48
- FreeHand Menus — 49
- Viewing Modes — 49
- View Pop-up Menus — 50
- Magnification Tool — 53
- Custom Views — 54
- New Window — 58

4. Drawing Basics — 61
- Primitive Shapes — 63
- The Rectangle Tool — 63
- The Ellipse Tool — 64
- The Polygon Tool — 65
- Composition of Your Artwork — 67
- The Pointer Tool and Object Inspector — 69
- Moving Objects with the Pointer Tool — 72
- Using the Line Drawing Tools — 75
- Curve Basics — 77
- Combining Straight Lines with Curves — 82

5. Creating and Editing Text — 85
- The Text Inspector — 88
- Typographic Settings — 90
- Text Special Effects — 92
- Working with Text Outlines — 97
- Importing Text — 100
- Linking Text Blocks — 101

6. Layers, Grids, and Guides — 103
- Layers — 105
- The Layers Options — 106
- Managing Layers — 107

Layer Priority	110
Rearranging Layer Order	111
Settings for Work Efficiency	113
Grids & Guides	116
The Page Rulers	116
Guides	117
Creating Guides	118
Controlling Guides	120
Setting the Zero Point	130

Review #1 — 133

7. Arranging, Aligning, and Distributing Objects — 135

Arranging Objects	137
Arranging Objects	138
Locking/Unlocking Objects	141
Grouping/Ungrouping Objects	142
Aligning/Distributing Objects	145
Align to Page	149

8. Path Operations — 155

Path-altering Operations	159
Operations that Combine	168

9. Painting FreeHand Objects — 175

Fill	178
Fill Inspector	178
Stroke Inspector	180
Applying Colors to Paths	182
The Color Mixer	183
Predefined Colors	183
Tints	184
Gradients	189

10. Anchor Points, Paths, and Segments — 193

Connecting Anchor Points	197
The Knife Tool	208
The Freeform Tool	208

11. Transformation Tools — 213

The Three Transformation Modes	215
Rotate	216
Reflect	218
Scale	220
Skew	222
The Interactive Transformer	224

12. Xtras — 227

The Xtras	229
Xtra Tools	230

13. Importing, Exporting, and Printing — 243

Getting Information into FreeHand	245
Vector Images	245
Editing Vector EPS Images	247
Raster (bitmapped) Images	248
Linking and Embedding Imported Graphics	251
Exporting	254
Printing Documents	259
Options (Macintosh)/Properties (Windows)	260

Review #2 — 263

Projects

Project A: Steaming Coffee (Chapter 4)	*A-1*
Project B: Last Mango Cafe Logo (Chapter 5)	*B-1*
Project C: Last Mango Business Cards (Chapter 6)	*C-1*
Project D: Java Jungle (Chapter 8)	*D-1*
Project E: Coffee Du Jour Ad (Chapter8)	*E-1*
Project F: Tropical Fish Art (Chapter 9)	*F-1*
Project G: Ball and Mirror (Chapter10)	*G-1*
Project H: Joker's Wild (Chapter 11)	*H-1*
Project I: Tropical Treasure Logo (Chapter 12)	*I-1*
Project J: Tropical Treasure Mailer (Chapter 12)	*J-1*
Project K: Grocery Ad (Chapter 13)	*K-1*

Glossary

Index

Preface

PURPOSE

The Against The Clock series has been developed specifically for those involved in the graphic arts field.

Welcome to the world of electronic design and prepress. Many of our readers are already involved in the industry — in advertising and design companies, in prepress and imaging firms, and in the world of commercial printing and reproduction. Others are preparing for a career somewhere in the profession.

This series of courses will provide you with the necessary skills to work in this fast-paced, exciting, and rapidly expanding business. Many people feel that they can simply purchase a computer, the appropriate software, a laser printer, a ream of paper, and begin designing and producing high-quality printed materials. While this might suffice for a barbecue announcement or a flyer advertising a local hair salon, the real world of four-color printing and professional communication requires a serious commitment.

THE SERIES

The applications presented in the Against The Clock series stand out as the programs of choice in professional graphic arts environments.

We've used a modular design for the Against The Clock series, allowing you to mix and match the drawing, imaging, and page layout applications to exactly suit your specific needs.

Titles available in the Against The Clock series include:

Macintosh: Basic Operations
Windows: Basic Operations
Adobe Illustrator: An Introduction to Digital Illustration
Adobe Illustrator: Advanced Digital Illustration
FreeHand: An Introduction to Digital Illustration
FreeHand: Advanced Digital Illustration
Adobe PageMaker: An Introduction to Electronic Mechanicals
Adobe PageMaker: Advanced Electronic Mechanicals
QuarkXPress: An Introduction to Electronic Mechanicals
QuarkXPress: Advanced Electronic Mechanicals
Adobe Photoshop: An Introduction to Digital Images
Adobe Photoshop: Advanced Digital Images
File Preparation: The Responsible Electronic Page
Preflight: An Introduction to File Analysis and Repair
TrapWise: Trapping
PressWise: Imposition

How to Use This Workbook

We've designed our courses to be "cross-platform." While many sites use Macintosh computers, there are an increasing number of graphic arts service providers using Intel-based systems running Windows (or Windows NT). The books in this series are applicable to either of these systems.

All applications covered in the Against The Clock series are similar in operation and appearance both on a Macintosh or Windows system. When a particular function differs from machine to machine, we present both.

Icons and Visuals

Pencil icon indicates a comment from an experienced operator. When you see the pencil icon, you'll find corresponding sidebar text that augments or enhances the subject.

Bomb icon indicates a potential problem or difficulty. For instance, a certain technique might lead to pages that prove difficult to output. In other cases, there might be something that a program cannot easily accomplish, so we might present a workaround.

Pointing Finger indicates a hands-on activity — whether a short exercise or complete project. This will be the icon seen most often throughout the course.

Key icon is used to indicate a keyboard equivalent to a menu or dialog box option. Key commands are often faster than using the mouse to select a menu option. Experienced operators often mix keyboard equivalents with menu/dialog box selections to achieve optimum speed.

If you are a Windows user, be certain to refer to the corresponding text or images whenever you see this **Windows** icon. Although there isn't a great deal of difference between these applications on a Macintosh or a Windows-based PC, there are certain instances where there's enough of a difference worth noting.

COURSE WALKTHROUGH

CHAPTER OPENINGS *provide the reader with specific objectives.*

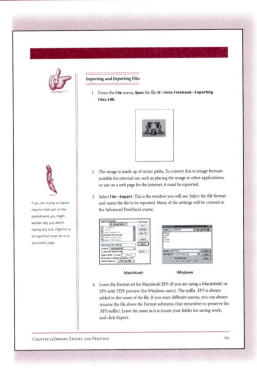

SIDEBARS and HANDS-ON ACTIVITIES *supplement concepts presented in the material.*

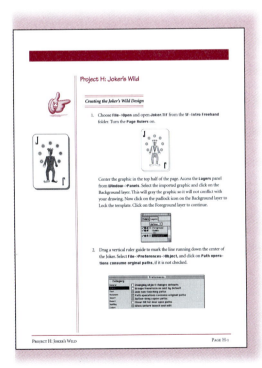

SUPPLEMENTAL PROJECTS *offer practice opportunities in addition to the exercises.*

PROJECT ASSIGNMENTS *will result in finished artwork — with an emphasis on proper file construction methods.*

The Projects You Will Work On

The Against The Clock course materials have been constructed with two primary building blocks: exercises and projects. Projects always result in a finished piece of work — digital imagery built from the ground up, utilizing photographic-quality images, vector artwork from Illustration programs, and type elements from the library supplied on your student CD-ROM.

This course, *FreeHand 8, An Introduction to Digital Illustration*, uses several projects that you will work on during your learning sessions. You will find the projects that you will have completed by the end of the course displayed on the inside front cover of the book. Here's a brief overview of each:

Project A: Steaming Coffee

The *Steaming Coffee* project makes use of simple closed paths to create the puffs of steam. The cup is constructed using the pen tool, setting paths to no fill and ensuring that the end caps are properly configured to simulate the end of a pen stroke. FreeHand's default end cap is a sharp, square edge – not suitable for most drawings of this type.

Project C: Last Mango Cafe Logo

The *Last Mango Cafe* logo combines type and linework to create a balanced, fun visual. The creation of the umbrella makes use of reflecting, editing, and modifying paths to create symmetrical shapes.

Project J: Last Mango Business Card

The *Last Mango Business Card* project requires careful attention to detail and the use of precision alignment. Business cards are often typeset in multiples based upon your printer's requirements. This project makes use of visuals created in previous projects and stresses the importance of precise object placement.

Project B: Java Jungle Logo

Selecting and drawing objects that you, as a beginning illustrator, see around you every day can prove to be a very effective teaching tool. To build the *Java Jungle* coffee cup, you will cut an ellipse to create symmetrical shapes for the lower portion of the opening and the bottom of the cup. You'll also be required to place type on the object. You might try the cup with several different typefaces as the logo.

The Projects You Will Work On

PROJECT H: COFFEE DU JOUR

Utilizing FreeHand as a page-layout tool, the *Coffee Du Jour* ad uses elements from previous projects as the components of a display advertisement. We create the headline, the deck, and then import text from a file that is supplied with this course. As a page-layout tool, FreeHand offers sophisticated type controls as well as drawing tools all in one package.

PROJECT D: TROPICAL FISH ART

Tropical Fish is built out of several primitive elements, including ellipses, freehand shapes, and random objects used for stylized shadings in the sand. To properly construct the artwork, you should use the Layers function – a critically important tool in the experienced artist's repertoire.

PROJECT F: BALL & MIRROR

The *Ball & Mirror* image uses the Freehand tool extensively for a hand-drawn look. The frame and the reflection are created using a linear gradient while the ball uses a radial gradient.

PROJECT G: JOKER'S WILD

A playing card is an excellent example of an illustration that takes advantage of FreeHand's powerful tool set. Throughout the project, you will create accurately spaced and mirrored elements. The stars around the Joker figure are repeated elements around an invisible circle created by the use of Repeat Transformation. This complex (and fun) drawing makes extensive use of templates, controlled cloning, layers, and guides.

PROJECT E: TROPICAL TREASURE LOGO

Designing a logo that speaks elegantly of a company isn't easy. Here, you will create a retailer's logo block called *Tropical Treasure* using type, an illustration of the little treasure chest in the copy line, bordering rules, and a "deck" ("*Gifts from the Sea*"). This is a type-intensive project, with shadow techniques derived from using layers of overlapping type.

PROJECT I: TROPICAL TREASURE MAILER

Another page-layout advertisement, the *Tropical Treasure Mailer* incorporates layers, imported copy files, and logos and visuals created in previous projects. This job emphasizes proper file construction for efficient output.

Support Materials

For the Student

On the CD-ROM you will find a complete set of Against The Clock (ATC) fonts, and a collection of data files used to construct the various exercises and projects in this course book.

The ATC fonts are solely for use with the Against The Clock materials. These fonts will be used throughout both the exercises and projects, and are provided in both Macintosh and Windows format.

A variety of student files has been included. These files, necessary to complete both the exercises and projects, are also provided in both Macintosh and Windows formats.

For the Instructor

The Instructor Kit consists of an Instructor's Manual and an Instructor's CD-ROM. It includes various testing and presentation materials in addition to the files that come standard with the student books.

- **Overhead Presentation Materials** are provided to enhance the instructor's presentation of the course. These presentations are prepared using Microsoft PowerPoint and are provided in both "native" PowerPoint format and Acrobat Portable Document Format (PDF).

- **Extra Projects** are provided with the data files. These projects may be used to extend the course, or to test the student.

- **A Test Bank of Questions** is included within the Instructor Kit. These questions may be modified, reorganized, and administered throughout the course.

- A **Review** of the material that the student has completed is provided midway through the course, with a **Final Review** at the end.

ACKNOWLEDGMENTS

I would like to give thanks to the writers, illustrators, editors, and others who have worked long and hard to complete the Against The Clock series. Foremost among them are Dean Bagley, David Broudy, Gavin Nagatomo, and Michael Barnett, whom I thank for their long nights, early mornings, and their seemingly endless patience.

Thanks also to the dedicated teaching professionals whose comments and expertise contributed to the success of these products, including Renée Prim of Central Piedmont Community College, Ron Bertolina of The Graphic Arts Technical Foundation, and Rainer Fleschner of Moraine Park Technical College.

A big thanks to Judy Casillo, Developmental Editor, for her guidance, patience, and attention to detail.

A special thanks to my husband for his unswerving support and for living in a publishing studio and warehouse during the three years it took to develop the ATC series of courses.

Thanks to my original partner and friend Steve Tripp for his faith and patience in the early days. Thanks, too, to Jung Mills, who was with me each and every day — making Against The Clock a household name.

Thanks to my "Fishin' Buddies" EW Spencer and Jeannie Pugh. And special thanks to my dogs, Spike (who left for the big rawhide factory in the sky before the project was completed), Boda, and Chase.

Ellenn Behoriam, June, 1998

About Against The Clock

Our Story

Against The Clock (ATC) was founded in 1990 as a part of Lanman Systems Group, one of the nation's leading systems integration and training firms. The company specialized in developing custom training materials for such clients as L.L. Bean, *The New England Journal of Medicine, Smithsonian Magazine*, National Education Association, *Air & Space Magazine*, Publishers Clearing House, National Wildlife Society, Home Shopping Network, and many others. The integration firm was among the most highly respected in the graphic arts industry.

To a great degree, the success of Systems Group can be attributed to the thousands of pages of course materials developed at the company's demanding client sites. Throughout the rapid growth of Systems Group, founder and General Manager Ellenn Behoriam developed the necessary expertise to manage technical experts, content providers, writers, editors, illustrators, designers, layout artists, proofreaders, and the rest of the chain of professionals required to develop structured and highly effective training materials.

Following the sale of the Lanman Companies to World Color, one of the nation's largest commercial printers, Ellenn embarked on a three year project to fully redevelop a library of training materials designed specifically for the professional graphic artist. The result of this effort is the ATC training library.

Ellenn lives in Tampa, Florida with her husband and her dogs Boda and Chase.

About the Authors

Every one of the Against The Clock course books was developed by a group of people working as part of a design and production team.

Dean Bagley is an experienced marketing and advertising expert. Dean is a professional cartoonist, well-known for his imaginative and entertaining "Baggy Gator" series of comic characters. Dean lives in Winter Haven, Florida with his cat Nuci.

David Broudy is an experienced prepress professional and works on many of the ATC projects. David lives in Rochester, New York, and is a graduate student in the College of Imaging Arts and Sciences at the Rochester Institute of Technology.

Gavin Nagatomo works on many of the Against The Clock projects in a wide range of roles. Gavin lives in Palatine, Illinois.

GETTING STARTED

Platform

The Against The Clock series is specifically designed to apply to both Macintosh and Windows systems — the courses will work for you no matter what environment you find yourself in. There are some slight differences in the two, but when you're working in an actual application, these differences are limited to certain types of functions and actions.

Naming Conventions

In the old days of MS-DOS systems, file names on the PC were limited to something referred to as "8.3," which meant that you were limited in the number of characters you could use to an eight-character name (the "8") and a three-character suffix (the "3"). Text files, for example, might be called *myfile.txt*, while a document file from a word processor might be called *myfile.doc* (for document). On today's Windows-based systems, these limitations have been somewhat overcome. Although you can use longer file names, suffixes still exist. Whether or not you see them is another story.

When your system is first configured, the Views are normally set to a default that hides these extensions. This means that you might have a dozen different files named *myfile*, all of which may have been generated by different applications and be completely different types of files.

On a Windows system, you can change this view by clicking on *My Computer* (the icon is on your desktop) with the right button, and choosing View ->Options. From this dialog box you may choose whether or not to display these older, MS-DOS file extensions. In some cases, it's easier to know what you're looking at if they're visible. This is a personal choice.

To ensure that the supplied student files are fully compatible with both operating systems, we've named all the files using the three-character suffix — even those on the Macintosh.

Key Commands

Key commands are fairly consistent between the Macintosh and the Windows versions of Macromedia FreeHand. The major difference lies in the names of special function keys. The Macintosh has a key marked with an Apple and an icon that looks like a clover leaf. This is called the Command key. Whenever you see this icon, you will need to hold this key down. The Command key is a *modifier* key; that is, it doesn't do anything by itself, but changes the function of a key pressed while it's being held down. A good example is holding Command while pressing the "S" key: this Saves your work. The same thing applies to the "P" key; hold down Command and press it to Print your work.

On Windows-based systems, the Control key is almost always the equivalent of the Command key on the Macintosh. (This is sometimes confusing to new users, since the Macintosh also has a Control key, although, on the Macintosh, it's hardly ever used in popular applications).

Another special function key on the Macintosh is the Option key. It's also a modifier key, and you'll need to hold it down along with whatever other key is required for a specific function. The equivalent modifier key on a Windows system is called the ALT key (for alternative). Besides these two nomenclature issues, there isn't really a lot of difference between using a Windows system and a Macintosh system (particularly when you're within a particular application).

The CD-ROM and Initial Setup Considerations

Before you begin using your Against The Clock course book, you will have to set up your system so that you have access to the various files and tools you'll need to complete your lessons.

Student Files

This course comes complete with a collection of student files. These files are an integral part of the learning experience, as they're used throughout the course to help you construct increasingly complex elements. Having these building blocks available to you throughout your practice and study sessions will ensure that you will be able to experience the exercises and complete the project assignments smoothly and with a minimum of time spent looking for the various components required.

In building the Student Files folders, we've created sets of data for both Macintosh and Windows users. Locate the appropriate version of the "SF-Intro FreeHand" folder for your platform of choice and simply drag the icon onto your hard disk drive. If you have limited disk space, you may want to copy only the files for one or two lessons at a time.

Creating a Project Folder

We strongly recommend that you work from your hard disk. However, in some cases you might not have enough room on your system for all of the files that we've supplied. If this is the case, you can work directly from the CD-ROM.

Throughout the exercises and projects, you'll be required to save your work. Since the CD-ROM is "read-only," you cannot write information to it. Create a Project Folder on your hard disk and use it to store your work-in-progress. Create your project folder using Command-N (Macintosh) or Control-N (Windows) while you're looking at your desktop. This will create the folder at the highest level of your system, where it will be easy to find.

Fonts

Whatever platform you're working on — Macintosh or Windows — you will have to install the ATC font library to ensure that your lessons and exercises will work as they're described in the course book. These fonts are provided on the student CD-ROM. There is a version for Windows and one for Macintosh.

Instructions for installing fonts are provided in the documentation that came with your computer. If you're using a font utility such as Suitcase or Font Juggler, then be sure to refer to the instructions that came with the font management application for installing your ATC fonts onto your system.

Prerequisites

This book assumes that you have a basic understanding of how to use your system. Whether you're working on a Macintosh or a Windows workstation, the skill sets are basically the same.

You should know how to use your mouse to point and click, and how to drag items around the screen. You should know how to resize a window, and how to arrange windows on your desktop to maximize the space you have available. You should know how to access pull-down menus and how check boxes and radio buttons work. Lastly, you should know how to create, open, and save files.

If you're familiar with these fundamental skills, then you know all that's necessary to utilize the Against The Clock courseware library.

Notes:

Chapter 1

An Introduction

Chapter Objective:

To provide you with an introduction to Freehand's user interface, basic controls, and customization ability. In Chapter 1, you will:

- Understand that FreeHand is both a powerful tool for creating commercial art and graphic illustrations, as well as a comprehensive layout program.
- Learn that images are created digitally, falling into two categories: Object-oriented and Bitmap (Raster).
- Learn that FreeHand is an object-oriented program with which your artwork is created using objects drawn as lines or curves.
- Understand what bitmap images are and begin to learn how they relate to the designs you will be creating in FreeHand.

Projects to be Completed:

- Steaming Coffee
- Last Mango Cafe Logo
- Last Mango Business Cards
- Java Jungle
- Coffee Du Jour Ad
- Tropical Fish Art
- Ball & Mirror
- Joker's Wild
- Tropical Treasure Logo
- Tropical Treasure Mailer
- Grocery Ad

An Introduction

FreeHand is a powerful application for creating commercial art and graphic illustrations. It is also a comprehensive page layout program that you can use to complete entire layouts. FreeHand 8's versatility is especially important for artists creating designs for printed publications, multimedia projects, and internet content.

Graphic design, even with a computer, should begin traditionally with a few pencil sketches (called *thumbnails*). Thumbnails offer several ideas and concepts for presentation to your client. Once a design is chosen, it's easy for a skilled designer to bring the sketch to life in FreeHand. The finished project (called a *comp* or *mechanical*) can then be incorporated into other projects, or used as is.

Digital Graphic Images

Images that are created digitally fall into one of two categories:

- Object-oriented
- Bitmap (Raster)

FreeHand is an *object-oriented* drawing program. Object-oriented drawing programs create artwork with graphic objects drawn as lines or curves. These lines and curves are known as *vectors*, and can be combined, colored, and modified in many ways to produce the desired effect that you require. Object-oriented images can also be scaled and printed in any size without a loss of quality.

Bitmap images can be created either by scanning a photograph, or by creating them in programs that use the raster format, such as Adobe Photoshop. As a designer, you will be working frequently with bitmapped images.

A bitmap image is a *map* composed of *pixels*, the simplest of which is one bit of information. Each pixel contains information in a *bit depth* that ranges from 1 to 32 bits. More information can be stored to represent the color of a specific pixel the higher the bit depth is. The most common bitmap image formats are TIFF, GIF, and JPEG. A common format on Windows computers is the BMP format; a common format on Macintosh computers is the PICT format, which

A *bit* is the smallest unit of information that can be stored in a computer. It is always either 1 or 0, or on and off. In a 1-bit image, bits with a value of 0 represent white, and bits with a value of 1 represent black.

can also store object-oriented images. Bitmaps cannot be scaled or printed in varying resolutions without a significant loss of quality, making them much less versatile than object-oriented images.

Step by Step

We feel very strongly that to train you, the aspiring designer, properly and efficiently in FreeHand 8 is by guiding you through a structured and creative course with practical, hands-on exercises accompanied by annotated, lecture-style information. This introductory course moves step-by-step through the workings of FreeHand 8 with many exercises to help you understand, by practice, how to use the many unique features of the software. When you have completed this course, you will have a firm grasp on creating complex documents and be ready to begin developing your own designs.

Follow the exercises; study them closely. This is your career, and it is our desire to train you to be the best designer you can possibly be. And when you've completed this Introduction to FreeHand 8, there are even more complex operations and additional material covered in the Advanced FreeHand 8 course from Against the Clock.

If your computer already has FreeHand 8 installed, you're ready to begin. If not, install the program from the CD-ROM following the installation instructions included with your software package.

Chapter 2

Freehand Workflow

Chapter Objective:

To become familiar with FreeHand's operating environment, tools, and controls. In Chapter 2, you will:

- Begin to understand Freehand's tools — panels, menus, Inspectors, toolbars, and document windows.
- Learn how the Toolbox can be modified and positioned.
- Understand why the most important tool in Freehand is the Pointer tool, and learn where and how it is used.
- Review one of the most basic commands an artist must remember when working in a graphic application: how to create, open, and save.
- Learn how to create or customize toolbars.
- Learn how to access the Inspector's numerous panels, sub-panels, and other panels that FreeHand offers.
- Explore Freehand's menu structure — view what selections Freehand provides, and explore its submenus.
- Learn about FreeHand's defaults, and how to customize them to your own specific tastes and standards.
- Learn a few basic drawing commands, and how to create custom views and windows of your document.
- Learn about Freehand's four viewing modes.
- Learn how to navigate your way through a Freehand document.
- Learn to utilize Wizards (Windows version only).

Projects to be Completed:

- Steaming Coffee
- Last Mango Cafe Logo
- Last Mango Business Cards
- Java Jungle
- Coffee Du Jour Ad
- Tropical Fish Art
- Ball & Mirror
- Joker's Wild
- Tropical Treasure Logo
- Tropical Treasure Mailer
- Grocery Ad

FreeHand Workflow

This section guides you through some of the fundamental operations of Freehand: creating and opening documents, saving them, and adjusting Freehand's defaults to suit your preferences. You'll also learn how to navigate through a document and examine how Freehand's tools are displayed and accessed.

The FreeHand Environment

In Freehand you work with panels, menus, Inspectors, toolbars, and document windows, which include the pasteboard.

At the top of the screen is the Menu Bar, where most of Freehand's major functions are accessed. The main document window (which only appears if you create a new document or open an existing one) contains all the document's pages and the Pasteboard.

Here's a representative look at Freehand's environment for the Macintosh. Your screen might look a little different because many things such as panels and the Inspector can be placed anywhere on the screen, or may not appear by default in a new document unless you modify the FreeHand Preferences (explained later in this section).

Imagine the pasteboard as a storage area for anything you might want to use in your artwork. Things on the pasteboard won't print or otherwise appear in your document, but can be moved onto the page at any time.

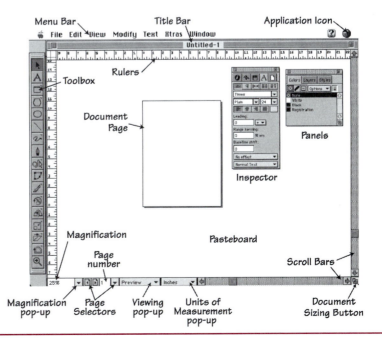

CHAPTER 2/FREEHAND WORKFLOW

Here's the Windows representation of the FreeHand environment. Most Freehand operations are identical between the two versions, but there are subtle differences in their appearance.

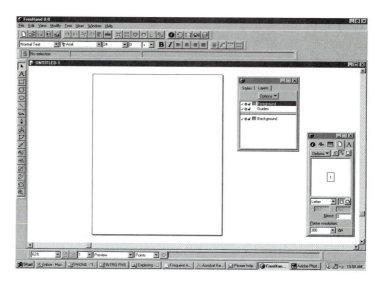

The Pointer Tool

The pointer tool (the arrow that moves with your mouse) is the most fundamental tool in FreeHand, and the one you'll probably use the most. It is selected at the top of the toolbar and is used within a document to select and move objects; and in the rest of FreeHand is is used to make selections from menus, inspectors, and other controls.

Saving a Document

It is important to develop the habit of saving early and saving often, as any financial advisor will tell you. Hours of work can be lost in an instant if your computer locks up or the power fails and you forgot to save your work, which can happen easily if you get really wrapped up in a design. By saving the document often, such as every five minutes, at worst you'll have to recreate five minutes worth of work if the power goes out. The easiest way to save is to take half a second and press Command-S (Macintosh) or Control-S (Windows).

Press Command (Macintosh) or Control (Windows) + S to save a document.

Both the Macintosh and Windows versions of FreeHand can open files created on either platform. Adding ".FH8" to the end of document file names ensures maximum compatibility across these two different computer platforms. The same applies for the ".FT8" file extension for FreeHand templates, which we will cover shortly. Refer to the **Getting Started** section for more information about file naming conventions.

Creating and Saving a FreeHand Document

1. Choose **File->New** to create a new document.

2. To save the document, choose **File->Save As**. Navigate to your **Work in Progress** folder that you created to save your work (you should have created this folder in the *Getting Started* section).

   The **Save As...** dialog appears. Click and hold on the **Format** pop-up menu to see the three formats for saving documents.

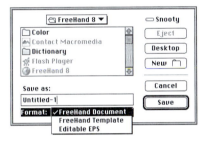
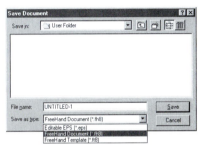

              Macintosh   **Windows**

3. Select **FreeHand Document**. In the **Save As** section, name the file "FreeHand Document.FH8" and click **Save**.

4. This will save the original document and create a copy. The new document name will appear in the Title Bar across the top of the document. Choose **File->Save As** again. This time, choose the **FreeHand Template** format. Name the file "FreeHand Template.FT8" (Macintosh and Windows). Choose **File->Save**. Notice how the name did not change in the Title Bar. The template was saved as an external copy of the document.

5. Choose **File->Save As** again. Click on the **Format** submenu to choose the **Editable EPS** option. Name the file "Editable.EPS" (Macintosh and Windows). Click **Save**. You have now saved the same document in three different formats. These file formats may not make much sense now, but we will cover them in later sections.

6. **Close** this document without saving.

CHAPTER 2/FREEHAND WORKFLOW

Opening a Document

To open an existing document, choose **Open** from the **File** menu.

Opening a FreeHand Document

1. In the File menu, choose **Open**.

2. In the **Open Document** dialog box, navigate to the SF-Intro FreeHand folder. When you click on a document name in this box, a preview of the document appears.

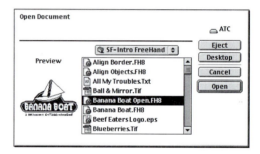

Randomly click on files that have an FH8 or FT8 extension — these are FreeHand documents and templates. This allows you to preview the file before opening it.

Press Command-O (Macintosh) or Control (Windows)-O (the letter "O," not zero) to show the Open Document dialog.

3. Select **Banana Boat.FH8** and click **Open**; the document opens and you can see the artwork inside.

Choose **File->Close** to put the document away.

Press Command-W (Macintosh) or Control-W (Windows) to close a document.

An EPS file is a universal format used to exchange artwork between different programs and different computers. It is one of the standard means of information interchange in the graphic arts industry.

4. Choose **File->Open** again and open **HoneyDo Logo Ad.EPS**. You will see a logo that you will use later within the Projects section of this course book. Because this file is in the EPS format, it can be placed in other applications such as PageMaker or QuarkXPress.

5. The upper left (Macintosh) or right (Windows) square in the document's Title Bar is the **Close** box. Click on it to close the document.

6. Choose **File->Open** and select **FreeHand Template.FH8** — you created this file in the previous exercise.

   When the document opens, look at the Title Bar. What do you see? Why the "Untitled" name? Templates allow a document to be saved with graphics, type, and attributes set for use in the untitled copies of the original. This eliminates accidentally changing or ruining the original you worked so hard to produce.

7. Let's assume you want to make changes to an existing template. Choose **View->Magnification** and select 25%. While in the **View** menu, select **Page Rulers**. Now choose **Save As** and save this file in **FreeHand Template** format, naming it "FreeHand Template.FT8". You will be asked if you want to replace the existing file of that name. Click **Replace**.

8. Close the untitled document without saving. If FreeHand complains about closing an unsaved file, click **Don't Save**.

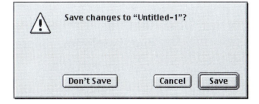

CHAPTER 2/FREEHAND WORKFLOW

Exploring the FreeHand Document

1. Choose **File->Open** to open **SF-Intro Freehand->Document Views.FH8**.

2. In the menu bar, click on each menu and view what selections it contains. If any selections have a triangle, highlight them to see the submenus and what they offer.

3. With the Pointer tool, click on the black square. Click on the magnification pop-up menu (see pages 1-2) at the bottom of the document window and try selecting different percentages. Observe how the document page enlarges or reduces.

   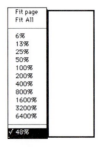 

              Macintosh   **Windows**

Press Command-K (Macintosh) or Control-K (Windows) to switch from Preview to Keyline mode.

4. To the left of the magnification pop-up menu is a field that shows the current percentage. Highlight this number with the mouse and type in 177. Press Return (Macintosh) or Enter (Windows) to apply; you will see the document change to this percentage. This is the way to achieve the exact magnification that you prefer.

5. Click on the Viewing pop-up menu (see pgs 1-2) at the bottom of the screen to see your four options. Select Keyline and observe how the square appears. Ignore Fast Preview and Fast Keyline, which are for more complex, color-intensive art. Return to **Preview** mode.

6. The Viewing pop-up menu is not the only way to go from Preview/Keyline modes. You can select either in the **View** menu. Do this now by choosing **Keyline** from the **View** menu. When you select a mode, the menu item changes to show the other mode. Choose **Preview** from the **View** menu to see the change.

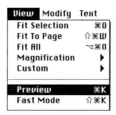

7. Page Rulers are very important for achieving exact measurements of objects and distances. If the rulers are not present on screen, choose **View** ->**Page Ruler**s to display them.

   Ruler increments have five measuring units from which to choose. To change to a different measuring unit, access the Units pop-up menu at the bottom of the document window. Click on this pop-up menu to observe the units. Choose Inches and watch the rulers on screen change as well. Now select Points and observe the rulers. Reset the pop-up menu back to Inches.

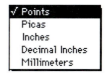

CHAPTER 2/FREEHAND WORKFLOW

8. From the **File** menu choose **Save As**. When the dialog box appears, navigate to the your **Work in Progress** folder and type in the name "FreeHand Sample.FH8" and click **OK**.

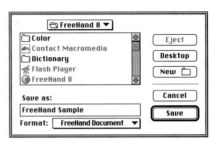

Now look at the Title Bar of the document; the name has changed to the new title you saved.

9. Sometimes the page needs to be moved away from the panels and dialog boxes to better view the image. This is done either by the scroll bars or the Hand tool.

The scroll bar consists of up/down arrows, the bar itself, and the scroll button on the bar.

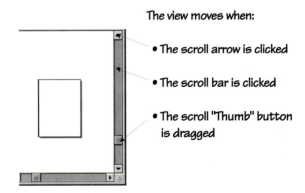

10. Hold the spacebar down; the Pointer tool changes to a hand. Drag the hand across the document page. This lets you move the document around in the window without using the scroll bars.

Hold the Spacebar to activate the scrolling Hand tool. It stays active as long as the Spacebar is held down.

11. Choose **Window->Inspectors** and select **Document**. Click on the **Options** feature and select **Add Pages**.

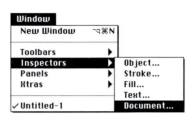

12. In the dialog, set the **Number of pages** to 4. Click **OK**.

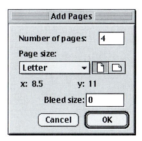

Press Command-5 (Macintosh) or Control-5 (Windows) to switch to 50% magnification.

13. Use the Magnification pop-up menu at the bottom of the screen to view at 50%.

14. The page selection features at the bottom of the screen offer two ways to go to a page, and tell you the page number you are currrently on.

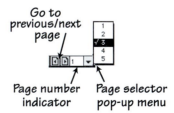

15. You have added four pages, and are looking at a single page on the screen. What is the number of this page? Click on the Previous and Next page buttons to scroll through your pages.

Observe how the page number changes as you do. Use the selector pop-up menu to access different pages.

16. **Close** the document without saving.

Document Inspector

Bleed is the area around the page that will be trimmed off after the document is printed. This way, you can have artwork extending off the page and when the page is trimmed, the art will appear to extend exactly to the edge of the page.

The Document Inspector is where you make most of the settings for the document's size, page orientation, *bleed*, and the number of pages in the document. You can also add, duplicate, and remove pages in the Inspector.

The Document Inspector presents a miniature view of the pasteboard with small icons (*thumbnails*) that represent each page of your document. Magnification settings for the pasteboard view are located at the top right of the Inspector. If your document contains lots of pages, they may not all fit within the pasteboard viewer at the larger viewing sizes.

 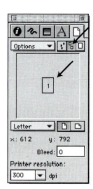 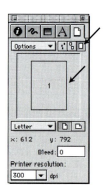

Using the Document Inspector

1. Create a new document by choosing **File->New**.

2. In the Magnification pop-up menu, set the page view for 25%. Choose **Window->Inspectors->Document**. The Inspector will appear on screen. Move the Inspector to the upper right corner of the document. Set the measurement Units to Inches from the Measurements pop-up menu.

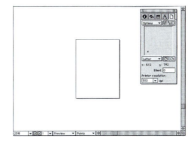

3. The three thumbnail options allow you to move the page around on the pasteboard.

4. The default thumbnail view is the left one, next to the Options submenu. Click on the middle thumbnail. In the Viewer, move the page around watching how the actual page on the pasteboard moves.

5. Click on the right thumbnail. In the viewer, move the page around to see how the document page moves.

6. Click on the Options submenu and select **Add Pages**. In the **Add Pages** dialog box, enter 5 and click **OK**.

Double-clicking on a page in the Document Inspector viewer brings the page in the document to the center of the drawing screen.

In the Document Inspector, click on the left view thumbnail. Five pages will appear on the pasteboard and in the Document Inspector, making six in all, counting the original. In the Document Inspector, the thumbnails will show one page that is darker than the others; this represents the current page.

7. Click on this darker page in the viewer and move it up slightly. Notice how the corresponding page in the document moves up too.

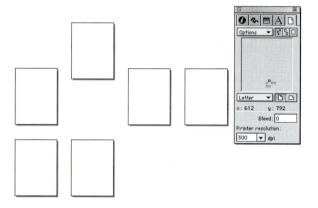

8. On the pasteboard, click on a different page. Notice how the corresponding page in the Inspector viewer becomes darker.

9. Select the Options pop-up in the Inspector and select Remove. What happened to the page on the pasteboard? Another page became the selected, darker page.

10. Navigate to the Page Size pop-up and select Legal.

11. Did all the pages become Legal size, or just the selected one?

12. Click on the other pages in the Inspector viewer. Each clicked page becomes darker, indicating it as the working page.

13. Click on the Landscape (horizontal) Orientation in the Inspector.

The corresponding page on the pasteboard responds to the change in page orientation.

14. Click on the middle viewing icon in the Inspector; the selected page goes to the center of the viewer.

15. Click on each page and Remove it in the Options submenu of the Inspector. Leave one page.

16. Choose **View->Fit To Page**. In the Status Bar, set the Units pop-up menu to Inches.

17. In the Inspector, enter 0.25 (inches) for Bleed. Press Return (Macintosh) or Enter (Windows) to apply. This will draw a gray outline around the page to show you how far the bleed extends.

    You have now experimented with the Document Inspector and observed how its various features work.

18. **Close** the document without saving.

FreeHand Defaults

Freehand's default settings are stored in a file on your computer called Freehand Defaults (Macintosh) or Defaults.FT8 (Windows). You might want to copy this file to a diskette should you ever want to revert back to the original settings. Freehand uses this settings document each time you create a new file. But you can create your own settings file, set up the way you want to work, and Freehand will use it for all new documents, instead of the original default settings file.

The way this default file is selected for use is in the **Preferences->Document** window, listed in the New document template box. FreeHand also uses this template file for all its settings when you create a new file. If you have other templates created with different settings they will be used if you type the document name in this box, then close Preferences.

Customizing Your Default Files

You can change nearly all Freehand settings to be used as a default. For example, if you create a set of base colors that you will often use, you can create a new settings file that contains those colors, and all of your new documents will contain them. A settings file is simply a Freehand template, the same as any other Freehand template.

Changing FreeHand Defaults

1. Choose **File->Open**. In the **Open Document** dialog, navigate to the FreeHand 8.0 application folder and open the file **FreeHand Defaults**.

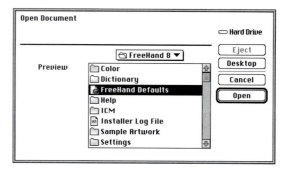

Macintosh

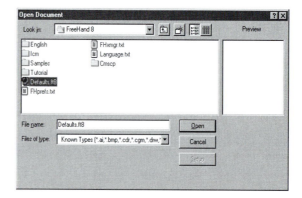

Windows

2. When you open the Defaults file, a new Untitled document is created, because the Default file is a template. All templates open as new, Untitled documents. You can save this as a new template, then tell Freehand to use it as a basis for all new documents by specifying the new template in the **Preferences->Document** settings.

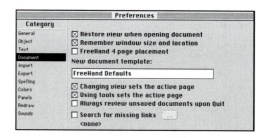

Macintosh

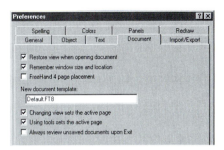

Windows

3. In this Untitled document, make these changes:

   - Go to the View menu and toggle on Page Rulers so the default document will automatically appear with rulers.

   - In the Units of Measurement pop-up menu at the bottom of the screen, set the units for Inches.

   - In the Magnification pop-up menu, set the percentage for 12%.

4. Your document should look something like this:

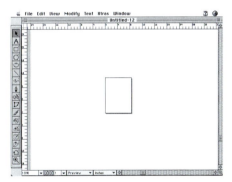

5. Choose **File->Save As** and select the FreeHand Template format. Be certain to save this in the FreeHand 8.0 folder. Name the file with your own name: "(Your Name) Defaults.FT8". Click **Save. Close** the Untitled file without saving. The Default file with your name is now available along with the FreeHand Defaults document in the FreeHand 8.0 folder.

6. FreeHand will still use the FreeHand Defaults file as a guide to create new documents. How do you change to your own defaults?

7. Choose **File->Preferences** and click on the Document option. See **New document template** in the list? Underneath this heading is where you type the name of the file you want used as the default file for new

CHAPTER 2/FREEHAND WORKFLOW

documents. In this input area, replace FreeHand Defaults with "(Your Name) Defaults.FT8". Close the Preferences window by clicking **OK**.

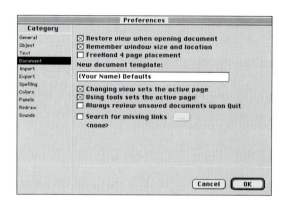

8. You do not have to restart the FreeHand application. Choose **File->New** to create a new document. When the document appears on your screen, what do you see?

   Creating default documents is useful for customizing features you want in all new documents. You can create and store as many as you want, using Preferences to select which one to use.

9. Return to **File->Preferences->Document** and type "FreeHand Defaults". Click **OK**.

10. **Close** the untitled document without saving.

The Status Bar (Windows)

The Windows version of FreeHand adds a floating Status Bar that incorporates Magnification, Page Selector, View, and Units pop-up menus. It also displays the status of any actions in progress, menu selections, and which tool is currently active.

Wizards

FreeHand's Wizard buttons accesses its help menus, and allows you to quickly select and create basic page layout and panel content options for commonly used types of documents.

The first menu screen that appears when you open FreeHand is the Welcome Wizard. This uses menus for creating or finding documents, or for launching the FreeHand Help menu.

The Welcome Wizard

The Welcome wizard buttons launch the Help system, helps you find previously created FreeHand documents, and assists with creating new documents.

The templates on the FreeHand CD-ROM are pre-built documents that you can use for many types of layouts, such as business cards, forms, stationery, and other types of documents. These always open as new, untitled documents to preserve the orginal. Templates have the extension ".FT8".

The Welcome wizard buttons are:

- **New** — Creates a new document, uses the FreeHand page default set. This is the same as choosing **File->New**.

- **Previous File** — Finds and opens the last FH8 document that was open. Previous files can also be found under the main File menu just above the Exit command.

- **Open** —Displays the Open Document dialog menu.

- **Template** — Asks for the FreeHand Template folder on the FreeHand CD-ROM, unless you copied it to your hard drive, and displays the Open Document dialog menu (looks for FT8 files).

- **FreeHand Help** — Displays the FreeHand 8 interactive help menu. This is the same as choosing **Help->FreeHand Help**.

FreeHand Help

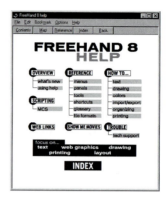

The FreeHand Help menu displays button links to FreeHand's interactive help menus. Clicking on **Overview**, **Reference**, **How To...**, or **Trouble** opens a selection list of related help or information topics.

- **Scripting** — explains how to access Macromedia Script Editor to create Java Scripts, which can automate frequently-used operations.

- **Web Links** — displays Macromedia's home page web address.

- **Show Me Movies** — plays the movies *Using the Color Main Menu* and *Using the Layers Main Menu* provided on the FreeHand application CD-ROM.

- **Focus on...** Text, Drawing, and Layout buttons — displays sample screens with interactive components that link to content area information or procedures. Click on any of the page components with the hand icon to display the list of related help topics.

- **Index** — opens the Help Index window. Help topics are listed by Contents books, general topic categories, a word based Index, and a word(s) Find listing that displays the desired word or phrase information and lists of related help topics.

Choose A Wizard

If you decide not to use the Welcome wizard to create a Freehand document, there is a second Wizard menu available to help make your document setup quick and easy. The **Choose a Wizard** menu, found under **Help->Wizards**, offers four new buttons for the creation of special content-based documents.

- **Welcome** — opens the Welcome wizards menu.

- **Setup** — creates an illustration-based document, either freehand or technical. Select colors for the Colors List, color mode, default unit of measurement, page size, and orientation.

- **Screen-based** — creates a document optimized for either Internet or multimedia/image graphics. Choose colors for the Colors List and set on screen page size and orientation.

- **Stationery** — creates common business page layouts including letterheads, envelopes, business cards, diskettes, and mailing labels. Select colors for the Color List and browse through several layout samples.

- **Publication** — creates multiple-page documents. Select the pager size, number of pages and orientation, colors to be included in the Colors List, the default unit of measurement, and preformatted type and graphic styles available in the Colors/Layers/Styles panel.

Each wizard document topic directs you through a series of interactive screens that allow you to select page options and panel contents specific to the document type of your choice.

The Stationery Wizard

1. From the **Choose a Wizard** dialog, click the **Stationery** wizard button. Select **Letter** for your page size and click **Next**.

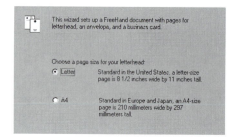

2. Click **Yes**, but don't select a color for the Color list. Click **Next**.

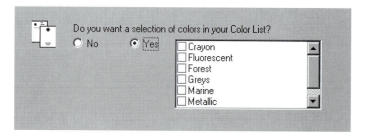

3. Select **Layout Ideas** and **Corporate** as your display sample, then click **Next**.

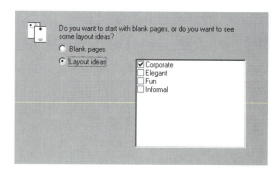

4. The **Attributes** menu should look like this:

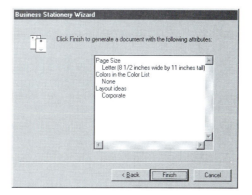

5. Your document screen should display the following:

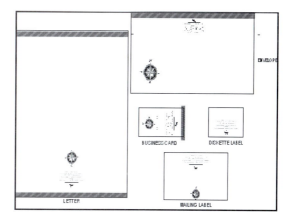

You just created a FreeHand document called Corporate. Any of the objects on the pages (text or graphics) can be selected and altered. Zoom in on the letterhead title at the bottom of the letter page. Use picas for your measurement unit and Newsletter-based graphic and text styles.

You should see five pages of varying sizes. Use the Text tool to highlight the dummy text and replace it with your own information.

6. Open the Color List panel. Note there are three spot colors used in this document. If you edit and change one of these colors, all the objects on all pages with that color applied to them will automatically reflect the change.

7. Open the Document Inspector. Click on any of the page icons displayed in the panel. The screen fills with that particular page.

The Publication Wizard

1. In the **Choose a Wizard** dialog, click **Publication Wizard** and create a four-page, letter size, tall document. Set your Units of measurement for Picas. Use Newsletter-based graphic and text styles. Your attributes should contain the following:

   ```
   Number of pages
       4
   Colors in the Color List
       Black plus 3 spot colors
   Finished page size
       Letter
   Document unit measurement
       Picas
   Graphic and text styles
       Newsletter
   ```

2. Open the Styles panel and examine the list of predefined type styles listed. Select Normal text from the Styles list and open the Edit menu under the Options button. Most of the text styles are based on the Normal text style. Select a typeface from the Font menu and click **OK**.

3. Select Article from text styles are based on the Normal text style. Select a typeface from the Font menu and click **OK**.

4. Select Article from the Style list and open the Edit menu. Examine the Style/Parent/Next relationship; the same Normal text-based font is selected.

5. **Close** the document without saving.

Chapter 3

The FreeHand Working Environment

Chapter Objective:

To become familiar with FreeHand's operating environment, tools, and controls. In Chapter 3, you will:

- Begin to understand FreeHand's working environment and the tools that you work with in FreeHand (panels, menus, Inspectors, toolbars, and document windows), and where to access them.

- Learn how the Toolbox can be modified and positioned, and how tool defaults can be changed.

- Understand why the most important tool in FreeHand is the Pointer tool, and learn where and how it is used.

- Review one of the most basic commands an artist must remember when working in a graphic application: how to create, open, and save.

- Learn how to create or customize toolbars.

- Learn how to access the Inspector's numerous panels and sub-panels.

- View what selections FreeHand provides, and explore its submenus.

- Learn about FreeHand's defaults, and how to customize them.

- Learn a few basic drawing commands, and how to create custom views and windows of your document.

- Learn about FreeHand's four viewing modes, and how to enlarge or reduce your document view.

Projects to be Completed:

- Steaming Coffee
- Last Mango Cafe Logo
- Last Mango Business Cards
- Java Jungle
- Coffee Du Jour Ad
- Tropical Fish Art
- Ball & Mirror
- Joker's Wild
- Tropical Treasure Logo
- Tropical Treasure Mailer
- Grocery Ad

The FreeHand Working Environment

FreeHand contains a powerful workshop of tools, panels, operations, and features. Once you become familiar with something's operation, it usually becomes second nature. For example, if you have a car, you jump in, start it up, and take off. You don't think too much about shifting, braking or steering — you just do it. The same principle applies to learning an application such as FreeHand.

The most important features of FreeHand are the:

- Panels
- Inspectors
- Toolbars
- Menus

The Toolbox

The toolbox is one of FreeHand's panels. It contains many tools used for drawing lines and shapes, placing text, reshaping and sizing objects, and otherwise modifying your artwork. The toolbox contains 17 tools:

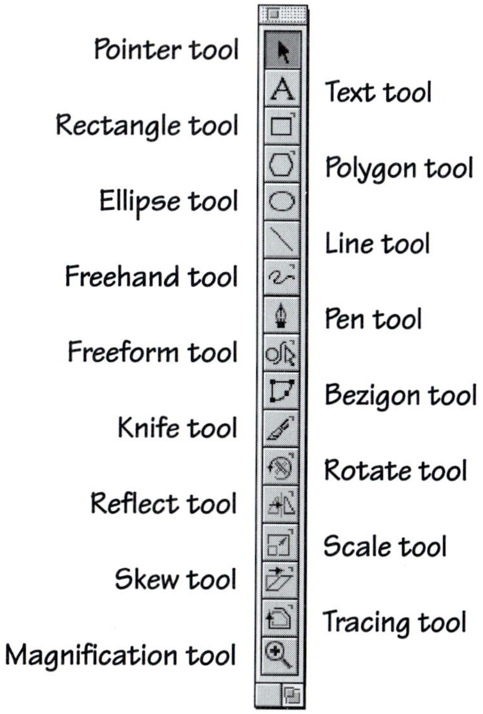

- Pointer tool
- Text tool
- Rectangle tool
- Polygon tool
- Ellipse tool
- Line tool
- Freehand tool
- Pen tool
- Freeform tool
- Bezigon tool
- Knife tool
- Rotate tool
- Reflect tool
- Scale tool
- Skew tool
- Tracing tool
- Magnification tool

Toolbox Options

Some tools, such as the Rectangle, Polygon, and Freehand tool, have small triangles in the corners of their tool icons. Double-clicking this icon will display a dialog box.

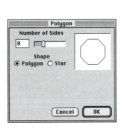  

The transformation tools all have this triangle symbol, but this brings up the Transform panel, set for the tool you double-clicked on.

The Toolbars

Toolbars are useful for accessing features and functions found in the menus and Panels. Toolbars are accessed in the Window menu.

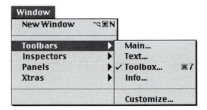

The Windows version also lists the Status Bar in the Toolbars menu.

These are the available Toolbars:

- Main Toolbar
- Text Toolbar
- Toolbox Toolbar
- Info Toolbar
- Status Bar (Windows only)

Flexibility of Toolbars

Toolbars can be maneuvered around the FreeHand environment, positioned at the extreme top or left side of the screen, or as a floating unit in the document.

When positioned at the top of the screen, the Toolbars are accessible, but out of the way, so you can get your work done without constantly moving them. They have different appearances, depending on their position. When at the extreme top or left side of the screen, they look like this:

Drag on these areas to maneuver toolbar on screen

When you drag on either end of the toolbar and move it into the document window, the appearance changes to look like the picture below. The top box closes the toolbar; the bottom box resizes it to several other configurations.

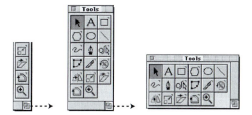

Main Toolbar

The Main Toolbar gives you immediate access to the menu functions by clicking on the icons located there. To avoid guessing games, you can select **Preferences->Panels->Show Tool Tips**. With this option on, a tool identifier appears when the Pointer passes over the tool.

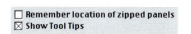 

Shown below is the Main Toolbar with its default icons that are present when FreeHand is first installed and launched; they can be customized with **Window->Toolbars->Customize**.

This is how the Main Toolbar looks when located out of the way across the top of the document window:

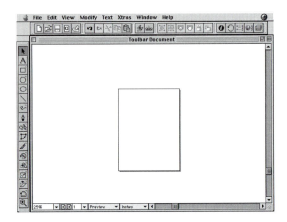

The Toolbox

The Toolbox, defined as a Toolbar, has traditionally been positioned on the left side of the FreeHand screen. It is best positioned on the left, but you can move it to the top of the screen.

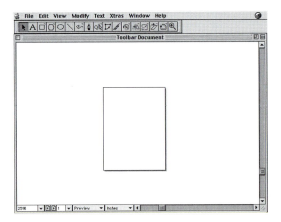

Managing the Toolbox

1. From the **File** menu, select **New** to create a new document.

2. A single page untitled document will appear. The Toolbox should be on the left side. If the Toolbox is not present, navigate to **Window->Toolbars ->Toolbox**.

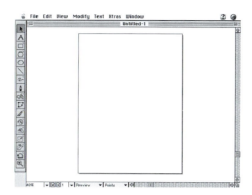

3. In the Toolbox, click-hold on the border just above the Pointer tool and drag the cursor up to the top of the document window. Release the mouse button. You have now moved the Toolbox to another postion across the top.

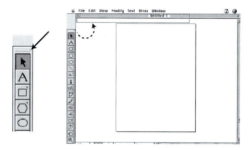

4. Click-hold on the area to the left of the Pointer tool and move the cursor downward to the left to return in to its original position.

5. With the Toolbox located on the left side of the screen, it is difficult to see its bottom portion. The top border above the Pointer tool is the area you click to drag the Toolbox. Click here and drag to move the Toolbox into the document area. You want to see the bottom of the Toolbox, so that when moving the outline of the Toolbox, make certain that the top of the Toolbox touches the Title Bar of the document. This is tricky because if you go too high, the Toolbox will try to go to Horizontal position.

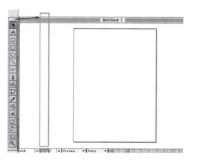

If you can't see any portion of the Toolbox, click on the Sizing button at the bottom right corner of the document; this will bring the Toolbox into view.

CHAPTER 3/THE FREEHAND WORKING ENVIRONMENT

6. When positioned, release the mouse button. Be careful. If the Toolbox disappears, don't panic. For some reason, it has become hidden by the document window itself. Click on the bottom right sizing box, and it will suddenly come forward.

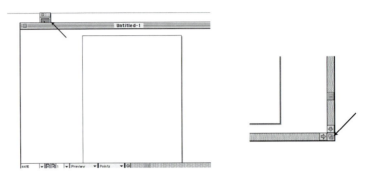

7. With the Toobox located away from the left side of the screen, it takes on a different look. Click-hold on the bottom right box and drag to the right. You will see the moving outline change on screen. Release the mouse button to see the new configuration. Experiment with using this box to reshape the Toolbox. Leave the Toolbox reshaped for the next step.

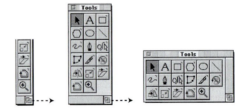

8. By clicking on the Title Bar of the Toolbox, you can drag it to any location of the document window. Don't click the Toolbox's close box; it puts the Toolbox away. Drag the Toolbox to other areas of the document, release the mouse button, then drag again.

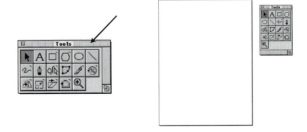

9. Drag the Toolbox back to the left side of the screen so that it snaps to the vertical position without any buttons.

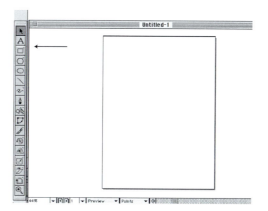

10. Navigate to the **Window->Toolbar** menu and select **Toolbox** to toggle it off, removing it from the screen.

11. Return to the same menu and toggle the **Toolbox** on, bringing it back to the screen.

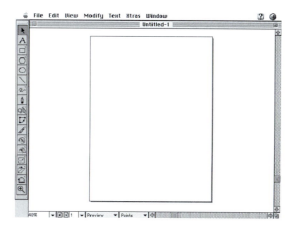

12. You have now seen the various ways to manage the Toolbox. **Close** the document without saving.

The Text Toolbar

The Text Toolbar offers the basic typographic settings you can apply to all selected text.

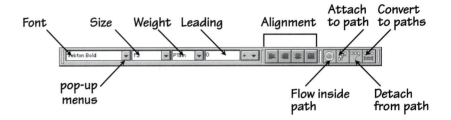

Along with the Main Toolbar, the Text Toolbar positions in the extreme top of the screen. They both can fit in this location above the document window.

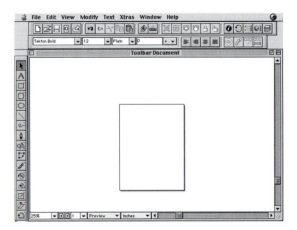

The Info Toolbar

The **Info Toolbar** shows what type of object is selected, its Lock status, and the x,y page location of the cursor.

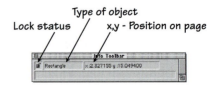

Text blocks, as well, are listed in the **Info Toolbar**.

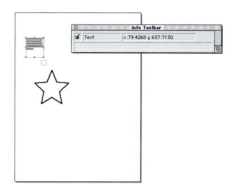

Customizing the Toolbars

Choosing **Windows->Toolbars->Customize...** lets you modify the Toolbars. Customization is available through the lists (A) on the left side of the window. Features of the chosen list appear as icons in the right side of the window (B).

You can add features by dragging the desired icon up into the Toolbar. You can remove features by dragging their icons out of the Toolbar.

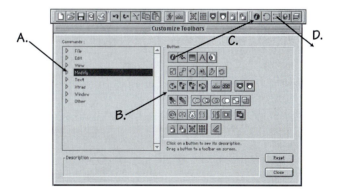

A. Menus are selected in this list
B. The menu items are represented by icons
C. Icons are dragged to add to Toolbar
D. Toolbar items are removed by dragging icon out

If you do not have **Preferences->Panels->Show Tool Tips** selected, you can click on the icon and the menu list will go to this name. Also, the function of the icon will appear at the bottom under Description.

Customizing the Main Toolbar

1. Choose **File->New** to create a new document.

2. Choose **File->Preferences->Panels** and make certain that **Show Tool Tips** is clicked.

3. If the Main Toolbar is not on screen, choose **Window->Toolbars->Main**.

4. Display the customizing dialog box with **Window->Toolbars->Customize**.

5. In the left side of the window you will see the menu names. Click on any of these menu names to see the icons representing the features in the menu that appear on the right side.

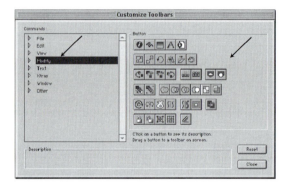

6. Click on the name **Other** in the list of menus; this is for functions other than those found in the menus ranging from the pop-up menus at the bottom of the document screen to tools found in the Toolbox. Touch the Pointer tool to the first icon at the top and leave it there a few seconds. A Tool Tip will pop out, identifying the icon.

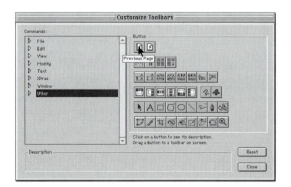

44   CHAPTER 3/THE FREEHAND WORKING ENVIRONMENT

7. As you can see, the Main Toolbar is full of icons. To remove any icon from a Toolbar, you simply click and drag it out of the Toolbar. Do this now. Click on the Find Graphics icon and drag it out of the Toolbar. Release the mouse button: it is no longer in the Toolbar.

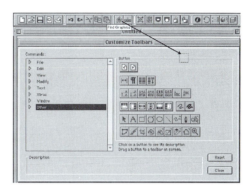

8. Click on the **Edit** menu name in the left side list. In the second row of icons, touch (don't click) the Pointer tool to the fourth icon to see its name, Paste in Front. Drag this icon up to the Toolbar to the left of the icon with the padlock symbol (Lock).

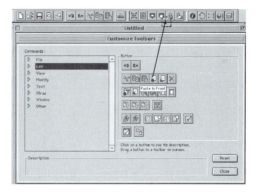

9. Click on the **View** menu name in the list. Click and drag the 400% View icon up to be next to the Lock icon.

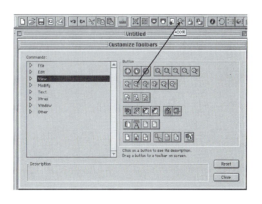

Preferences->Panel->Show Tool Tips must be selected if you want to know the names or functions of icons in the Toolbars.

10. You have now received an introduction to customizing the Toolbars. Drag the Paste in Front and 400% View icons out of the Toolbar to return the Main Toolbar to it original state. From the View list, drag **Find Graphics** back into the toolbar. **Close** the document without saving.

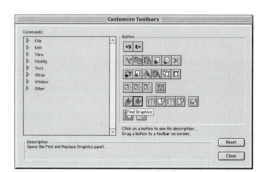

The keyboard shortcuts to access the panels are:

Layers:
Command-6 (Macintosh) or Control-6 (Windows).

Styles:
Command-3 (Macintosh) or Control-3 (Windows).

Color List:
Command-9 (Macintosh) or Control-9 (Windows).

Color Mixer:
Shift-Command-C (Macintosh) or Shift-Control-9 (Windows).

Tints:
Shift-Command-Z (Macintosh) or Shift-Control-3 (Windows).

Halftones:
Command-H (Macintosh) or Control-H (Windows).

Align:
Option-Command-A (Macintosh) or Alt-Control-A (Windows).

Transform:
Command-M (Macintosh) or Control-M (Windows).

Panels

Panels float on top of the pasteboard and can be dragged and placed anywhere on your screen. Panels are customizable tabbed windows that can be moved, separated, or combined by dragging their tabs.

All panels can be moved and hidden. To hide all panels, choose **View->Panels** or press F12. Press F12 to show all the panels again.

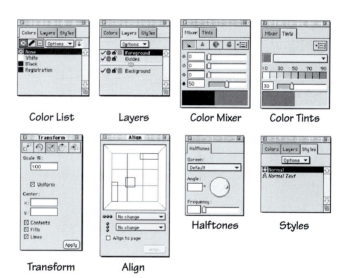

- **Color List** — is the main color palette where colors are accessed. The Options pop up menu manages colors and external libraries of color.

- **Layers** — is where layers are created, managed, and maneuvered for increasing the productivity of your design.

- **Color Mixer** — creates colors for storage in the Color List.

- **Color Tints** — creates tint percentages of existing colors and stores them separately in the Color List.

- **Transform** — is used to access the transformation tool dialog boxes.

- **Align** — is where selected objects are aligned and distributed.

- **Halftones** — control the resolution and halftone screens of raster images.

- **Styles** — holds text styles that you create and store.

Inspectors

Most tasks that you perform in Freehand involve the use of the Inspector panels. The Inspector is a multi-panel, floating control center from which you select a particular Inspector panel by clicking on the panel's tab.

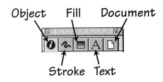

When an Inspector tab is clicked, one of the following Inspectors appears:

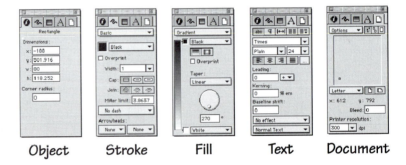

The keyboard shortcuts to access the Inspectors are:

Object Inspector:
Command-I (Macintosh) or Control-I (Windows).

Stroke Inspector:
Option-Command-L (Macintosh) or Alt-Control-L (Windows).

Fill Inspector:
Option-Command-F (Macintosh) or Alt-Control-F (Windows).

Text Inspector:
Command-T (Macintosh) or Control-T (Windows).

Document Inspector:
Option-Command-D (Macintosh) or Alt-Control-D (Windows).

- **Object Inspector** — tells what type of object is selected, and gives dimensions, x,y locations, and closes paths.

- **Stroke Inspector** — applies colors and special visual effects, assigns thickness to the selected path, and creates arrowheads and dashed lines.

- **Fill Inspector** — applies colors and special visual effects, and creates and alters gradients.

- **Text Inspector** — assigns typographic settings to selected text, from fonts, size, leading, and has four other windows that apply settings for paragraph, horizontal spacing, rows and columns, and copy fitting.

- **Document Inspector** — lets you control the pages of a document, such as its quantity, size, orientation, bleed, and printer resolution.

FreeHand Menus

You have seen Toolbars, Panels, and Inspectors and observed their uses and customizing qualities. Some of these functions possess a few features that are not available in a menu, such as setting the Stroke width of a path, which can only be performed in the Stroke Inspector.

Other than these few exceptions, many of the panel and Toolbar features are found in corresponding menus. For example, if you want to apply a font, point size, alignment, or other specifications, you could easily pull down the Text menu and find many text features.

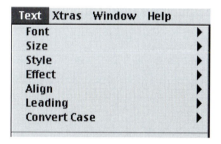

Submenus

Some menu selections have a triangle to the right of its name indicating that there are more available options. When the triangle is selected, its submenu appears. You can then drag the mouse into this menu to make a selection.

Viewing Modes

FreeHand allows you to see your documents and designs in a variety of different views. Aside from simple page magnification, there are: the View menu selections, four viewing modes, Custom Views, and New Window.

If Fast Preview is still taking too long to paint the screen, going to Keyline mode will allow you to move objects around faster without the repainting that occurs in Preview mode.

The four viewing modes are the most important for seeing what you are designing, making certain that you are achieving the colors and effects you desire, and to give you a reasonable idea of how the job will look when printed. They are:

- Preview
- Fast Preview
- Keyline
- Fast Keyline

View Pop-up Menus

The view pop-up menu in the lower part of the document window accesses the four viewing modes. The different view modes affect the on screen representation of your artwork, not data or print quality.

Preview

When you work in Preview mode, the display shows you most all Fills as they will look when sent to the printer. The only exceptions to this are the PostScript Fills and Strokes that must be printed for viewing.

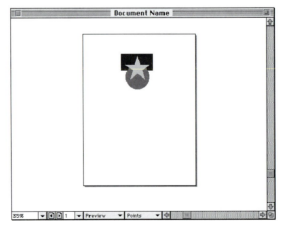

Image in Document

The Printed Page

Fast Preview

Certain features, such as Gradients, can take a lot of time to paint on the screen, especially if there are many objects colored with these features. To expedite seeing the colored image, and not having to wait as the screen paints, FreeHand has added the Fast Preview.

Fast Preview works on Gradients, which will be covered in a later chapter. But be aware that Fast Preview affects how Gradients are viewed on screen to decrease the time it takes for the screen to redraw when changed.

Preview mode

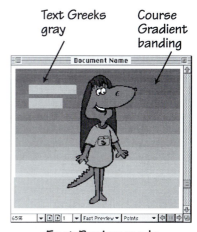
Fast Preview mode

Press Command-K (Macintosh) or Control-K (Windows) to switch between Preview and Keyline views.

Keyline View

It is possible to see a path's anchor points and segments in Preview mode, but for fine-tuning of paths it is best to view them in Keyline mode. This viewing mode very clearly shows the points and segments without their fills or strokes.

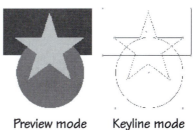
Preview mode   Keyline mode

The ability to isolate individual aspects in a complex drawing is very important. You can see the constructing anchor point and segments of the paths, and click on them easily in Keyline mode when they might be obscured in Preview.

The keyboard shortcut for switching from Preview or Keyline mode is Command-K (Macintosh) or Control-K (Windows).

The Plus (+) and Minus (-) symbols can be toggled by pressing the Option (Macintosh) or Alt (Windows) key when using the Magnification tool.

Fast Keyline

Fast Keyline shows grayed (*greeked*) text below 50 points.

Keyline mode   Fast Keyline mode

Using the Four Viewing Modes

1. **Open** the file **SF-Intro Freehand->Preview.FH8**.

2. When first opened, the document will be in Preview mode.

3. Use the Viewing pop-up menu at the bottom of the screen to navigate to Fast Preview.

4. What changes did you see? Can you read the headline type? What about the Gradient background?

5. Go back to Preview mode. Does it look better?

6. Select Keyline mode in the pop-up menu.

7. Now you have a better look at the creating paths, but what happened to the colors? In Keyline mode you will never see colors of any kind. This is a look at the raw structure of anchor points and segments.

8. In the pop-up menu, go to Fast Keylinc. What changes did you see take place?

9. Return to Keyline mode, observe the images, then switch to Fast Keyline.

10. Use the pop up menu to select Preview mode. You have now experienced the four main viewing modes of FreeHand.

11. **Close** the document without saving.

Magnification Tool

The Magnification tool enlarges (plus sign) or reduces (negative sign) the view of your artwork on the page. Specific objects or locations can be isolated and magnified by dragging a *marquee* around the object.

A marquee is the visual representation of a selection, represented by a dashed line.

Press Command (Macintosh) or Control (Windows) plus one of the following numbers to zoom in or out:

5	50%
1	100%
2	200%
4	400%
8	800%
0	fit in window

Using the Magnification Tool

1. Select **File->New** to create a new document.

2. With the Magnification tool, click on the page. Observe how the view enlarged; look at the magnification percentage in the lower left corner of the document to see how much it has enlarged.

3. Hold the Option (Macintosh) or Alt (Windows) key so that the magnifying tool has a negative (–) symbol in it and click again; the view will reduce in size. Observe its percentage in the lower left.

4. Drag a marquee around the upper left corner of the page. It will zoom up to an enlarged view. What was its enlarging percentage?

5. Hold the Option (Macintosh) or Alt (Windows) key and drag another marquee around the page corner. The view will reduce in size. Observe its percentage in the lower left.

6. You have now seen the various uses of the Magnification tool and how it works.

7. **Close** the document without saving.

Custom Views

You can create a Custom View in the View menu if there are certain locations or magnifications of a document that you access often. When accessed, custom views go instantly to this created view when needed, rather than clicking the Magnifying tool and repositioning the screen each time.

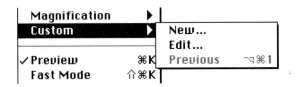

Creating Custom Views

The procedure to create a Custom View is simple enough. After you've arranged the document window to a view you like, choose **View-> Custom->New**.

The **New View** window appears in which you can name the view appropriately for the view's function.

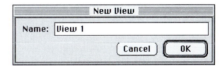

The advantage to this feature is that regardless of the magnification percentage or the location of the document on which you are working, you will instantly be taken to that exact location and viewing percentage if you choose **View ->Custom** and select the named view.

You can create multiple views and select them this way at any time.

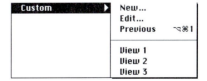

Whether you apply a Custom View to a New Window, or just use Magnification tools to zoom in to a location, you can have several of these windows on screen for design purposes.

Editing Custom Views

There might be times that you want the custom view to be modified slightly so you can work or see the design better. This is done by going to the view in the **View->Custom** menu. For example, we will go to View 2.

You then would rearrange the screen to your new desired view. Then, **View->Custom->Edit** would be selected. The **Edit Views** dialog box would appear. The **View 2** would be clicked on in the view list, and **Redefine** clicked, then **OK**. After this modification, **View 2** would be set to your new changes.

Deleting Custom Views

The **Edit Views** dialog box is also used to delete any views you do not want. You do not need to go to the custom view before accessing the dialog box; you would merely go to the **Edit Views** dialog box, select the view in the list you no longer want, and click Delete, then **OK**.

Creating, Modifying, and Deleting Custom Views

1. Open the file **SF->Intro Freehand->Custom Views.FH8**.

56 Chapter 3/The FreeHand Working Environment

2. Use the Magnifying tool to draw a marquee around the large top star to zoom in on it.

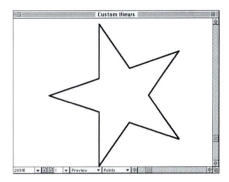

3. Select **View->Custom->New**, and in the New View window, name the view "Stars Closeup" and click **OK**.

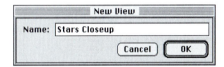

4. Select the Magnification pop-up menu at the lower left of the screen and set the view for 13%.

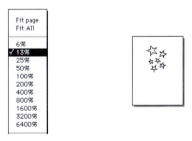

5. Select **View->Custom->New** and name this view "Stars 13%". Click **OK**.

6. Use the Magnification pop-up menu to go to 50% view.

7. Go to **View->Custom** and select the **Star Closeup** view.

8. What do you see on the screen? Haven't you seen this view before?

9. Select **View->Custom** and select the **Stars 13%** view. Now what do you see on screen?

10. You can make as many Custom Views as you want, but your document will only show one view at a time. If you need to see multiple views at the same time, you must use New Window.

11. **Close** the document without saving.

New Window

If you use Custom views, you can only see one custom view at a time. The New Window feature allows you to create other view windows of the same document and assign one of the custom views to each. You can then view the same document in many different perspectives on screen at the same time.

New Window, though, is not dependent upon Custom Views. Each of the New Window views appears in a different document window, but is a representation of the original document. Any changes made to these extra viewing window objects will affect the actual document.

In this example, three new windows were created and zoomed to different viewing levels. Notice that they are named appropriately. The original document will have a "1" after its name. The second window has a "2", and so on.

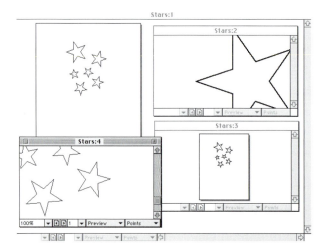

Creating New Windows is convenient when you want to see the same document in both Preview and Keyline mode at the same time.

If you have several new windows active, and they get lost behind other document windows, it is simple to access them. Select the **Window** menu and the active new windows will be listed for selecting.

Managing New Windows

1. Select **New->Open** and open **SF->Intro Freehand->Custom Views.FH8**.

2. From the **Window** menu choose **New Window**. A new window representing this same document will appear. Notice that it completely covers the original window.

3. With the Magnification pop-up menu go to 25% view. Resize the window down to a smaller size and move it to the upper right corner of the first window.

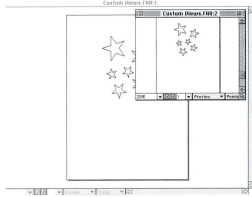

CHAPTER 3/THE FREEHAND WORKING ENVIRONMENT

4. From the **Window** menu select **New Window** again. A new window will appear, but it covers the second window. New windows always appear in front of the active window, and it will always be the same size as the source window.

5. This is New Window "3". Drag it down under number 2 and use the Magnification pop up menu to go to 200% screen view.

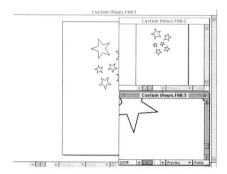

6. Select **Window->New Window** again. The new window will appear in front of window 3. Drag new window 4 over to the left. Use the Magnification pop-up menu to go to 50% screen view. Also, use the Viewing pop-up menu to go to Keyline view.

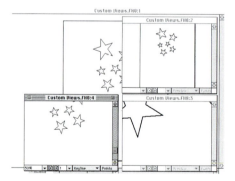

7. You have now created three different windows of the same document, all viewed at the same time. Each window shows a completely different display of the same document.

8. **Close** the document without saving.

Chapter 4

Drawing Basics

Chapter Objective:

Learning more about drawing basics briefly covered in Chapter 3, and expand the material to cover most aspects of Freehand illustration techniques. In Chapter 4, you will:

- Learn the fundamentals to create, edit, and compose basic shapes — the first step in drawing with Freehand.
- Learn about primitive shapes, the most basic shapes used in commercial art, design, printing, or advertising.
- Understand how your artwork can exist on the many different planes of layers, and what objects you can place in layers.
- Learn how to create a closed path with straight lines and curves.
- Learn how to use the Line tool, where to access it, and its many features.
- Learn about using the two movement methods.
- Learn about paths and path segments.
- Understand to fill closed paths with a wide variety of styles.
- Understand about strokes and how to alter them.
- Learn to use the Object Inspector.
- Learn how to draw curves and straight lines.

Projects to be Completed:

- **Steaming Coffee**
- Last Mango Cafe Logo
- Last Mango Business Cards
- Java Jungle
- Coffee Du Jour Ad
- Tropical Fish Art
- Ball & Mirror
- Joker's Wild
- Tropical Treasure Logo
- Tropical Treasure Mailer
- Grocery Ad

Drawing Basics

Now that you know how to work with Freehand, we can finally start drawing something. This section teaches you how to create basic shapes, how to edit them, and how they are composed.

Primitive Shapes

The most basic shapes used in commercial art, design, printing, or advertising are known as "primitive" shapes. They are the easiest to draw, and are sometimes taken for granted.

For instance, you might have created an ad that needs a border. If you had to do this by hand with a ruler, you would have to do a lot of measuring, mark corner points, then draw each line separately and move the page around to make certain that you are drawing accurately. All this for a simple border?

With FreeHand, your ad would already be laid out using the Page Rulers. You would simply select the Rectangle tool, begin dragging from the upper left corner, and release the mouse when the cursor reached the bottom right corner of the ad.

There are three tools in the Toolbox that draw primitive shapes by merely dragging the tool cursor on the page. They are the:

- Rectangle tool
- Ellipse tool
- Polygon tool

The Rectangle Tool

The Rectangle tool draws either one of two shapes:

- **Rectangle**

Press the number keys 1, 2, or 3 (you can use the number keys across the top of the keyboard or the ones on the keypad) to quickly select these tools. Press other numbers to see which tools get selected.

These tools will begin drawing from the center if you hold the Option (Macintosh) or Alt (Windows) key before you start to draw.

The Corner radius increments you apply will be set in the Units of measurement applied in the pop-up status bar.

- **Square** — created when you hold the Shift key while drawing the object.

Rounded Corners

If you double-click on the Rectangle tool icon in the Toolbox, you will see a dialog box where you can customize the corner radius of the drawn object.

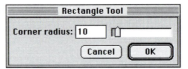

When you set the roundness of the corner radius, the tool will draw objects with this setting, and do so until you change the dialog box again.

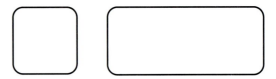

The Ellipse Tool

The Ellipse tool draws shapes that fall into two categories are:

- **Ellipse**

- **Circle** — created when you hold the Shift key while drawing the object.

64   Chapter 4/Drawing Basics

The Polygon Tool

The Polygon tool lets you draw a variety of shapes based upon geometric polygons.

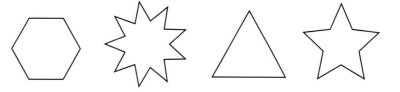

Double-clicking on the Polygon tool in the Toolbox shows the Polygon control dialog:

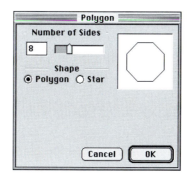 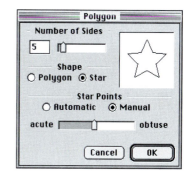

You can experiment with these settings to draw many different shapes.

The Primitive Shape Drawing Tools

1. Choose **File->New** to create a new document.

2. At the top of the Toolbox, below the Pointer tool, are a variety of drawing tools that produce paths and objects using different techniques.

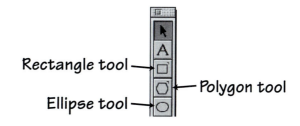

Holding the Shift key while using the Polygon tool will constrain the polygon in increments of 15 degrees.

3. Click on the Rectangle tool. Click and drag the crosshair cursor on the document page to draw a rectangle. Draw another rectangle on the page, but this time hold the Shift key as you drag. This will make it a square. Hold the Option (Macintosh) or Alt (Windows) key to draw the rectangle/square from the center outward.

4. Click on the next tool, which is the Polygon tool. Click-drag the cursor across the page, which draws an unconstrained ploygon. Draw another polygon, holding the Shift key to constrain the image.

5. Double-click on the Polygon tool in the Toolbox.

6. The Polygon dialog box appears. Set the polygon for Star with 5 points. Click **OK**.

7. Now click-drag the Polygon crosshair across the page and see what sort of star you are creating. Experiment by holding the Shift key to constrain the star as you draw the star shape.

Objects drawn with the Rectangle, Ellipse, or Polygon tools can be originated from the center by holding the Option (Macintosh) or Alt (Windows) key.

8. Click on the next tool in the Toolbox, which is the Ellipse tool.

9. Click-drag the Ellipse crosshair across the page to see the oval shapes that you can create. Add the Option (Macintosh) or Alt (Windows) key to draw the ellipse starting from the center.

10. Draw an ellipse holding the Shift key to constrain it to a circle. Draw another circle from the center.

11. **Close** the document without saving.

Composition of Your Artwork

Your artwork can exist on many different planes called Layers. Within each layer you can have placed images, drawn vector paths, text, and other objects. Most objects in FreeHand are made of points, segments, and fills.

Segments connect points that define an outer border of an object (easily seen in Keyline mode) that can be filled (easily seen in Preview mode) with a multitude of different colors and patterns. All points that make up an object rest on a single layer within FreeHand.

FreeHand uses mathematical equations to place the object at the specified location. This location is determined by its Cartesian coordinate (x,y). This x and y can be anywhere on the 222-inch by 222-inch pasteboard. The measurement system used is the system you choose from the Units pop-up menu.

Points

As previously mentioned, all objects contain points. These individual points determine the boundaries of an object.

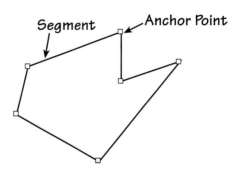

There are three types of points: a Corner point, a Curve point, and a Connector point:

You place points by drawing with the various tools in FreeHand. Each tool results in different objects:

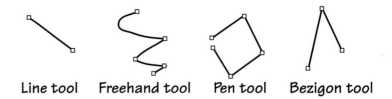

Segments

When you connect two points, a segment occurs. Segments are defined by the relationship between two points. There are only two types of segments: the straight segment, and the curved segment. In FreeHand, segments are called paths.

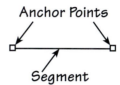

An object can be considered either open or closed. If an object is open, there is not a common beginning and end point. An example of an open path would be a straight line. When an object is closed there is a common beginning and end point. Fills can only be applied to a closed path.

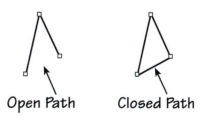

Fills

The third component of an object is its fill. Fills are set from the Fill Inspector. There are many types of fills that can be applied. Fills are only visible when in a Preview mode.

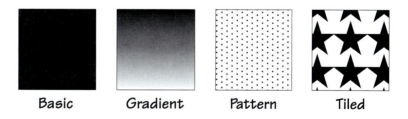

The Pointer Tool and Object Inspector

The Pointer tool and the Object Inspector work hand in hand. When an object is selected with the Pointer, its data is displayed in the Object Inspector.

The Pointer tool can be toggled on when using other tools by pressing the Command key (Macintosh) or Control key (Windows).

Pointer Tool

The Pointer tool is used to select and/or drag objects. To select something, click the pointer on a path. You can select multiple objects by drawing a selection *marquee* around the objects.

Object Inspector

Path information is shown in the Object Inspector, where you can make alterations. The Object Inspector shows the object type, dimensions, point types, number of points, and open/closed path status.

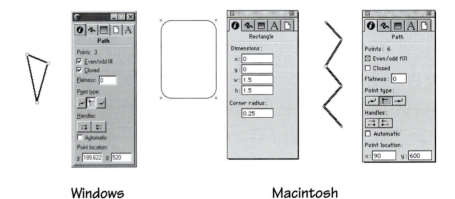

Windows   Macintosh

Using the Pointer Tool

1. Open the file **SF-Intro Freehand Pointer->Tool.FH8**.

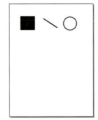

2. Select **Window->Inspector->Object** to access the Object Inspector.

3. With the Pointer tool, click on the black square. The Object Inspector displays the object's coordinates, width, and height.

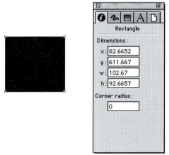

The keyboard shortcut to the Object Inspector is Command-I (Macintosh) or Control-I (Windows).

4. Click on the black square and hold the mouse button down, without moving, until the cursor becomes a cross with arrowheads.

5. Move the square slightly to the left. Observe how the coordinates change in the Object Inspector.

6. Click on the middle object — the single line. See how different its information is in the Object Inspector. Remember, the path is not closed.

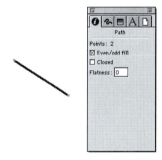

7. With the Pointer tool, draw a marquee around this middle object.

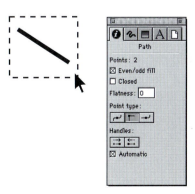

CHAPTER 4/DRAWING BASICS

71

8. Click on the circle object. Observe how similar its information is to the square; however, circles do not have a corner radius.

9. You have now seen how the Pointer tool and the Object Inspector can show you information about objects that would not readily be visible. You will learn to apply changes in upcoming exercises.

10. Keep the document open for the next exercise.

Moving Objects with the Pointer Tool

There are two ways to select and move objects with the Pointer tool. They are very different in appearance, and give you more control over positioning the object when you move it. The two methods are:

- Click-hold mouse on object

- Quickly moving the Bounding Box

The Click-Hold Method

When you click on an object without moving it and hold the mouse button down for a few seconds, the cursor turns into a cross with arrowheads.

The object is ready to relocate, and the advantage to this method is that you can see the object as you move it.

In this example, the circle was clicked and held until the cross appeared (a), then the circle was moved (b).

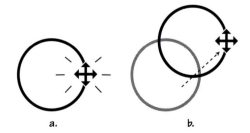

The Quick-move Method

Every object or group of objects has a *Bounding Box*. The Bounding Box shows the outer perimeter of the objects, but it doesn't appear until you move the object with the quick-move method.

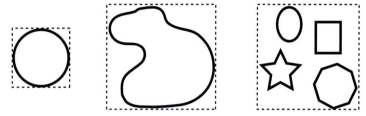

Bounding Boxes of various objects

The secret to moving objects and seeing only their Bounding Box is tricky. You must be comfortable with using a mouse. The idea is to begin the move as soon as you click on the object in one sweeping movement.

When you succeed in selecting the object this way, you will only see its Bounding Box, not the paths of the object. This is used mostly for more precision alignment. When the edge of the Bounding Box touches a target path or guide, you know the object's extreme dimensions are in place.

In this example, the circle was quickly clicked on and moved in one sweep. The cursor remained a Pointer arrow, and the moving object became the Bounding Box. When the mouse is released, the object will be moved.

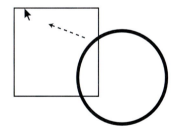

CHAPTER 4/DRAWING BASICS

Using the Two Movement Methods

1. Continue working in the open Pointer Tool document.

2. Click on the black square with the Pointer tool but do not move it. Hold the mouse button down for a few seconds and you will see the cursor turn into the cross with arrowheads.

3. Continue holding the mouse button and move the square around on the page. Drag the square over the other two objects on the page to see how the dragged image alters when it touches other objects. End this move with the square under the line and the circle. Release the mouse button.

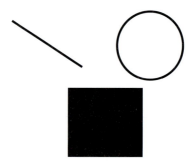

4. Click-hold on the square again and move it toward the circle. Notice how the original image remains as you move the object. Also notice the visual effects seen on screen as the various objects touch and overlap.

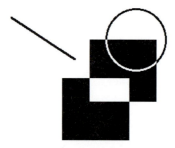

5. Release the mouse and select **Edit->Undo**.

6. With the Pointer tool, perform a quick select-move on the line object; the Bounding Box appears as the moved object. Release the mouse to see how the line was moved. Select **Edit->Undo**.

7. Quickly select-move the circle so that you see only its Bounding Box. Move this around on the page and over other objects to see how the appearances do not change.

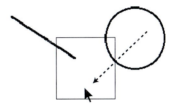

8. Release the mouse.

9. You have now experienced and observed the two methods of using the Pointer tool to move objects.

10. **Close** the document without saving.

Using the Line Drawing Tools

A simple way to think of drawing with the Pen tool is as a game of connect-the-dots. First, you click to create your first Anchor Point (first dot). You then select where you want the next point to be and click again. When the second point is made, FreeHand connects the points with a line segment. This is called a *path*. As mentioned earlier, a path can be lines, curves, or a combination of both. You will be working with creating curves in the next section.

Drawing Lines

1. Select **File->New** to create a new document.

2. Click on the Line tool.

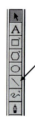

3. Click and drag a line to the length you desire and release the mouse. Drag the crosshair at an angle to draw a single line. By holding the Shift key, the line will be constrained to a 45° angle as you drag.

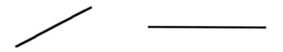

4. Click on the next tool, which is the Freehand tool. Using this tool is like drawing with a pencil, totally unrestricted, and cannot be constrained with the Shift key.

   With the Freehand tool selected, click-drag it onto the page to experiment with its drawing technique.

5. The next tool in the Toolbox is the Pen tool. Make single clicks with this tool in a zigzag pattern. This is an open path. Deselect the path. With the Pen tool, click three times to create a triangle, making a fourth and final click on the first point made. This last click will close the path.

6. The next drawing tool in the Toolbox (after the Freeform tool) is the Bezigon tool. This tool's technique is to click with it the same way you clicked the Pen tool. It can create both open and closed paths but will not draw curves like the Pen tool. It is also very similar to the Line tool, creating straight lines. If you hold the Shift key while clicking, it will constrain the lines. Experiment with the Bezigon tool, creating a variety of shapes.

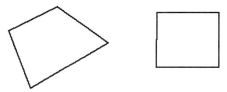

7. You have now been introduced to the drawing tools in FreeHand. Take time to experiment with these tools.

8. **Close** the document without saving.

Curve Basics

You use the pen tool to draw curves as well as straight lines, but the big difference, as the saying goes, is all in the wrist. Curves are created when you click to create a new anchor point and drag the mouse to "pull" curve handles out of the point. The acuity and direction of the curve depends upon how you move the curve handles. Curves drawn with the Pen are mathematically represented as *Bézier* ("bez-yay") curves, named after the French mathematician Pierre Bézier, who developed them for automobile design.

Curve, Corner, and Connector Points

FreeHand can create three different types of points: Curve Points, Corner Points, and Connector Points.

- **Curve Points** — drawn by click-dragging the Pen tool in the direction of the curve, and identified by hollow circles when selected.

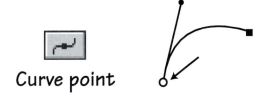

Curve point

It's a good idea to have Smart Cursors selected in **Preferences->General**. With this option on you can observe the crosshair when it touches the point where the path began. When the path touches, the small square dot will appear on the crosshair.

- **Corner Points** — created by clicking (do not drag) the Pen tool on the page, and identified by hollow squares when selected.

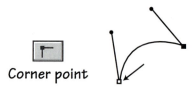

- **Connector Points** — creates transitions between curved and straight path segments, identified by hollow triangles when selected.

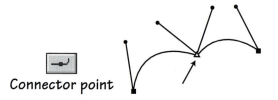

Drawing Curves

1. Create a **New** FreeHand document. Select the Pen tool and click-drag it to create an anchor point.

2. Move the mouse to the right. Hold the Shift key (to constrain) and single-click (don't drag). Click-hold on this second point and drag a control handle downward to the right. Release the mouse. Move the Pen tool crosshair to the right, then single-click a third point. Press the Tab key to deselect. You should have an object looking something like this:

3. With the Pointer tool, click on the path to select it, then click directly on the second point; its control handle will appear. Drag the handle so that the curve bends downward. Experiment with moving the handle to see how it affects the curve of the segment.

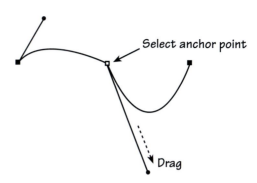

4. With the Pointer tool, click on the first point drawn; its control handle will appear. Drag the handle so that the curve bends upward, making the curve uplift to make a continuity of the curve from the other segment. Experiment with moving the handle to see how it affects the curve of the segment. You should have a curving object that looks similar to this:

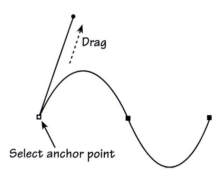

5. You have now had an opportunity to draw and alter curving segments.

6. **Close** the document without saving.

Creating Consecutive Curved Lines

1. In the **File** menu, select **New** to create a new document.

2. Select the Pen tool and click-drag the crosshair on the page, pulling out direction handles. Release the mouse button.

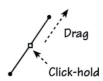

Move the crosshair to the right and click-drag direction handles on this point. Release the mouse button.

Move the mouse to the right and click-drag direction handles on this point. Release the mouse button.

Move the mouse to the right and click-drag direction handles on this point. Release the mouse button. Move the crosshair to the right and make one final click. Select the Pointer tool for modifying the curves.

3. Each anchor point has direction handles that allow you to change the curves by moving them around. Select the different points and their handles. Pull and rotate the handles to see how the curves respond. When finished, delete the path.

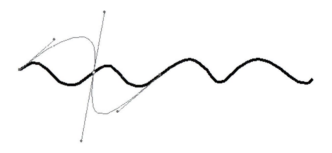

4. Select the Pen tool to create a new path. Click-drag the crosshair on the page to make the beginning point. Release the mouse. Move the crosshair to the right and, holding the Shift key to constrain, single-click the second anchor point.

5. Click-drag the crosshair on the endpoint you just made. This will continue the selected path. You will see a direction hand that will extend out of the clicked anchor point. Release the mouse.

   The next click will make a curving segment. Move the mouse slightly to the right, hold the Shift key and single-click an endpoint.

6. With the Pointer tool, click the middle anchor point and drag its direction handle upward.

7. With the Pointer tool, click the first anchor point and drag its direction handle upward.

   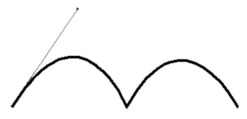

8. You have now created one path with two independent curves. When their direction handles are moved, they do not affect the adjoining curve.

9. **Close** the document without saving.

Combining Straight Lines with Curves

Many times, you'll want to create artwork that contains both straight lines and curves. This is easy to do by using Freehand's ability to constrain an anchor point's curve handles to zero, 45, 90, or 180°.

Creating a Closed Path with Straight Lines and Curves

1. Create a **New** FreeHand document.

2. With the Pen tool, single-click on the page to establish a beginning point. Move the mouse up a ½ inch, then, holding the Shift key to constrain to a straight line, click again.

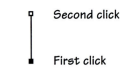

3. Move your mouse up and to the left of the second point. Click-drag upward to create a curve point.

4. Move the mouse to the right, past the straight segment. Click and drag again to create the fourth point.

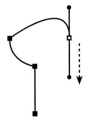

5. Move down and left, next to the second point you drew, and single-click.

6. You need one last point. To draw this, move down, level with the first point, and click again while holding the Shift key.

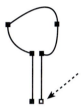

7. To finish your object, click the cursor on the first point you clicked with the Pen tool. You have now created a closed object that can be filled. Click on the curve points to access their control handles and fine-tune the object to look more rounded, as if it were an abstract tree to be used in an illustration or architectural design.

 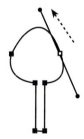

8. **Close** the document without saving.

Complete Project A: Steaming Coffee

Notes:

Chapter 5

Creating and Editing Text

Chapter Objective:

To gain an understanding of how to work with text in FreeHand. In Chapter 5, you will:

- Begin to understand Typography, and how to kern and perform leading — two of the most important functions used in design.
- Begin creating and formatting text as both an indepent design, or for incorporation into a design complete with graphics and other elements.
- Learn about the text tool and the two types of text containers.
- Learn the importance of the Text Inspector's five sub-panels.
- Learn how to work with text outlines to create distinctive special effects such as headline.
- Import text from Freehand, complete with the Typography and effects you have created.
- Understand how to create tints of colors.
- Learn about several typographic special effects.
- Understand how to convert selected text into editable paths.
- Learn how to import text from word processing files.
- Learn how to link one text container to another.

Projects to be Completed:

- Steaming Coffee
- **Last Mango Cafe Logo**
- Last Mango Business Cards
- Java Jungle
- Coffee Du Jour Ad
- Tropical Fish Art
- Ball & Mirror
- Joker's Wild
- Tropical Treasure Logo
- Tropical Treasure Mailer
- Grocery Ad

Creating and Editing Text

FreeHand offers sophisticated typographic features. Because of the small increments of size and letter spacing available, words and text lines can be adjusted to fit practically any layout. Text can be created in two ways:

- **Point text** — created by clicking the Text tool cursor on the page. This type of container has no defined right margin. As long as you continue to type, the container will get wider and wider and you will need to press Return or Enter to create lines of type. However you use the Pointer tool to adjust the size and shape of the container, the text will not wrap. This is also known as an auto-expanding text box.

- **Area Text** — created by dragging the Text tool cursor onto the page, creating a text block of a finite size. An Area text block can be resized to smaller or larger dimensions by moving the corner handles of the block with the Pointer tool. This is the type of text container you should create if you have a lot of text and require a right margin from which to wrap the text.

There are two ways to select the text in text blocks:

- With the Text tool cursor (I-beam)

- With the Pointer tool

The Text Tool Cursor

The Text tool cursor is an I-beam with which you can highlight text to isolate letters, words, or paragraphs. Type that is highlighted with this cursor can have any text attributes applied. When you want to see the Text Ruler, you must click in the text block with this tool cursor.

The Text Ruler is visible when the Text tool cursor is clicked inside the Text Block.

The Text tool cursor can highlight isolated letters and words in the text.

Selecting with the Pointer Tool

The Pointer tool can select the entire text block. This is also the only way to select and apply attributes to several text blocks at once. When the Pointer tool is used to select a text block, all text is affected by changes. Use the Pointer tool on the handles of an Area text block to resize it.

The Link box can flow text into other text blocks.

The Text Inspector

Once text has been selected, its attributes can be modified in the Text Inspector. You make choices for applying Size, Font, etc., to the text.

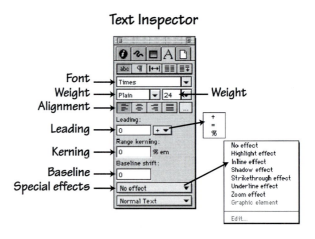

You can further adjust the formatting of type with the Text Inspector. From alignment and indentations to word and letter spacing, you can adjust settings to make type appear the way you want. Across the top of the Text Inspector are five icons that, when clicked, give you more panels in which to make typographic changes.

The icons in the Text Inspector are:

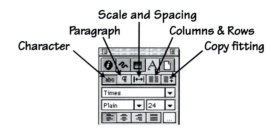

Character — where you choose a type font, the weight (regular, plain, medium, bold), the size (measured in points), alignment, leading, kerning, and special effects.

Paragraph — allows you to make setting changes to the paragraph.

Horizontal Scale — changes the horizontal width of the letters, and adds/subtracts spacing between letters and words.

Columns & Rows — configures the selected text block into columns or rows.

Copy Fitting — allows you to adjust the text to fit specific layout dimensions of the page.

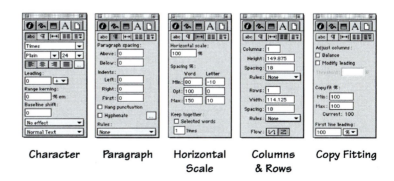

Character   Paragraph   Horizontal Scale   Columns & Rows   Copy Fitting

The keyboard shortcut to increase/decrease the point size is:

Macintosh

Hold the Command-Shift keys then press the Greater Than (>) key to enlarge the size or the Less Than (<) key to reduce the size.

Windows

Hold Control-Alt keys then press the Up Arrow key to enlarge the size or the Down Arrow key to reduce the size.

Typographic Settings

Typography is a very broad subject, but the basics can be used quite proficiently in FreeHand. If you have not studied or had experience with typography, we will give you an overview of what the various terms — such as kerning — mean when setting type.

Point Size

The height of a letter is called the Point Size because it is measured in point increments. Show below is an anatomy of letters in typographic terms:

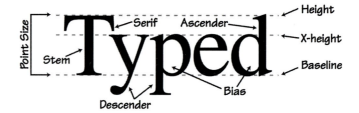

Leading

The spacing between lines of type is called leading. Depending on the font used and its characteristics, as well as the look you are attempting to achieve, the leading can be very tight or very loose.

When you read magazines or books, the standard leading is 2 pts. larger than the point size of the actual type. In other words, if the body text is set for 10 pt., the leading should be set for 12 pt. When handwriting their shorthand notes to specify type settings, typographers will use the slash (/) to divide the point size and the leading. For example, "10/12" means that the text should be set for 10 pt. size over 12 pt. leading.

Here are some samples of leading:

Sirens screamed and emergency lights flashed as firemen arrived on the scene and began unwinding yards of fire hose, donning their gas	Sirens screamed and emergency lights flashed as firemen arrived on the scene and began unwinding yards of fire	Sirens screamed and emergency
10 pt. type 12 pt. leading	9 pt. type 18 pt. leading	18 pt. type 22 pt. leading

Kerning can also be achieved by clicking on the text block with the Pointer tool to see the handles, and dragging on either of the side handles. Dragging wider increases the spacing between letters.

Kerning

Kerning and tracking are the adjustment of spacing between letters. Kerning is the adjustment of spacing between two letters; tracking is the adjustment of space in a range of characters. Positive values increase space between letters; negative values decrease space. All characters can be kerned or tracked, including punctuation.

Sometimes letters do not always fit up to each other aesthetically. This makes readability and attractiveness of the text somewhat unappealing. The answer is to kern the text, either as individual pairs, or applied to a range of text.

Each letter has a width that butts up against other letters.

Kerning tightens the spacing between letters

Kerning can be performed two ways:

- **Manual** — place the text cursor between the two letters or select a range of text and hold the Option (Macintosh) or Control-Alt (Windows) key while pressing the Left or Right Arrow key. The Left Arrow key decreases kerning; the Right Arrow key increases kerning.

- **Text Inspector (Character)** — enter the numeric amount of kerning the letter pair or selected text should receive. Negative numbers decrease kerning; positive numbers increase.

Baseline Shift

Sometimes you might need to adjust the Baseline Shift of a letter or letters, such as in the creation of logos or creative headlines for ads. The shifting adjusts the letter above or below the Baseline.

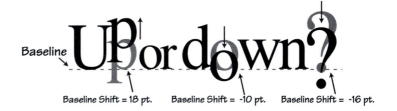
Baseline Shift = 18 pt. Baseline Shift = -10 pt. Baseline Shift = -16 pt.

The keyboard shortcuts for aligning text are to hold Shift-Option-Command (Macintosh) or Shift-Alt-Control (Windows) then adding one of the following alignment keys:

Left = L

Right = R

Center = M

Justified = J

Alignment

Most reading material on the newsstands is aligned left, called "flush left" by typographers. "Ragged Right" is another term meaning the right margin is uneven, or ragged, as opposed to justified type. Justified means that both the left and right margins are flush, or evenly lined.

The Text Inspector shows these icons for you to click to set the text alignment.

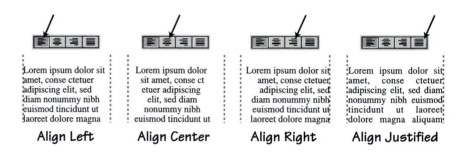

Text Special Effects

At the bottom of the **Text Inspector->Character** window is a pop-up menu that offers special effects to your selected text.

Here are some samples of what the effects look like. You should experiment with this feature to see how all the effects appear. Remember that these special effects work only on type in text format.

If you apply a special effect to text, then convert the text to paths, you will destroy the effect.

CHAPTER 5/CREATING AND EDITING TEXT

Creating and Formatting Text

1. Select **File->New** to create a new document.

2. Select the Text tool in the Toolbox.

3. In the upper left corner of the page, click the Text cursor to create a Point text block. The Text Ruler will appear to show the text container.

4. Type this text:

   "To sit in solemn silence, on a dull, dark dock. Awaiting the sensation of a short, sharp shock."

5. What did you notice? Did the test wrap at any time? If you had continued to type, how wide would the text block become?

Most type fonts have stylized components; for example, bold, italic, or bold italic. Some specialized fonts, such as Zapf Dingbats, Wingdings, Zapf Chancery or display fonts like Adobe Trajan do not contain these styles. Freehand recognizes this, and these style options will be grayed-out in the Text ->Style menu.

6. Click on the text block with the Pointer tool. Where did the Text Ruler go? Use the Pointer tool to move the corner handles of the text block to try to resize it. Did you succeed?

7. Select the Text tool and click after the word "dock." Press Return (Macintosh) or Enter (Windows) to create a line return.

The shortcut to using the Grabber hand is to press the Spacebar. But watch out! You might have text selected, the Text cursor located in a Text block. Then, when you press the Spacebar, you will get unwanted effects, such as deleted text, or a series of empty spaces.

8. Click on the text block with the Pointer tool. Select **Edit->Cut**.

9. Select the Text tool. Click-drag an Area text block that is approximately 3-inches square. Click the Text cursor in the block, then **Edit->Paste**.

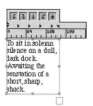

10. Click on the text block with the Pointer tool. In the Text Inspector apply the settings: **Font** = ATC Sands, **Size** = 9 pt., **Leading** = 11 pt. (Fixed "="). Notice how all the text is affected when selected in this manner.

11. Click on the Text tool, then highlight only the words "dull, dark, dock." In the Text Inspector apply these settings: **Font** = ATC Coconuts Extra Bold, **Size** = 12 pt., **Leading** = 14 pt. (Fixed "="). With the Text tool you can isolate words or letters for modification.

12. Click on the text block with the Pointer tool. Click on and drag any of the corner handles to resize the block wider, then taller.

13. Click-hold on the text block with the Pointer tool so that you can move the block to other locations on the page. Move the block around the page.

14. Click on a side handle of the text block and drag it wider. What happened to the spacing of the text? This is another way to manually perform kerning. Select **Edit->Undo**.

15. Click on a side handle of the text block and drag it wider. What was the spacing result? — You increased the letter spacing. Drag again, but hold the Option (Macintosh) or Alt (Windows) key. What was the spacing result? This is how you manually adjust spacing between words.

16. Select the Text tool and click its cursor in the text block. Select **Edit->Select->All**. This is yet another way to select all the text.

17. **Close** the document without saving.

Applying Typographic Settings to Type

1. Select **File->Open** and navigate to **SF-Intro Freehand->Text Inspector Type.FH8**. Set the measuring Units to Points.

2. With the Pointer tool, click on the text block. Select **Window->Inspectors ->Text** to access the Text Inspector.

3. Apply these settings: **Font** = ATC Colada, **Size** = 10 pt., **Leading** = 14.5 pt. (Fixed "="), **Alignment** = Align Left.

"All My Troubles
Seemed So Far Away"
by Dean Bagley

Sirens screamed and emergency lights flashed as firemen arrived on the scene and began unwinding yards of fire hose, donning their gas masks and chopping down a tall fence to get to the blaze. The neighbors who had called them peered over their wooden fences, gaping and pointing at what was surely the most horrifying spectacle ever to appear in their neighborhood.
Their adjoining neighbor, Walter Melon, had created a blazing bonfire in his backyard that was a veritable funeral pyre of books from his library. Self-help books he prized more than anything and read ravenously. And to make this entire scene seem even more like some fire-dance in a voodoo ritual, Walter was dancing around the inferno with a can of barbecue lighter fluid, sprinkling here and there and laughing a maniacal laugh that sent chills through the hearts of onlookers.
His light blue shirt was ripped and totally unbuttoned, stained with dark, hideous blotches. His stained white pants were becoming grayer by the minute from the smoke and ashes, all of which combined to make him look like the lone survivor of an airliner crash.

4. Use the Text tool to highlight the title and author's by-line name.

5. In the Text Inspector, apply these settings: **Font** = ATC Coconuts, **Size** = 14 pt., **Leading** = 18 pt. (fixed "="), **Alignment** = Align Center.

6. With this text still selected, click on the Horizontal Scale icon in the Text Inspector. In the panel, set the Horizontal scale for 120%. Press Return (Macintosh) or Enter (Windows) to apply.

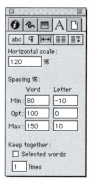

7. Highlight the title and apply these settings: **Size** = 18 pt., **Leading** = 27 pt.

8. Highlight the author's by-line name, then apply a Baseline shift of –10. This will drop this line down without changing the leading.

"All My Troubles
Seemed So Far Away"
by Dean Bagley

9. Now highlight the body text. Click on the Paragraph icon in the Text Inspector. In the Paragraph spacing Above, type 10pt. Go down to Indents and type 10pt. for First. Apply this to the text.

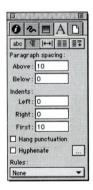

10. The text block should look like this:

"All My Troubles
Seemed So Far Away"
by Dean Bagley

Sirens screamed and emergency lights flashed as firemen arrived on the scene and began unwinding yards of fire hose, donning their gas masks and chopping down a tall fence to get to the blaze. The neighbors who had called them peered over their wooden fences, gaping and pointing at what was surely the most horrifying spectacle ever to appear in their neighborhood.

Their adjoining neighbor, Walter Melon, had created a blazing bonfire in his backyard that was a veritable funeral pyre of books from his library. Self-help books he prized more than anything and read ravenously. And to make this entire scene seem even more like some fire-dance in a voodoo ritual, Walter was dancing around the inferno with a can of barbecue lighter fluid, sprinkling here and there and laughing a maniacal laugh that sent chills through the hearts of onlookers.

His light blue shirt was ripped and totally unbuttoned, stained with dark, hideous blotches. His stained white pants were becoming grayer by the minute from the smoke and ashes, all of which combined to make him look like the lone survivor of an airliner crash.

11. You have now been introduced to basic typesetting as performed in FreeHand's Text Inspector.

12. **Close** the document without saving.

Working with Text Outlines

If you want to get really creative with text, such as making a distinctive headline, you may first want to convert the text to an outline or a set of paths. Some effects like the Transparency Lens won't work on text until it is converted to paths.

You can Fill and Stroke standard text, but you won't be able to use anchor points for stretching, distorting, and curving the outline of the letters in creative ways. Before you can do this, text must be converted to paths by selecting **Text->Convert to Paths**.

Creating Type Outlines

1. Create a **New** document. Click the Text tool cursor on the page to create a text block.

2. On two lines type the words:

    TROPICAL

    TREASURE

3. Highlight the type with the text cursor. Apply these settings in the Text Inspector: **Font** = ATC Jamaica, **Size** = 72 pt., **Leading** = 72 (Fixed "=").

4. Click on the text block with the Pointer tool. In the Text menu, choose the Convert to Paths option; the text letters will become outlines. Select Keyline viewing mode to view the new path outlines.

Remember, the Special Effects found in the Text Inspector work only on type in text format. Once you use these effects on text, and then convert them to outline paths, the Special Effects disappear.

Converting text to outlines is sometimes necessary when you want to achieve certain looks.

TROPICAL TREASURE

5. Click on this object with the Pointer tool. The conversion has automatically grouped all the letters into one object indicated by the four corner handles of the group. Select **Edit->Copy** to duplicate it for later use.

6. Select **Modify->Ungroup**.

7. Even though you ungrouped the object, notice how each word is individually grouped. Select **Modify->Ungroup** again.

8. The letters are now separate objects. Click on any of the various letters to see how their anchor points are visible to work with.

9. With the Pointer tool, click on the letter "T" in TROPICAL; you will see its anchor points. Select any one of the points and drag it to distort the path. Do this to other points of the "T."

10. Click on the "O" in TROPICAL with the Pointer tool. Why don't you see anchor points? — It looks grouped, with corner handles. Certain letters in the alphabet are actually made up of two paths. The internal path is see-through, not white. This is a compound effect called a *composite* path. Letters such as "A, B, D, O, P, Q, and R" possess this internal path. How do you split up the "O" to change it?

11. With the "O" highlighted, select **Modify->Split**. This removes the compounding effect. You can now see both paths.

12. Click on the anchor points of the "O" paths with the Pointer tool to select and distort them.

13. You have now observed the outline paths of text that has been converted. Select **Edit->Select->All** and delete all the paths.

14. Select **Edit->Paste** to paste the original outlines you copied previously.

15. Use the Color List to paint the outines: **Fill** = White, **Stroke** = 1 pt. Black.

16. Keep the document open for the next exercise.

Creating a Drop Shadow to Path Outlines

1. In the open file, select the letter outline group, and select **Edit->Copy**.

2. Select **Edit->Paste Behind** to paste the duplicate behind the group.

3. Once pasted, the duplicate will be the selected object. Press the Right Arrow twice, then the Down Arrow twice.

4. In the Color List, use the Options pop-up menu to access the **Crayons** library. Select Gray and click **OK**. Paint the copy: **Fill** = Gray, **Stroke** = None.

5. You have now created one of the Special Effects in the Text Inspector by using path outlines. Now if someone requires you to give them the job in outline format, you will be able to include your own special effects.

6. **Close** the file without saving.

Importing Text

When putting a job together, there will be times that you will be supplied with text created in other applications and residing in external text files. Text can be imported for use within FreeHand documents. Once imported, you can apply fonts, point sizes, leading, and other text attributes within the FreeHand document.

Importing Text

1. Select **File->New** to create a new document.

2. From the **File** menu select the **Import** option.

3. The Import dialog box allows you to select the file you want.

4. Navigate to the **SF-Intro FreeHand folder** and select the file **Import Text.TXT**. Click **Open**.

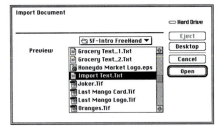

5. This has returned you to the document page. With the Import cursor, draw an area text block that is approximately 5 inches wide x 7 inches high. When you release the mouse, the text will appear in its own text block.

6. Press Command-A (Macintosh) or Control-A (Windows) to **Select->All** of the imported text.

7. Using the **Text Inspector**, apply these settings to the text: **Font** = ATC Colada, **Size** = 10 pt., **Leading** = 12 pt. (Fixed "=").

8. Keep the document open for the next exercise.

Linking Text Blocks

When a text block is not big enough to show all the type, a small box with a dot will appear at the bottom right corner.

This is the *text overflow* indicator, letting you know that more text is in the text box but that there is not enough room to display it. You can choose to enlarge the box or link the text into another text block.

Using Link with Text Blocks

1. In the open document, select the Rectangle tool and draw a rectangle about the same size as the text block. Set the Fill and Stroke of the rectangle to None.

2. With the Pointer tool, select the text block. Click on the overflow box and drag its marker over to touch the empty rectangle.

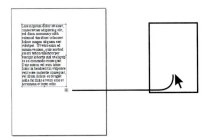

3. The overflow dragging will convert the rectangle into a text block and fill it with more type, continuing the flow.

4. Draw more rectangles and continue to flow the text this way until there are no more overflow boxes.

5. **Close** the file without saving.

Project B: Last Mango Cafe Logo

Chapter 6

Layers, Grids, and Guides

Chapter Objective:

To learn how FreeHand's Layers can help you to organize your document, and how Guides and Grids are a designer's best friend as they help simplify the creation of complex layouts. In Chapter 6, you will:

- Learn about layers — one of FreeHand's most useful design aids and understand the various controls in the Layers panel.
- Learn the importance in how layers are arranged, and the different methods in which they can be arranged and modified.
- Understand how to lock, hide, and otherwise customize layers to suit your personal needs.
- Learn how to reassign objects to other layers — a task frequently necessary for successful and appealing design.
- Learn the importance of guides; how to show and hide guides, create and modify guides, and understand how guides relate to layers.
- Learn to use the Guide Manager to precisely position guides.
- Learn to use and modify the document grid; learn to modify the grid from its plotted and set size.
- Understand how to reset rulers and the zero point.

Projects to be Completed:

- Steaming Coffee
- Last Mango Cafe Logo
- **Last Mango Business Cards**
- Java Jungle
- Coffee Du Jour Ad
- Tropical Fish Art
- Ball & Mirror
- Joker's Wild
- Tropical Treasure Logo
- Tropical Treasure Mailer
- Grocery Ad

Layers, Grids, and Guides

Layers

Layers are one of FreeHand's most useful design aids. Imagine a three-story building, layered vertically. Each floor has its own objects: people, offices, furniture and such, and these are independent of the same things on the other floors. If you tip the building over, the floors are now layered horizontally and everything on each floor is stacked closer to or farther away from what was once the floor (assuming everything and everyone is nailed down).

Layers are conceptually similar. If three layers are used in a document, each layer can have its own objects that can be created, modified, and manipulated independently of objects on other layers.

Layers are created and controlled in the Layers panel, by choosing **Window->Panels->Layers**.

The graphic below shows the controls in the Layers panel:

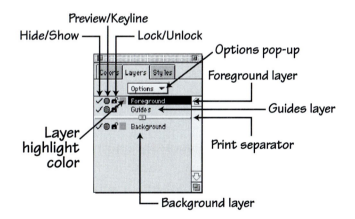

Press Command-6 (Macintosh) or Control-6 (Windows) to show the Layers panel.

The Layers panel is one of FreeHand's most convenient features for controlling objects. You can manipulate locking, hiding, viewing, guides, and templates, all in one panel.

- **Hide/Show** — The check mark icon at the far left of the Layers panel field indicates if the objects on that layer are Shown (visible) or Hidden (invisible). When you click the check mark, it toggles the Hide/Show feature of the layer.

Chapter 6/Layers, Grids, and Guides　　　　　　　　　　　　　　　105

- **Preview/Keyline** — a circle icon that when clicked changes the viewing mode of a layer. To change the view of an individual layer to keyline, change the solid Preview icon to a hollow Keyline icon by clicking once. A layer can be returned to Preview mode again by a single click, returning the icon to a solid circle.

- **Layer hightlight color** — This allows you to change the default selection color for each layer to help differentiate them.

- **Lock/Unlock** — locks a layer from editing functions by clicking the padlock icon. When clicked again, the padlock is open, or unlocked.

- **Options pop-up** — This menu offers several selections to create, delete, duplicate, and/or Hide/Show the layers.

- **Foreground layer** — the default layer created in all new documents.

- **Guides layer** — a default layer that is used to create and manipulate page guides. Any vector path assigned to this layer turns into a guide. Ruler guides are shown, hidden, and locked on this layer.

- **Print separator** — The Separator bar divides the layers into two groups: printing layers (above the bar) and dimmed non-printing layers (below).

- **Background layer** — used to hold objects that you want to appear grayed out for use as templates. Any object, whether vector or raster, will appear dimmed.

New layers automatically appear at the top of the layers list, making it the frontmost layer. You can relocate the new layer by dragging it above or below other layers.

The Layers Options

Use the Options pop-up menu for adding, removing, duplicating, and viewing layers.

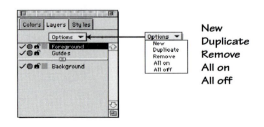

The Options pop-up menu offers these selections:

- **New** — adds a new layer to your document.
- **Duplicate** — duplicates the currently selected layer.
- **Remove** — deletes the current layer and all objects on that layer.
- **All on** — shows all layers.
- **All off** — hides all layers.

Managing Layers

When you begin working in a new document, all objects drawn will be placed on the Foreground Layer. The Foreground Layer is one of the three default layers. When you begin a new document, a Foreground, Background, and Guides Layer are created. All guides are assigned to the Guide layer by default.

As a FreeHand operator you have the ability to change and manipulate these defaults, as well as defining your own working system. You can name and rename a layer at any time, place a layer in any order you want, or view layers as needed. The versatility of the environment is a plus for any situation.

To change the name of a layer, double-click its name. Type a new name, then press Return (Macintosh) or Enter (Windows) to apply the change.

Adding, Removing, and Duplicating Layers

1. Select **File->Open** to open **SF-Intro Freehand->Layers Options.FH8**.

CHAPTER 6/LAYERS, GRIDS, AND GUIDES

2. Press Command-6 (Macintosh) or Control-6 (Windows) to access the Layers panel.

3. The objects, by default, are on the Foreground layer; they need to be organized to be on separate layers.

4. In the Layers Options pop-up menu, select New to create a new layer.

5. Do this two more times to create new layers.

All on and *All off* are useful for hiding/showing all the layers at once without having to click each layer individually.

6. Double-click on Layer-3, rename it "Rectangle", then Return/Enter to apply the change. Double-click on Layer-2 and rename it "Circle", pressing Return/Enter to apply. Double-click on Layer-1 and rename it "Star". Press Return/Enter to apply the change.

7. With the Pointer tool, click on the star that is peeking out from behind the top of the circle on the page. Click on the Star layer in the Layers panel. Click on the circle on the page, then click the Circle layer in the Layers panel. Now click on the rectangle on the page, and click on the Rectangle layer in the Layers panel. Press the Tab key to deselect everything.

8. Click on the Foreground layer, then go to the Layers Option pop-up menu and select Remove to delete the layer.

9. Click on the Rectangle layer, then go to the Layers Option pop-up menu and select Remove to delete the layer. What warning did you get? Click **No** so you don't delete the layer and its object. This is FreeHand's way of watching out for accidental deleting of useful objects.

10. Click on the rectangle on the page and the Rectangle layer in the Layers panel will become highlighted to show that this is the layer it is assigned to. Click on the star and observe the Layers panel change.

11. With the Star layer still highlighted, go to the Layer Options menu and select Duplicate. A new layer appears with the word "copy" in its name. Click on the star on the page and move it off to the right. What do you see? The Duplicate option not only duplicated the Layer, but it made a copy of the object assigned to it.

12. Select **Edit->Undo** twice to undo the move and layer duplication.

13. You have now succeeded in using selections in the Layer Options menu, and observed how they affect the layers and objects in the document.

14. Keep the document open for the next exercise.

Layer Priority

The order in which the names appear in the Layers panel determines which layers are in front of or in back of others. The priority of layers is from the top of the layers list to the bottom. The layer at the top of the list contains the foremost objects. As the layers go down the list, the objects assigned to them are behind the objects belonging to the layers above them. The layer at the bottom of the list contains objects that are behind all others.

In this example the four objects are each assigned to their own layer. At the top of the layer list is the Circle layer. It is in front of the other objects.

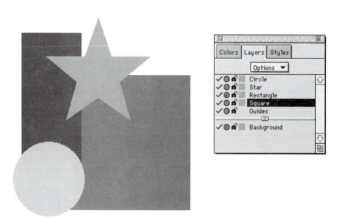

If the Circle layer was dragged down to the bottom of the list, its object, the circle, will be behind the other objects.

If the Square layer was dragged up to the top of the list, its contents would be in front of all the other objects. Notice where the square is now.

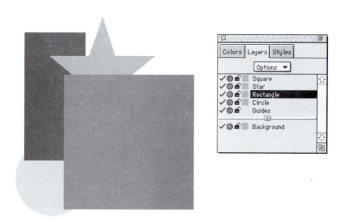

Rearranging Layer Order

It is quite easy to change the order of the layers. There will be many times that one layer will need to be moved in front of another. Simply drag a layer to the location within the Layers panel that works best for your design.

It this example, it was desired to place the square object behind the star but in front of the rectangle. This was done in the Layers panel by dragging the Square layer below the Star layer, but above the Rectangle layer.

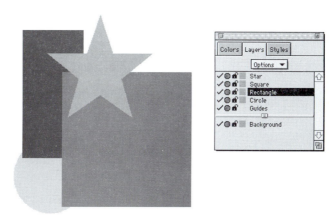

Using Layers to Organize Objects

1. Continue working in the open document.

2. In the previous exercise, you assigned the objects to their own layer, but they still are not organized in layer priorities.

3. Drag the Star layer up to the top of the layer list.

4. Drag the Rectangle layer down, just under the Circle layer.

5. You have now succeeded in rearranging the objects in relation to their Front/Back positions by dragging the layers into a different order of priority.

6. Keep the document open for the next exercise.

Reassigning Objects to other Layers

As easily as layer order can be rearranged, so can the layer to which an object is assigned. Frequently an object will need to be moved to another layer. When an object is selected, the layer to which it is assigned becomes highlighted in the Layers panel. With the object still selected, click the other layer to which you want to move the object; the new layer will become highlighted to indicate the change.

In this example the star was selected, showing the highlighted Star layer. The Rectangle layer was clicked to reassign the star to this layer, changing the star's position.

Be careful when you are clicking various layers in the Layers panel. If any objects are selected, you will unknowingly reassign them to other layers.

Settings for Work Efficiency

FreeHand allows individual layers to be hidden, viewed, locked, or modified. Learning when to change views and lock status is critical. Changing views too often leads to lost time; changing views too infrequently also equals poor productivity. The same goes for locking layers. It will eventually become instinctive to know when to change settings.

Hide/Show

Change the visibility of a layer to see what it obscures. Toggle the check mark on to show the layer; off to hide the layer.

Preview/Keyline

Use the keyline/preview toggle to easily select objects in complex drawings. The solid grey dot indicates that a layer is currently being viewed in Preview mode; an empty circle with a tiny "x" indicates Keyline mode.

In this example, the Star layer Preview/Keyline circle icon was clicked, which puts the star's layer into Keyline viewing mode.

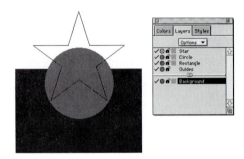

The **Modify->Lock** feature still allows the object to be clicked on, while the Layers locking feature totally isolates the layer objects and will not allow them to be clicked on and selected.

Lock/Unlock

If you find yourself constantly selecting the wrong object, altering it by accident, then undoing, it's time to lock your layers. Plan ahead and use the Layers panel and its functions to your benefit. Allow yourself room to make changes. Sometimes locking entire layers is the only way to edit that one path that you can't ever seem to select. Click the padlock to the left of a layer to lock it; click again to unlock it.

In this example, the Star layer padlock icon was clicked to Lock the layer. All objects were selected and moved, but the locked star was not affected.

114   CHAPTER 6/LAYERS, GRIDS, AND GUIDES

Locking, Viewing, and Previewing Layers

1. Continue working in the open document.

2. In the Layers panel, click the padlock icon for the Circle layer.

3. Click the Hide/Show checkmark on the Rectangle layer to hide the object.

4. Click the Preview/Keyline circle icon for the Star layer to toggle the star to Keyline viewing mode.

5. The design should look like this:

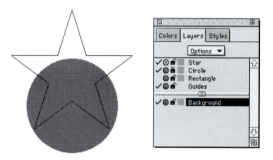

6. Try to click on the locked circle object and move it. What happened? Click on the padlock on the Circle layer to unlock the circle. Now try to click on the circle and move it.

7. Click on the Preview/Keyline icon of the Star layer; the star's layer returns to Preview mode.

8. Click on the Hide/Show checkmark of the Rectangle layer; the rectangle's layer returns to view.

9. You have now used the Layers panel to control the objects and their attributes on the page.

10. **Close** the document without saving.

Grids & Guides

Non-printing Grids and Guides are extremely useful in keeping measurements and laying out your page. These measurement tools make alignment consistent in design work. When laying out an ad, logo, or complex page, these measuring features are essential in visually orientating objects on the page.

The Page Rulers

Press Command-Option-M (Macintosh) or Alt-Control-M (Windows) to turn page rulers on or off.

The Grid and Guides are directly referenced to the Page Rulers, which you can turn on or off by selecting **View->Page Rulers**.

The Page Rulers directly reflect the Units of measurement set in the status bar pop-up menu. Change the Units of measurement to fit your desired method.

The Ruler Zero Point

The Zero Point of the rulers can be moved to any part of the document, and is not a permanent change. You can move it when the rulers are on by clicking in the upper left corner of the document where the two rulers meet and dragging to the desired location.

The intersection of the two rulers, the *zero point*, moves along with the rulers, which is useful for referencing measurements not based on the page boundaries.

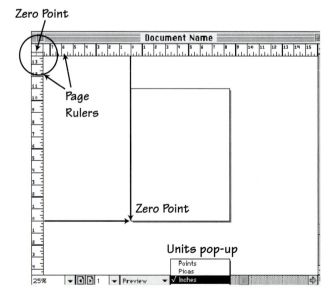

116   Chapter 6/Layers, Grids, and Guides

Guides

Use guides to lay out your page or designate measurements to follow. These non-printing blue lines (the color can be changed in **Preferences->Colors**) can be located anywhere on the document page.

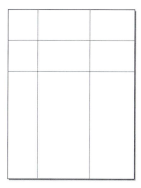

Show/Hide Guides

When you create a new document, the guides are visible by default. You can Show/Hide Guides by toggling **View->Guides->Show**. A check mark next to Show signifies that guides are on.

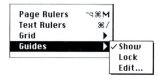

Guides and Layers

The guides can also be shown and hidden by clicking the check mark symbol on the Guides layer in the Layers panel. This the Show/Hide icon. When the check mark is not visible, the guides are Hidden. The padlock icon locks the guides.

The Guides layer in the Layer panel cannot be deleted.

CHAPTER 6/LAYERS, GRIDS, AND GUIDES

Creating Guides

Guides can be created using three different methods:

- **Page Rulers** — When Guides and Rulers are visible you can add new guides. Simply drag a guide from the horizontal or vertical Page Rulers to the desired position.

- **Converting Paths** — Paths created with the FreeHand drawing tools can be assigned to the Guides layer in the Layers panel.

- **Guides dialog box** — Accessed with the **View->Guides->Edit** menu, this dialog box allows you to create or modify the characteristics of existing guides. When you click on **Add**, the **Add Guides** dialog box will display to allow you to adjust your settings.

Use the Guides dialog box for exact positioning of new guides.

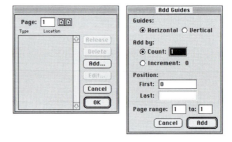

Guides Dialog Box

From the Guides dialog box you can add, delete, and modify guides. This box can be accessed by using **View->Guides->Edit**, or by double-clicking on any guide on the page.

The Guides dialog box displays guide data for only one page of your document at a time. Enter the page you wish to modify or use the next/previous page buttons. The Location that corresponds with the orientation (Horizontal, Vertical, or Path) of the guide will be in the Unit mode you selected. The orientation is listed under Type.

The guide you wish to change in this window should be highlighted; all buttons will now be available to use:

- **Release** — turns the selected guide into a path.

- **Delete (Macintosh) or Remove (Windows)** — deletes the guide.

- **Edit** — edits the location of the guide.

- **Add** — The Add Guide dialog box allows you to create your own guides numerically by specifying origin and quantity.

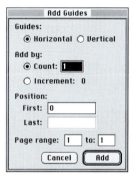

- **Guides** — Choose an orientation, either Horizontal or Vertical.

- **Add by** — Count allows you to choose how many guides will appear. Increment specifies the distance between multiple guides to create a grid or the basis for a form.

- **Position** — allows you to set the first and last measuring points for the number of guides specified.

- **Page range** — lets you select the pages in which you wish the guides to appear.

Removing Guides

Removing guides is as simple as creating them. To remove a guide manually, just click and drag it off the page. This is true for ruler guides as well as paths turned to guides.

Releasing a guide turns the guide into a FreeHand object. If you made an object into a guide, this will convert it back to an object for further editing.

To remove guides in the dialog box, click on the guide listed in the Type column. The dimmed buttons (Release or Delete) will activate and you can release the guide or delete it.

Controlling Guides

Guides come with a few more options that make them even more useful. You can have objects "snap" like a magnet when they are moved close to the guides, lock the guides from modification, and change the color from blue or to any color you desire.

"Snapping" is like a magnetic force that attracts the object to the guide when it is a certain distance away. Choose **View->Snap to Guides** or press Command-\ (Macintosh) or Alt-Control-G (Windows).

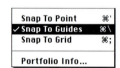

You can customize snapping by specifying a "Snap Distance" in screen pixels in **Preferences->General**. The default value is 3; smaller values decrease snapping, and larger values increase snapping.

Locking Guides

If you find yourself accidentally moving your guides after precisely locating them, Lock them from modification. Select **View->Guides->Lock** or lock the padlock for the Guides layer in the Layers panel.

Creating and Modifying Guides

1. Select **File->Open** and navigate to the **SF-Intro Freehand->Grid & Guides.FH8** file.

2. In the Magnification pop-up menu in the lower left of the screen, set the percentage for 50%.

3. Select **View->Page Rulers** to toggle the rulers on screen. Set the measurement Units for Inches.

4. Click on the vertical ruler at the left side of the screen and drag a guide onto the page, matching it to the 4.25 inch mark on the horizontal ruler at the top of the document. Click on the horizontal ruler and drag a guide down onto the page, matching the 5.5 inch mark of the vertical ruler. The place where the two guides meet in the middle marks the center of the page. This is the ruler-dragging method.

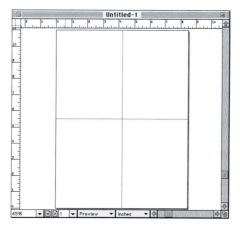

CHAPTER 6/LAYERS, GRIDS, AND GUIDES

5. Sometimes custom guides need to be created from paths. Select the square on the page.

6. Select **Window->Panels->Layers** to open the Layers panel. You will notice that it has three layers: Foreground, Guides, and Background.

7. With the square selected, click on the Guides layer to assign the square. Click the check mark on the Guides layer. This is the Show/Hide button. What happened to all the guides on the page? Click this button again.

8. Click on the square guide and move it around the page. Click on the padlock icon on the Guides layer. Try to move the square guide; try to move any of the guides. The clicked padlock Locked them. Click this again to Unlock the guides.

9. You now have three guides on the page — the vertical, horizontal, and the square. Let's assume you want the square turned back to a path for use in a design. How do you convert paths back? — You do this in the Edit Guides dialog box, accessed through either **View->Guides->Edit** or by double-clicking on the guide in question.

10. Double-click on the square guide to display the dialog box listing the guides by their type or measurement location; the Path option will be highlighted. Click Release, then click **OK**.

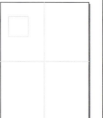

11. What happened to the guide? It reverts back to an object. Choose **Edit** ->**Undo** to make the path a guide again.

12. In the Layers panel, click on the check mark on the Guides layer. What happened to all the guides? Click this check mark again to Show the guides.

13. Click on the vertical guide and drag it off the page. What happened to it? Drag the horizontal guide off the page. Guides are deleted by dragging them off the page.

14. Click on the square object and assign it to the Guides layer to make it a guide. Now double-click on the square guide to display the **Edit Guides** dialog box.

15. Click on the Path item in the Type column. Click the **Delete** (Macintosh) or **Remove** (Windows) button, then click **OK**. What do you see on the page?

16. Keep the document open for the next exercise.

Creating Guides with Add Guides

1. Continue working in the open document.

2. You should be looking at a blank page with no guides or paths.

3. Select **View**->**Guides**->**Edit** to show the **Edit Guides** dialog box. Click on the **Add** button to display the **Add Guides** dialog box.

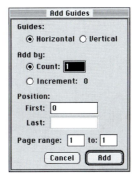

CHAPTER 6/LAYERS, GRIDS, AND GUIDES

4. Apply these settings:

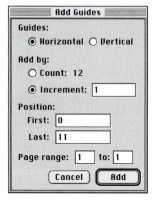

If you are not satisfied with the blue color of the guides, change the color. Locate the Colors section of your Preferences and change the "Guide color" by double-clicking on its swatch to bring up the system color palette.

- The Position starts at 0 for the Zero Point, wherever it is located.

- Horizontal is the guide's orientation.

- The Count is 12 because the page is 11 inches tall, so 12 guides must be made to go from the top of the page to the bottom.

- Increment is 1 for 1 inch since you have the Units set for inches.

- The Last is set for 11, because it is an 11 inch page.

- Page range is 1, because you are working on page 1.

  Click **Add**.

5. Here are the new guides in the Guides dialog box. Click **OK**.

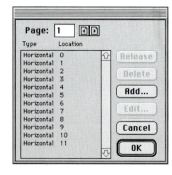

6. You will see the guides on the page.

7. Double-click on any of the guides with the Pointer tool to display the **Edit Guides** dialog box. Click the **Add** button.

8. Enter these settings:

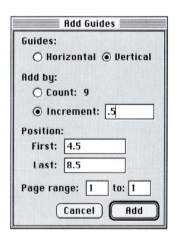

- The Position starts at 4.5 inches (you can start the guides anywhere you want).

- Vertical is the guide's orientation.

- The Count is 9, because the page is 8.5 inches wide.

- Increment is set for 0.5 inches.

- The Last is set for 8.5 inches, to stop at the edge of the page.

- Page range is 1, because you are working on page 1.

- Click **Add**.

9. You will see the Guides dialog box. Click **OK**.

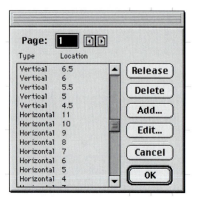

10. Here's the page with your custom-made guides:

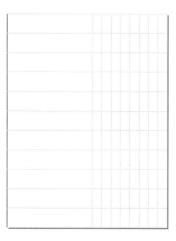

11. **Close** the document without saving.

Grids

The FreeHand Grid is a background of horizontal and vertical dotted lines set as a background (non-printing) alignment tool. The Grid is plotted at a set size, but you can alter these settings.

Show/Hide Grids

Like Guides, Grids can be toggled on and off by choosing **View->Grid ->Show**. When you launch a new document the Grid is off. Choose **View ->Grid->Show** to display the non-printing grid.

Editing the Grid

Think of a Grid as dotted lines that turns your page into graph paper. The increments between the horizontal and vertical parallels are exactly the same. The value can be set by selecting **View->Grid->Edit**.

Remember that the value entered into this box depends on what Unit of measurement you have set. Shown below is the default setting for inches:

The color of the grid defaults to red, but this can be changed by making a new color setting in **Preferences->Colors**.

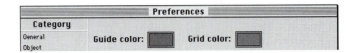

Snapping

Grids can snap objects, much like guides. You activate this feature by choosing **View->Snap to Grid** or press Command-; (Macintosh). Snapping attaches objects to the nearest intersection on the Grid. Everything from charts to business cards and logos to multimedia projects such as web graphics and marketing materials can benefit from using a grid for your layout. The grid is the most basic and powerful tool available to a designer.

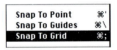

Using Grid and Guides

1. From the **File** menu, select **New** to create a new document.

2. Use the Magnification pop-up menu to set the view for 50%.

3. Select **View->Grid->Show**.

4. You will only see the Grid appear on the page.

5. Click on the Rectangle tool and drag the crosshair on the page while holding the Shift key to draw a square. Click on the square with the Pointer tool and slowly move the square around on the page. Do you see the grid lines "tugging" on the square? No? Then go to **View->Snap To Grid** to toggle this on, with a check mark next to it. Again, move the square around. Do you see it snapping to the grid now?

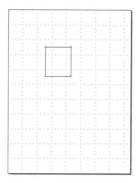
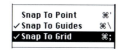

6. Select **View->Grid->Edit** to display the dialog box for customizing the grid's increments. Specify the Grid increment based on the measurement units selected in the Units pop-up menu.

7. Set the Units pop-up menu for inches. The **Edit Grid** defaults to 0.125 inches.

8. Experiment with this dialog box. Change this **Grid Size** to any other number you wish and click **OK**. View the Grid on screen.

9. After you have an idea of how the Grid can be changed, change the Grid Size back to 0.125 inches and click **OK**.

10. The Grid is useful for giving you a guide-like system to use for placement and measurements without having to drag out Guides to create one. Unlike Guides, you can't move the Grid.

11. Select **View->Grid->Show** to turn the Grid off. You can see how simple it is to control and edit the Grid.

12. **Close** the document without saving.

The default location of the Zero Point is the lower left corner of the document page. If you have changed the Zero Point and want it back to the default position, double-click on the Zero Point icon where the rulers meet in the upper left corner of the screen.

Setting the Zero Point

One of the most important reasons for using guides is to accurately exert control over the measuring system. To accurately measure, you must have a starting point from which to begin. Set your starting point with the Zero Point. The zero point is determined by the location of the intersection of the horizontal and vertical rulers.

If you closely observe the document window with the rulers turned on, you will see that documents are measured from the lower left corner of the page. Rulers are your basic guides. To move the zero point of your rulers to any location in the document, drag the zero point to the desired location.

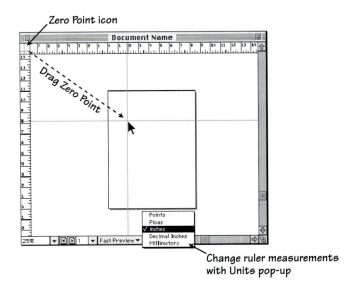

Setting the Zero Point

1. Select **File->New** to create a new document.

2. Select **View->Page Rulers** and turn on the page rulers. The zero point is in the upper left corner of the document where the rulers meet.

3. Click the mouse on the Zero Point and drag it onto the page. Observe the rulers' zeroes as you move the mouse around.

4. Choose a location where you want the zero point to be relocated, then release the mouse; the zeroes of the rulers have now changed.

5. You do not have to drag the zero point back to its original position. Double-click on the zero point in the upper left corner to reset the zero point back to the original position.

6. Notice how the zeroes of the rulers return to the default position.

7. You have now seen how you can drag the zero point to any other location in the document.

8. **Close** the file without saving.

Complete Project C: Last Mango Business Cards

Notes:

Review #1

Chapters 1 Through 6:

In Chapters 1 through 6, we learned the basic operation and layout of FreeHand, how to customize preferences, how to draw basic shapes, how to work with text, how to manage documents efficiently with layers, and how to enter and edit text. After completing the first part of this book, you should:

- Understand FreeHand's various panels, Inspectors, tools, and menu selections; understand how to open and save documents; set FreeHand preferences, and create a new default template.

- Understand how to use views and windows and add and remove pages in a document. Users of the Windows version of FreeHand should understand what Wizards are, and how to use them.

- Know the operation and function of basic drawing tools.

- Know how to draw primitive shapes; how to zoom in and out; how and when to use preview and keyline viewing modes.

- Know how to draw basic shapes with the pen tool; know the differences and uses of the three types of anchor points; fill objects and the various types of fills; use the fill Inspector; change stroke attributes with the stroke Inspector; the two ways of moving an object with the Pointer tool; how to draw lines and curves; and join lines and curves.

- Understand how to create text containers and edit text; know how to use the text Inspector panels; understand kerning and why it is sometimes important; understand how to create and apply text styles; apply special effects to text; convert selected text to editable outlines; import text from outside files; and link text containers together.

- Understand how to create layers and the reasons for using them; know how to arrange layers, rename them, and modify their attributes.

- Know the use of guides, and how to place guides precisely with the guide manager; set up and customize a grid, and know why a grid can be useful for layout purposes; understand the zero point, how to reset the zero point, and the use of rulers.

Chapter 7

Arranging, Aligning, and Distributing Objects

Chapter Objective:

To learn how FreeHand stacks objects in layers, and how to arrange objects and modify their attributes. In Chapter 7, you will:

- Learn about the stacking order of objects within a layer; how without layers, manipulation of objects could be an incredibly tedious task.
- Understand how to move objects forward or backward to change their relationship to each other.
- Learn to nest groups within groups, and how FreeHand will automatically remember how many nested groups exist in your document.
- Understand how to lock and hide objects for ease of editing.
- Understand how to group and ungroup sets of objects.
- Understand how use the Align panel to align objects relative to each other or to the page.
- Learn how to align and distribute with both the preview and pop-up methods.
- Learn how to make settings in the pop-up menu without visually manipulting the preview.
- Learn how to distribute a set of objects across a range of space.

Projects to be Completed:

- Steaming Coffee
- Last Mango Cafe Logo
- Last Mango Business Cards
- Java Jungle
- Coffee Du Jour Ad
- Tropical Fish Art
- Ball & Mirror
- Joker's Wild
- Tropical Treasure Logo
- Tropical Treasure Mailer
- Grocery Ad

Arranging, Aligning, and Distributing Objects

Without layers, manipulation of objects could be an incredibly tedious task. Since you now know how to create various objects, you need to know how to keep them organized. Objects in a layer are arranged in a stack. A layer can have many objects stacked on top of each other.

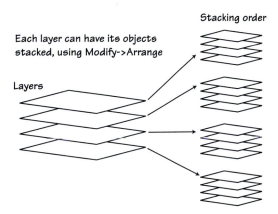

Arranging Objects

Every object in FreeHand has its own properties: its X and Y coordinates on the page, its Stroke and Fill, and its stacking order from Front to Back.

Every object in FreeHand either sits above or below other objects, even if the objects don't overlap. This order is determined by which object was drawn first. The sequence in which you draw objects will place them in a stacking order from bottom to top. Each new object drawn is automatically in front of all previous objects, unless the objects are created on other Layers.

If you created a rectangle first, then a circle followed by a star, the star would be in front of the others. The rectangle, created first, would be in back.

Objects can be arranged into any order by moving them Forward or Backward, to the Front or to the Back. The stacking order tools can be found in the **Modify->Arrange** menu.

In addition to stacking order, it is important to know an object's location in reference to the zero point. You can also align and distribute objects in reference to each other and their coordinate location. The Align panel allows you to align or distribute objects across a single axis or both axes.

You can Group multiple selected objects into a single combined object, and Ungroup them as needed. This has always been a very powerful feature in FreeHand.

Arranging Objects

There are four functions available from the **Modify->Arrange** menu. These four functions, called the Arrange commands, change the stacking order of objects. If you change the stacking order of objects that don't overlap, the change may not be apparent.

Move Forward, Move Backward

You can move an object forward or backward within a layer by choosing Move Forward or Move Backward. In this example, the rectangle (a) needs to be between the circle and the square in back. Without Move Forward/Backward, a lot of Send To Back and Bring To Front would have to be applied.

If the rectangle is selected, and **Modify->Arrange->Move Backward** is chosen, the rectangle moves backward one object (b).

a   b

Bring To Front, Send To Back

You can also move an object to the Front or Back of a layer by choosing Bring to Front or Send to Back in the **Modify->Arrange** menu.

In this example the circle is behind all other objects (a) and needs to be in front. It would be time-consuming to perform Move Forward as many times as needed. Instead, the circle was selected, then **Modify->Arrange->Bring To Front** chosen. This brought the circle all the way to the front (b).

a   b

These four functions are very useful in allowing you to arrange objects without having to create layers and assigning the objects to each one. Also, if a layer has several objects assigned to it, the Front/Back arranging can manipulate these objects on the layer.

Using Front/Back Movements

1. Choose **File->Open** and open **SF-Intro Freehand->Manipulating Objects.FH8** (Macintosh) or **Manipulating Objects.FT8** (Windows).

CHAPTER 7/ARRANGING, ALIGNING, AND DISTRIBUTING OBJECTS

Use these keyboard shortcuts to quickly arrange objects:
Cmd/Ctrl-F = move to front
Cmd/Ctrl-B = move to back
Cmd/Ctrl-[= move forward
Cmd/Ctrl-] = move backward

2. Click on the rectangle with the Pointer tool. Select **Modify->Arrange->Bring To Front** and notice what has happened to the rectangle.

3. Click on the star. Select **Modify->Arrange->Move Forward**. Now click on the circle and select **Modify->Arrange->Move Forward** again. Where is the circle in relation to the star and rectangle?

4. Click on the star and select **Modify->Arrange->Move Backward**. Where is the star located?

5. Select **Modify->Arrange->Move Backward** again. Where is the star now?

Locking items can be useful for a number of tasks, especially when you have finished with an object and want to protect it from accidental alteration. Another use for locking an item is if you have multiple objects stacked over each other and are having a hard time selecting the ones at the back. Locking the foreground object can make it easier to select the others. It's also useful when using the Align panel for forcing other objects to align with reference to a locked object.

6. Click on the circle and the rectangle. Select **Window->Arrange->Send To Back**.

7. You have now used the four arranging features available in the **Modify ->Arrange** menu.

8. Keep the document open for the following exercise.

Locking/Unlocking Objects

FreeHand allows you to lock and unlock the position of individual objects with the **Modify->Lock/Unlock** options.

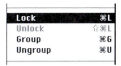

Locking an object doesn't mean you can't select it; you can click on the object and see its anchor points, but you cannot move or transform it. You can, however, still apply different fills or strokes to the locked object.

Locking/Unlocking Objects

1. Continue working in the open FreeHand file.

Chapter 7/Arranging, Aligning, and Distributing Objects

The keyboard shortcuts for Locking are Command-L (Macintosh) or Control-L (Windows).
To Unlock a selected object, press Shift-Command-L (Macintosh) or Shift-Control-L (Windows).

Objects must be selected to be Locked or Unlocked.

2. With the Pointer tool click on the star. Select **Modify->Lock**.

3. Drag a marquee around all three objects with the Pointer tool to select them.

4. Move the objects several inches to the right. What was the result? Did the star move with the other objects?

5. Choose **Edit->Undo** to undo the move. Deselect all the objects.

6. Choose **Modify->Unlock**. Why is it grayed out? If an object is Locked, shouldn't this feature be accessible?

7. Click on the star, then select **Modify->Unlock**. Unlock is now accessible.

8. You have now observed and experienced how Lock/Unlock can make objects immune to movement or modifications.

9. Keep the file open for the following exercise.

Grouping/Ungrouping Objects

The **Modify->Group** feature combines several objects together into a single object; this makes performing the same tasks on multiple objects easy and faster.

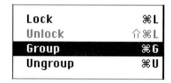

Nesting Groups

You can nest groups within groups. FreeHand remembers how many nested groups exist. If you need to Ungroup them, you can at any time.

In this example there are three ovals and three squares (a) that were Grouped together into their own groups (b). The two groups were then selected (c) and Grouped into a single object (d). Single and Grouped objects have four corner handles to select them.

The keyboard shortcuts for Grouping is Command-G (Macintosh) or Control-G (Windows).

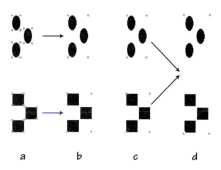

Ungrouping

Grouped objects can be ungrouped by selecting Group, then choosing **Modify->Ungroup**. Ungrouping will only undo the last Grouping performed. All other groups will stay together until Ungroup is selected again.

In this example, the nested grouped object was selected and Ungrouped (a). The two previous groups become evident (b). Both groups are selected, then Ungrouped, resulting in the original separate objects (c).

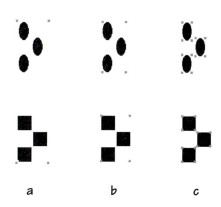

Grouping and Ungrouping Objects

1. Continue working in the open document.

2. Click on the three objects; you will see all their anchor points.

3. Select **Modify->Group**. You will now see only the four corners of the bounding box of the grouped objects.

4. With the Pointer tool, select the group and move it around the page to see how the three objects move as one.

5. If you want to select a single object or line segment to modify, hold down the Option (Macintosh) or Alt (Windows) key as you click on the circle; only the circle is selected.

6. Now add the Shift key as you click on the rectangle to select multiple objects. You can isolate objects in a group with these keys.

7. Release the keys and click away from the objects to deselect them.

8. With nothing selected, select **Modify->Ungroup**. Why isn't it accessible in the menu? Click on the grouped objects, then go back to **Modify->Ungroup**. You can now select **Ungroup**.

9. You have now seen how **Grouping** combines objects, and how certain keys allow you to select individual objects in a group. You have also learned to **Ungroup** combined objects.

10. **Close** the document without saving.

Aligning/Distributing Objects

The Align panel is accessed by selecting either **Window->Panels->Align** or **Modify->Align**.

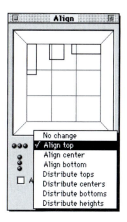

There are two ways to use the Align panel:

- **Preview** — by double-clicking the squares in the preview window.

- **Pop-up menus** — by using the pop-up menus in the panel.

Preview Method

If you prefer to work visually, you can single-click the regions to see alignments for selected objects. Double-click the region to apply the alignment. When each region is selected, you will see its specifications listed on the pop-up menus.

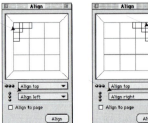

In this example, the three objects were selected (a). The preview window was clicked on to see a preferred alignment (b). The desired region was double-clicked, applying this alignment to the selected objects (c).

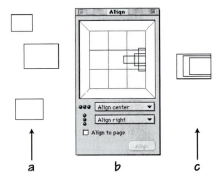

a   b   c

Pop-up Menu Method

If you prefer to make settings without visually manipulating the preview, make changes in the appropriate pop-up menu.

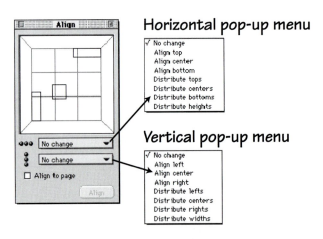

The keyboard shortcut for accessing the Align panel is Option-Command-A (Macintosh) or Alt-Control-A (Windows).

The Vertical align pop-up:

- **No change** — No changes are made to the vertical position of objects.
- **Align top** — All objects will align to the top of the highest object.
- **Align center** — The vertical center of all objects will become the alignment point.
- **Align bottom** — All objects align to the lowest point of the bottom object.
- **Distribute tops** — Determines the top of the highest and the lowest selected objects then distributes the tops of all other selected objects evenly between them.
- **Distribute centers** — Determines the centers of the highest and lowest selected objects then distributes the centers of all other objects evenly between them.
- **Distribute bottoms** — Determines the bottoms of the highest and lowest selected objects then distributes the bottoms of all other objects evenly between them.
- **Distribute heights** — Determines the bottom of the highest and the top of the lowest selected objects, then distributes the facing sides of the other objects between them.

The Horizontal align pop-up menu:

- **No change** — No changes are made to the horizontal position of objects.
- **Align left** — All objects will align to the left of the leftmost object.
- **Align center** — Aligns selected objects to the horizontal center of all objects.
- **Align right** — All objects align to the rightmost point of the furthest right object.
- **Distribute lefts** — Determines the leftmost and rightmost objects then distributes the lefts of objects between them.
- **Distribute centers** — Determines the leftmost and furthest right objects then distributes the centers of all objects between them.

CHAPTER 7/ARRANGING, ALIGNING, AND DISTRIBUTING OBJECTS

- **Distribute rights** — Determines the leftmost and rightmost objects then creates an equal amount of space between the right edges of the objects.

- **Distribute widths** — Determines the right edge of the leftmost object and the left edge of the rightmost object then creates an equal amount of space between the facing edges of objects.

Aligning

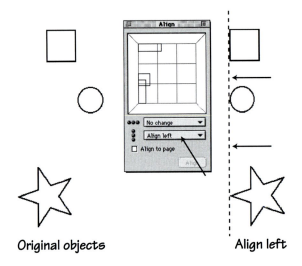

Original objects   Align left

Distribute

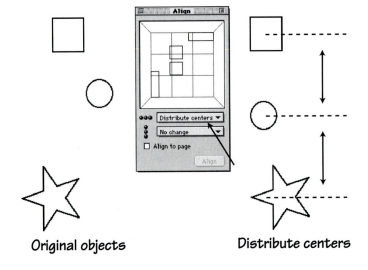

Original objects   Distribute centers

Align to Page

When Align to page is checked, all selected objects are aligned or distributed in relation to the current page dimensions. If only one object is selected, Align to page must be checked to apply an alignment.

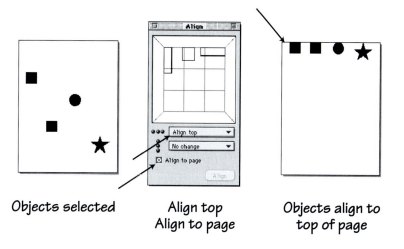

Objects selected   Align top   Objects align to
                    Align to page   top of page

Aligning and Distributing with Preview Method

1. Choose **File->Open** and open the file **SF-Intro Freehand->Align Objects.FH8**.

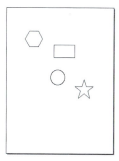

2. Click on each object, holding the Shift key to select them all, or choose **Edit->Select All**. Choose **Modify->Align** to display the Align panel.

3. Click on the various areas of the preview in the Align panel to see the alignments available. **Align** (Macintosh) or **Apply** (Windows) will apply these settings to the selected object, if clicked. Do not click for now.

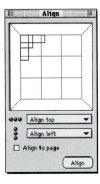 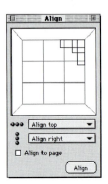 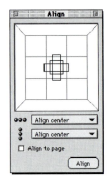

4. Double-click on any preview area you desire. Observe how the objects were affected by this method. Select **Edit->Undo**.

5. Double-click on a different area in the preview window. Note how the objects change with this alignment. Select **Edit->Undo**.

6. Click the Align to page option in the panel. Now double-click on a different area of the preview window. Notice how the alignment used the document page as a reference for its alignment. Select **Edit->Undo**.

7. Keep the document open for the next exercise.

Align and Distribute by the Pop-up Menu Method

1. Continue working in the open document with the Align panel on screen.

2. Select all the objects in the document.

3. In the Horizontal pop-up menu, select Align Top.

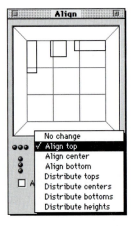

150 Chapter 7/Arranging, Aligning, and Distributing Objects

4. You might be puzzled as to why you see nothing happening on screen. You must click the Align or Apply button in the lower right corner of the Align panel; you will then see the objects align across the top.

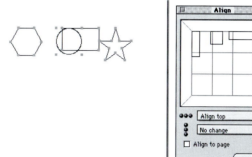

5. Select **Edit->Undo,** or Command (Macintosh) or Control (Windows)-Z.

6. With the objects still selected, navigate to the Vertical pop-up menu and select Align left. Set the Horizontal alignment for No change. Click Align.

7. The objects will vertically align their left sides.

 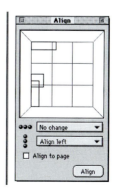

CHAPTER 7/ARRANGING, ALIGNING, AND DISTRIBUTING OBJECTS

8. Click on the star and drag it down to the bottom of the page.

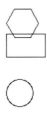

9. Select all the objects on the page. Set the Horizontal alignment for Distribute heights. This will distribute the objects up and down a vertical axis, evenly spaced based upon their heights.

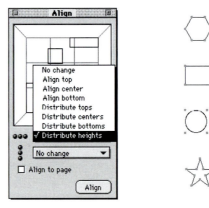

10. In the Align panel, there is an option called Align to page. If this is clicked, the objects will use the page as a guide for vertical or horizontal aligning. Select **File->Revert** to return the document back to its original state.

11. Select all the objects. In the Align panel, click on Align to page. In the Vertical pop-up menu, select Align left. In the Horizontal sub-menu, set No change. Click Align. The objects will align left, but against the extreme left side of the page.

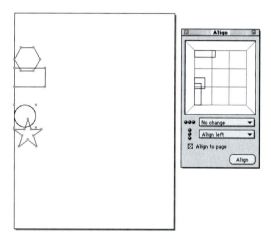

12. You have now experimented with the various aligning and distributing functions available in the Align panel. **Close** the document without saving.

Notes:

Chapter 8

Path Operations

Chapter Objective:

To learn the assorted tools and techniques for altering paths and creating new objects from operations on paths. In Chapter 8, you will:

- Learn how Path Operations are preprogrammed operations, styles, and features that automatically perform very complicated tasks.
- Review the Operations panel, its tools, and how quickly its tools automatically perform operations on paths.
- Learn how to use the Xtras and Modify menus, as well as understand the Xtras window.
- Understand Path- altering operations to simplify, reverse, and eliminate overlap in paths.
- Learn how to create a blend of two objects.
- Learn how to use Expand Stroke to create composite paths.
- Understand what a composite object is, and how you can use it to enhance your design.
- Learn how to use Inset Path to create scaled replicas of paths; understand the use of Inset Path from both the Operations panel and Inset Path dialog box.
- Understand how to combine paths to create new objects using the union, intersect, punch, crop, transparency, and blend functions.

Projects to be Completed:

- Steaming Coffee
- Last Mango Cafe Logo
- Last Mango Business Cards
- **Java Jungle**
- **Coffee Du Jour Ad**
- Tropical Fish Art
- Ball & Mirror
- Joker's Wild
- Tropical Treasure Logo
- Tropical Treasure Mailer
- Grocery Ad

Path Operations

Path Operations are preprogrammed operations, styles, and features that perform work that would be very complicated if attempted by hand. They're accessed in several locations in addition to the Path Operations sub-menu (Path Operations were never very well-organized in FreeHand) and some are located under the **Modify** menu. Many of them are actually FreeHand Xtras, but perform operations strictly on paths, so we're presenting them separately.

The following sub-menus will show small dialogs after they're chosen:

- **Xtras->Create**

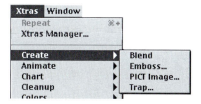

- **Xtras->Cleanup**

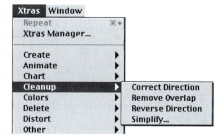

- **Xtras->Path Operations**

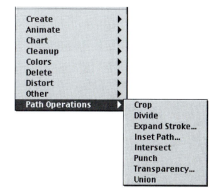

CHAPTER 8/PATH OPERATIONS 157

Press Command-Shift+I (Macintosh) or Control-Alt+O (Windows) to open the Operations panel.

- Window->Xtras->Operations

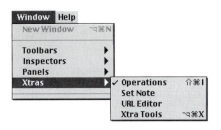
Macintosh

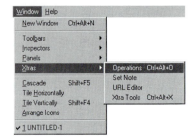
Windows

This will show the floating Operations panel. The majority of all the Path Operations tools appear on the Operations panel.

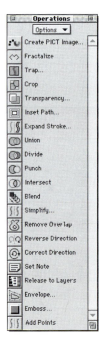

The Operations panel

These Path Operations tools perform operations on paths in seconds that would take considerable time if done manually.

Some Path Operations combine objects, create new objects, or modify objects. Using these operations may require some experimentation to obtain the desired effect.

158   Chapter 8/Path Operations

There are two results that you can get from using some of the **Path Operations**. You can either create a third object on top of the original objects, or the originals can be deleted during the operation if **Preferences->Objects->Path operations consume original paths** is turned on, which will leave you with a single resulting object.

Path-altering Operations

Located in the **Operations** panel, these tools alter paths offering several operations that work on the general makeup of a path, simplifying, or creating new paths based on the original. In this course we won't look at all of them, but we will examine some of the more commonly-used ones.

Remove Overlap

- With a closed path that overlaps itself, **Remove Overlap** eliminates the crossover and unites everything into one or more paths.

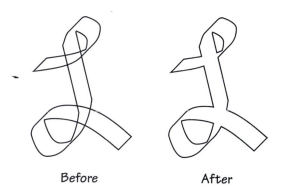

Before   After

Simplify

- Simplify removes unnecessary points that do not affect the look of the line; the amount of change can be controlled through its dialog. Double-click the Simplify Xtra to display the dialog box. Higher simplification values will result in more obvious changes in the object. You really only need to simplify a path if it contains an unmanageable number of points, or if your printer fails to print a complex path.

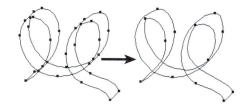 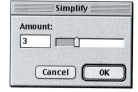

Press Command-Shift-B (Macintosh) or Control-Shift-B (Windows) to create a blend of two objects.

Blend

- A blend is a set of intermediate paths between two objects. You control the number of intermediate steps between the objects in the Object inspector. The starting object will "morph" into the ending object.

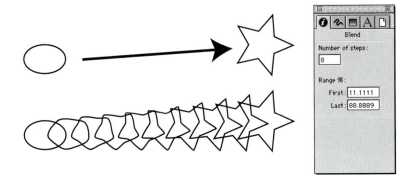

Expand Stroke

Expand Stroke converts selected lines (strokes) and converts them to closed, sometimes composite paths. It's useful if you have sketched in some lines to make a rough object and later decide to convert them from lines to closed paths. You can also use this function if you want to use a Fill type that is not available for a Stroke, such as Gradient, Radial, Custom, and Texture. This function lets you create a closed path that looks like a stroke, and then Fill it.

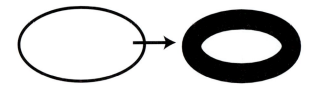

To expand a stroke to a closed path, select the object, choose Expand Stroke from the Operations panel, and set the **Width** of the new path in the dialog box.

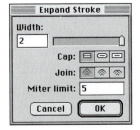

The result of using **Expand Stroke** on an already closed path is a composite object — an object that is made up of two paths.

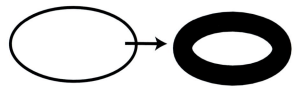

In Keyline mode, there is an inside and outside to the object. This is the same result you'd get if you used **Modify->Join** to combine the objects.

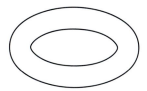

Composite objects have an inner path that is transparent. Background objects can then show through the opening.

You could **Modify->Split** the object to separate the paths, after which the inner path would no longer be transparent.

Here's a reminder of the Cap and Join options found in the Stroke Inspector:

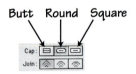

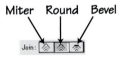

Expand Stroke Dialog Box

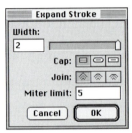

- **Width** — sets the thickness of the object that will be created. You can enter in a value in points, inches, or millimeters.

- **Cap** — controls how the endpoint of an *open* path to be expanded is shaped. There are three options — the same ones that are in the **Stroke Inspector**.

- **Join** — controls the shape where two path segments meet at a corner point. There are three options that are available: miter, round, and beveled, which work just like those in the **Stroke Inspector**.

- **Miter limit** — controls how far the **Stroke** will extend before it converts to a beveled join. It is the ratio between the length of the miter join and the stroke width.

Using Expand Stroke and Blends

1. Create a **New** document. Set the measurement unit for Points.

2. Choose **Preferences->Object**. Select **Path operations consume original paths** if it is not already on.

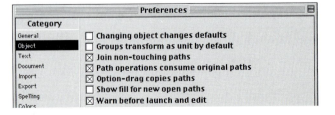

3. Draw an ellipse with the Ellipse tool. With the Color List set the **Fill** = None and **Stroke** = Black. Select Preview mode.

4. With the ellipse selected, select **Modify->Alter Path->Expand Stroke**.

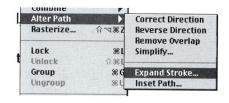

5. Enter 20 pt. for the **Width**.

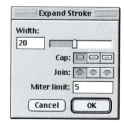

6. To see the object paths you have created, switch the view mode to Keyline to see the two outlines.

7. Go back to Preview view. Open the Fill Inspector and try different Fills on this object. Try some that you couldn't use with a stroke, such as a Gradient.

8. Use the Polygon tool to draw a star and give it a solid black fill. Move the star over to overlap the expanded ellipse and choose **Modify->Arrange->Send To Back**. The star will show through the opening in the expanded object, courtesy of the composite paths.

Press Command (Macintosh) or Control (Windows) -K to switch between Keyline and Preview modes.

Use these keyboard shortcuts to quickly arrange objects:
Cmd/Ctrl-F = move to front
Cmd/Ctrl-B = move to back
Cmd/Ctrl-[= move forward
Cmd/Ctrl-] = move backward

If you prefer to keep the original path along with the inset duplicates, make certain that **Preferences->Object->Path operations consume original paths** is turned off to avoid deleting the original.

9. Select the expanded ellipse and choose **Modify->Split**. This separates the two paths as shown below:

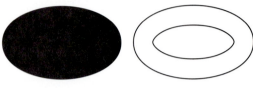

Split - Preview mode   Split - Keyline mode

10. Click on the outer path and choose **Modify->Arrange->Send To Back**. It ends up in front of the smaller path because the inner path of a composite object always goes to the back, and filling it would obscure the inner path.

11. You have now taken a single path and created two custom paths with Expand Stroke. Imagine how you could create your own images using this useful operation.

12. Select the outer path and the star and set both: Fill = None, Stroke = Black. Click the Blend Xtra in the Operations panel to "morph" between them.

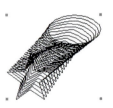

This blend shows 25 Steps, which you can change in the Object Inspector. With the blend selected, select the Object Inspector and change the Steps values to 5. See the difference? You can select as many steps between the objects as you like, but the practical limit is 256 steps or fewer.

13. **Close** the file without saving.

Inset Path

The Inset Path Xtra is also in the Operations panel. It allows you to create enlarged or reduced duplicates of a closed path. You can specify the number of duplicates in the **Inset Path** dialog box. Here the star was inset with 3 **Steps** (meaning 3 duplicates), sized **Uniform**, and **Inset** 4 pts. apart.

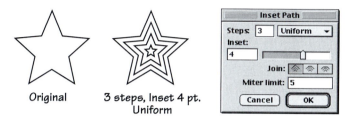

Inset Path, for some reason unknown to anyone except the original programmer, uses positive values to make the insets inside the original object, and negative values to make an *outset* of duplicates. In this example, the same star was inset with a –4 pt. "inset." The same **Join** and **Miter Limit** options found in the Stroke Inspector are available here.

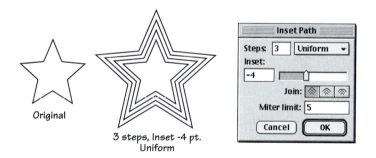

Inset Path Dialog Box

- **Steps** — the number of repeating paths that will be created.

- **Inset** — the distance, in the currently selected measurement units, that separates the steps as they repeat.

Here's a reminder of the Join options found in the Stroke Inspector:

- **Join** — controls the shape where two path segments meet at a corner point. There are three options: miter, rounded, and beveled.

- **Miter limit** — controls how far the Stroke will extend before it converts to a beveled join. It is the ratio between the length of the miter join and the Stroke width.

- **Uniform, Farther, Nearer** — are the distances each step is from the others. Uniform means that the repeating steps will all be an equal distance apart, set in Inset. Farther makes each step close up the distance, becoming smaller as the steps repeat. Nearer makes each step increase the distance, becoming wider as the steps repeat.

Uniform   Farther   Nearer

Using Inset Path

1. Create a new document. Set the measurement Units to Points.

2. Select **Preferences->Object**. For this exercise, the **Path operations consume original paths** option should be turned off.

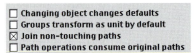

3. Double-click on the Polygon tool, and in the dialog box make its settings an 8-sided polygon. Click OK. Draw a polygon on the page that is approximately 2 inches wide.

166   Chapter 8/Path Operations

Press Command-Shift-I (Macintosh) or Control-Alt+I (Windows) to open the Operations panel.

4. Open the Operations panel by choosing **Windows->Xtras->Operations**. With the polygon selected, choose the **Inset Path** Xtra from the **Operations** panel. Set the **Steps** for 9, **Uniform**, the **Inset** for 8 and click OK.

5. With the Pointer tool, click on the middle of this object and move it to the right. The Inset Path operation creates the duplicates as a group, leaving the original polygon alone.

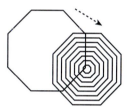

6. Select the Grouped duplicates and delete them. Select the polygon. Select **Modify->Alter Path->Inset Path** again. Now set the Steps for 3, Uniform, -4 for the Inset. Click OK. The negative number forced the inset outside of the original path.

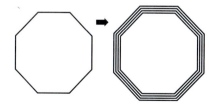

7. Select **Edit->Undo** and return to **Modify->Alter Path->Inset Path**. Make the settings of 8 Steps, Farther, 8 pts. Inset. Click **OK**.

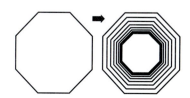

CHAPTER 8/PATH OPERATIONS

8. Select **Edit->Undo** and return to **Modify->Alter Path->Inset Path**. Make the settings of 8 Steps, Nearer, -6 Inset. Click OK. Notice how the paths became closer together as they are duplicated toward the center of the object.

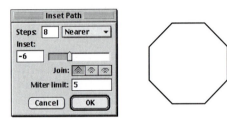

You have now seen how Inset Path works and observed its variations of path modification.

9. **Close** the document without saving.

Operations that Combine

There's a variety of operations that work with two or more objects to produce a single combined object. Here are some samples of what they create:

- **Join Blend To Path** — adheres a blend to a path, literally wrapping the blend along the contours of the path. This function is not in the Operations Panel but is chosen from **Modify->Combine->Join Blend to Path**.

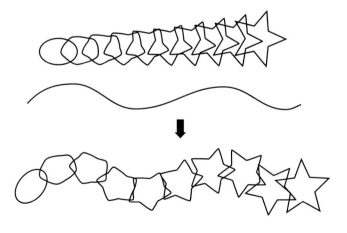

Press Command-Option-Shift+B (Macintosh) or Control-Alt-Shift+B (Windows) to join a blend to a path.

- **Intersect** — creates a path based on where two or more closed paths overlap each other. The stroke and fill of the new object is based on the rear most object's attributes.

Original objects   Intersect

- **Punch** — cuts the top path out of selected closed path(s) underneath it. Stroke and Fill attributes remain unchanged.

Original objects   Punch

- **Union** — creates a new path that is the combination of two or more closed paths. The stroke and fill of the new object is based on the rear most object's attributes.

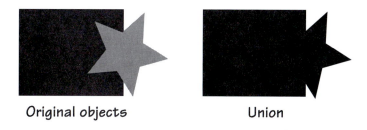

Original objects   Union

- **Crop** — removes the portion of selected, closed paths that are outside of the top most closed path.

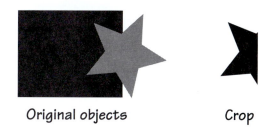

Original objects   Crop

- **Transparency** — operates on two or more closed paths, creating a third path that is an in-between percentage of the two colors filling the original paths. This new object really isn't transparent; it just looks that way because the color is an average of that of the other objects' colors.

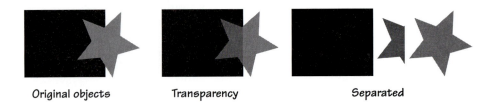

Original objects   Transparency   Separated

The percentage of transparency is controlled with the **Transparency** dialog. Select the Transparency Xtra in the **Operations** panel to show the Transparency dialog. Higher values increase the level of transparency.

Note that this Transparency operation differs quite a bit from a Lens applied in the Fill Inspector, which creates actual transparency in selected objects.

- **Divide** — cuts overlapping sections of selected paths into new paths defined by the area of overlap. The original paths can be open, closed, or both. Stroke and fill of any new paths is based on the top most object's attributes.

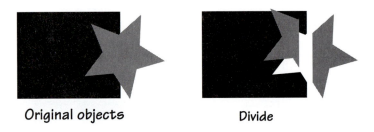

Original objects   Divide

Practicing Path Operations

1. Create a **New** document.

2. Select **Preferences->Object**. Select **Path operations consume original paths** if it is not selected.

3. Select the Rectangle tool and draw a rectangle. Use the **Color List->Options** pop-up menu to access the **Crayon** library and select several light and dark colors. Click **OK**. Fill the rectangle with a dark color.

4. Double-click on the Polygon tool and set it to draw a star; then draw a star. Paint it with a light color from the Color List, then move it in front of the rectangle, overlapping it slightly.

6. Shift-select both of the objects. Select **Window->Xtras->Operations** to open the Operations panel.

7. Click **Crop**. This should be your result.

8. Revert back to the two original objects with **Edit->Undo**.

CHAPTER 8/PATH OPERATIONS

9. Click on Transparency in the Operations panel. Enter 15 in the dialog box and click **OK**. The two objects will turn into three. Move them apart with the Pointer tool to see how the transparency was accomplished.

10. Select **Edit->Undo** to undo the moves and the Transparency operation until you are back to your original two objects.

11. With the two objects selected, click **Union** in the Operations panel. Set your view for Keyline to see the result more clearly.

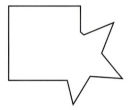

12. Select **Edit->Undo** to undo the operation. Return to Preview mode. Click on **Divide** in the Operations panel. To see the resulting paths more clearly, move them apart.

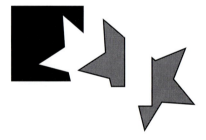

13. Select **Edit->Undo** to undo the moves and the Divide operation until you are back to your original two objects. Click **Punch** in the Operations panel.

14. Select **Edit->Undo** to undo the Punch operation. Click **Intersect** in the Operations panel. Its intersecting feature is very much like Crop.

15. Select **Edit->Undo** to undo the Intersect operation. To Blend the two objects, move the star about four inches to the right of the square.

Select both objects and click **Blend** in the Operations panel. Keep the object selected.

16. Select **Window->Inspectors->Object** to see the Object Inspector. See the **Number of steps** option? This is where you set the number of objects (steps) between the originals after the Blend is applied. Set the **Number of steps** for 5 and press Return (Macintosh) or Enter (Windows) to apply.

Press Command-Shift-B (Macintosh) or Control-Shift-B (Windows) to create a blend of two objects.

CHAPTER 8/PATH OPERATIONS

17. Use the FreeHand drawing tool to create a wavy line under the blend.

18. Select the two objects and navigate to **Modify->Combine->Join blend to path**. This is an operation, though not located in the Operations panel that attaches the Blended objects to the wavy line.

19. You've now received an introduction to Operations and how they affect selected objects. The possibilities to the objects you can create and then modify with Operations are almost endless.

20. **Close** the document without saving.

Complete Project D: Java Jungle Logo

Complete Project E: Coffee du Jour Ad

Chapter 9

Painting FreeHand Objects

Chapter Objective:

To learn many of the available techniques and methods for coloring and patterning objects. In Chapter 9, you will:

- Learn how to paint the objects that you have created in FreeHand, applying colors to enhance your design.
- Understand the many important functions of the Fill Inspector; become comfortable with Basic, Custom, Gradient, Lens, Pattern, PostScript, Textured, and Tiled effects on objects.
- Study the Fill Inspectors pop-up menu.
- Become comfortable with the Color List; how to use it, and how to access the Color List if you don't want to have to use Inspectors.
- Learn about End Caps and how they cap off the endpoint of open paths.
- Learn more about fills, strokes, and their Inspectors.
- Learn how to create new colors, and select colors from predefined libraries.
- Learn how to create tints of colors.
- Learn how to use and understand the color and tint Mixer panels.
- Understand what Gradients are, and how to create and apply them.

Projects to be Completed:

- Steaming Coffee
- Last Mango Cafe Logo
- Last Mango Business Cards
- Java Jungle
- Coffee Du Jour Ad
- **Tropical Fish Art**
- Ball & Mirror
- Joker's Wild
- Tropical Treasure Logo
- Tropical Treasure Mailer
- Grocery Ad

Painting FreeHand Objects

Using the many tools and operations of FreeHand to draw shapes is a lot of fun, but to create truly attractive designs, painting the objects is another step or two up the ladder of digital illustration.

The making, accessing, and applying of just colors is a small part of the picture. The painting procedure goes way beyond simple colors to the realm of textures, gradients, pattern tiles, transparent lens effects, and a host of other decorative visuals that can be applied to your paths.

Applying color to any path is based on two components of the object:

- **Fill** — fill the interior of a closed path with a color, tint, gradient, pattern, or PostScript fill. This is controlled in the Fill Inspector.

- **Stroke** — the attribute applied to the line of a path segment. This can be a color, tint, or a pattern, controlled in the Stroke Inspector.

Objects can have a Fill, a Stroke, or both a Fill and a Stroke. This star path below was painted three different ways.

Stroke only　　　　Fill only　　　　Stroke 3 pt. Black
3 pt. Black　　　　40% Black　　　　Fill 40% Black

Fill

If filling an object with only a basic color were the only decision that you would have to make when painting an object, life would be simple. But in the Fill Inspector you can choose from a wide variety of visuals that can fill paths.

Fill Inspector

When you access **Window->Inspectors**, you will find the Fill Inspector option. If chosen, the panel appears. It will default to None, meaning no fill, so the pop-up menu at the top of the panel must be selected to apply the desired fill.

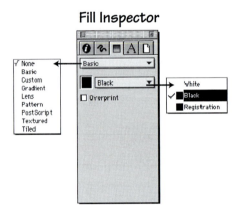

Remember, only closed paths can be Filled in FreeHand.

- **Basic** — applies a simple color, either Process or Spot. Libraries of colors, such as Pantone, can be accessed through the Color List panel, or you can create your own in the Color Mixer.

- **Custom** — a PostScript fill that can only be seen when the page is printed.

- **Gradient** — a blend of two or more colors that intersect where they meet in a range of tones. Gradients can be linear or radial. We will go over this in more detail later in this chapter.

- **Lens** — an assortment of six special effects that perform visual enhancements such as transparency, magnification, inverting, and others.

There are three Fills that you cannot see on screen. Objects painted with these fills must be printed out before you can see what they look like. The three Fills are: Custom, PostScript, and Textured.

Transparency   Magnify   Invert   Lighten   Darken   Monochrome

- **Pattern** — bitmapped patterns that can be customized pixel by pixel.

- **PostScript** — a special effect that requires knowledge of the PostScript language to apply the effect to the object. PostScript effects cannot be seen on screen but appear when printed.

- **Textured** — a variety of textures that can be applied to an object. It cannot be seen on screen, but the Inspector shows a sample of what the texture looks like.

- **Tiled** — Fills an object with multiple copies of another object, composed of something you create and paste into the Tiled Fill Inspector.

Here are four of the Fill Inspectors in the pop-up menu:

    Basic   Gradient   Texture   Tiled

Stroke Inspector

When you apply a color, pattern, custom, or PostScript visual effect to an object, it is applied to the defining path or segments that make the object. What determines the Stroke, when painted, is the visual effect applied, and the thickness or width of the stroke.

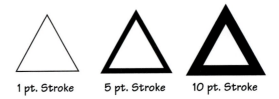

1 pt. Stroke   5 pt. Stroke   10 pt. Stroke

The Stroke Inspector offers a pop-up menu to select the type of Stroke. Width affects the thickness of the line, End caps are the ends of an open path, and Joins are the corners where paths meet at an anchor point. Dashed lines and arrowheads are other features that can be applied.

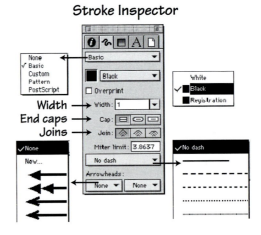

The Stroke Types

The Stroke pop-up menu offers five visual choices to apply to the path stroke:

- **Basic** — applies simple color, either Process or Spot. Libraries of colors, such as Pantone, can be accessed through the Color List panel.

- **Custom** — a PostScript fill that can only be seen when printed.

- **Pattern** — a variety of patterns that can be applied to the stroke.

- **PostScript** — is a special effect that requires knowledge of the PostScript language to apply the effect to the object. It cannot be seen on screen.

Stroke End Caps and Joins

End Caps are defined by how they cap off the endpoint of open paths.

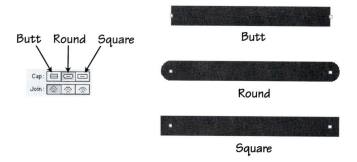

- **Joins** affect the corner where two segments meet at an anchor point.

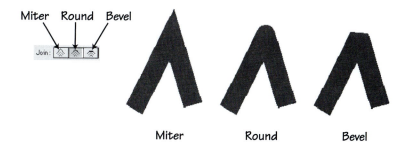

Applying Colors to Paths

A number of options can be applied to the objects that you have drawn in FreeHand. Understanding the available options enables you to add interest and detail to an illustration.

In both the Fill and Stroke Inspectors there is a Basic type of Fill and Stroke, which is the painting of the object with a color. Colors are created in the Color Mixer or selected from a predefined library of colors in the Color List's Options pop-up menu. Colors appear in the Color List panel after you add them.

The Fill and Stroke Inspectors list all colors in the Color List in their pop-up coloring menus. You can select the color and it will be instantly applied.

The Color List

If you want to apply colors to objects without constantly accessing the Inspectors, you can also use the Color List.

Clicking the Fill, Stroke, or Both buttons designate what part of the selected object will be painted.

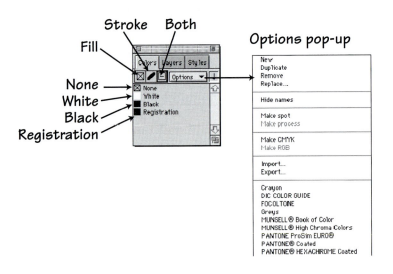

Selected objects can also be painted by clicking on the color name in the Color List.

How To Use The Color List

Despite all the buttons in the Color List, you only have to be concerned with the Fill, Stroke, and Both buttons. Any object you select, including text highlighted with the text cursor, will take on any color attributes when you drag the desired color swatch up to touch the appropriate button.

The Color Mixer

In conjunction with the Color List, the Color Mixer can both create or modify colors, determining whether the color is Spot or Process, and add colors to the Color List.

Here are the features of the Color Mixer:

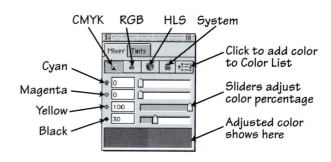

CMYK is short for the four process colors: Cyan, Magenta, Yellow, and Black.

Predefined Colors

FreeHand has libraries of predefined colors in the Color List's pop-up menu.

You can choose industry-standard colors from this list; we'll show you how in the next exercise.

Tints

Tints are shades of a color and are described in percentages of the original. The Tint panel can adjust these percentages and add the tint to the Color List.

There are three ways to modify the tints:

- Click on the percentage boxes listed in the panel.

- Enter numeric percentages in the field to the left of the slider.

- The slider can be dragged to achieve the desired tint.

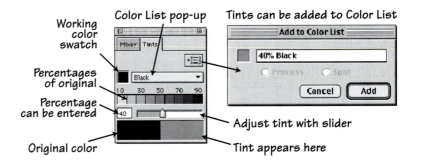

Using the Color List Panel

1. Select **File->New** to create a new document.

2. With the Rectangle tool draw a simple square.

3. Select **Window->Panels->Color List**.

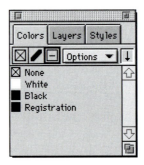

4. With the square selected in the Color List, drag the Black swatch (next to the color name) up to touch the Fill button; the square is now filled with solid black.

5. Click on the Both button. Click on the White name in the Color List. Where did your square go? — It's still there. You can see the selected handles. You painted both White by clicking the Both button, then the White name.

6. Click on the Black name. Both the Fill and Stroke turned Black.

7. Drag the White swatch up to touch the Fill button. The square is now Filled with White, and Stroked with 1 pt. Black.

8. Keep the document open for the next exercise.

Creating Colors

1. Continue working in the open document. Keep the square you drew selected. Select the **Color Mixer** from the **Window->Panels** menu.

2. In the dialog box make certain that the CMYK box is clicked in the upper left corner. Drag the M (Magenta) slider to 37 to mix a custom color.

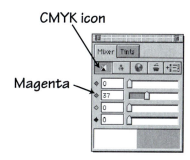

The notation "0c 37m 0y 0k" refers to the percentage of each process color used in the new color. 0c 0m 0y 100k is 100% black, 100c 100m 0y 0k is a bright red, 25c 0m 95y 5k is a yellowish-green color. Experiment with the Color Mixer to see what new colors you can create with different percentages of process colors.

3. **Open** the **Window->Panels->Color List** panel. With both panels open, click the Pointer tool in the **Color Mixer** color sample box (lower right corner) and drag the color to the area of the Color List that holds all the names.

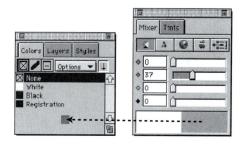

Chapter 9/Painting FreeHand Objects

Color Libraries contained predefined, industry-standard color swatches in the form of a Color System. In North America, the Pantome Matching System (PMS) is the most widely used color system; most of the others available in FreeHand are used in other parts of the world.

4. The color now appears in the list.

5. You can also add standard spot colors such as Pantone through the **Options** menu in **Color List**.

6. Click on the **Options** pull-down menu and select the **Pantone Coated** option to display a dialog box with a library of Pantone colors.

7. Scroll through the window. Type the number 105 in the box and click **OK**.

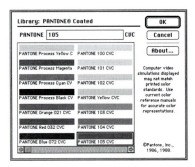

There are thousands of colors from which to choose. They're easy to access through **Libraries** in the **Color List Options** box. If you don't find what you're looking for, you can always create your own and name it whatever you like.

8. Return to the **Color List**. Notice that the Pantone color you selected is now listed.

9. Leave the document open for the next exercise.

Using Tints

1. Select the **Tints** tab in the **Color Mixer**.

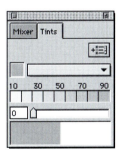

There are several ways to create tints in the Tints panel. There are the percentage buttons, and also the slider underneath them to adjust a desired tint.

2. In the **Color List**, drag Pantone 105 over to the Tint swatch at the bottom left of its panel; the color will appear.

 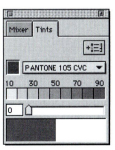

The numbered percentage boxes can be dragged to the lower right sample box.

CHAPTER 9/PAINTING FREEHAND OBJECTS   187

3. In the **Tint** panel, click on the 50% button in the middle. Watch the swatch in the lower right change to the 50% tint.

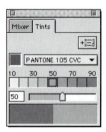

4. From the lower right Tint swatch, drag the new tint to the **Color List** names area.

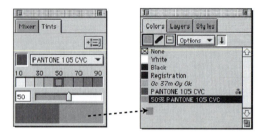

5. FreeHand adds the tint percentage to the name.

6. Draw some basic objects (squares, ovals). Create new tints and assign them to both the fills and strokes of these objects. **Close** the document without saving.

Gradients

Gradients can add to your artwork. The light-to-dark or color-to-color tones add depth and contour to two-dimensional art. To apply a gradient to an object, select it and choose the **Gradient** option in the **Fill Inspector**:

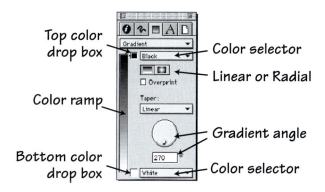

You can use the color pop-up selector to choose colors, or you can drag colors from the **Color List** to the color drop boxes to change the colors in the selected object.

Linear and Radial Gradients

There are two types of gradients:

- **Linear**

- **Radial**

Linear gradients are blends that go from side to side. Radial gradients radiate from a point outward. Select one or the other by clicking on the appropriate icon.

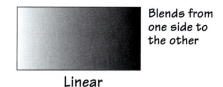

Linear

You also control the angle of gradients and the center point of radials from the Gradient dialog box.

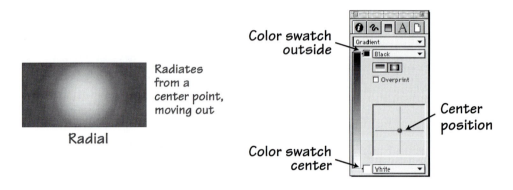

Radial

Radiates from a center point, moving out

Radial Gradient

Color swatch outside

Color swatch center

Center position

Creating Gradients

1. Create a **New** FreeHand document.

2. With the Rectangle tool, draw a rectangle. Click the rectangle with the Pointer tool to select it.

3. **Open** the **Fill Inspector**.

4. Click on the **Gradient** option in the pop-up menu. Be certain that the gradient is set to Linear.

5. Open the **Color List**. Use the **Options** menu to access the **Crayon** selection. Choose two colors of your choice (holding the Shift key) from this assortment. Click **OK**.

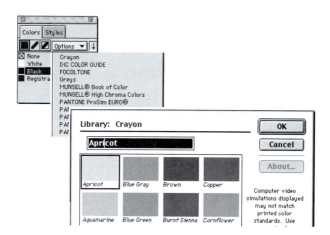

6. Drag one of the new colors from the Color List to the gradient's top drop box. Now drag the other color to the bottom drop box of the gradient. The rectangle gradient on screen is changed by applying these colors.

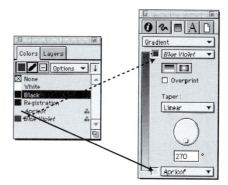

7. Select **Edit->Undo**. Repeat this operation with other colors and observe the effects on the rectangle.

8. Leave the document open for the next exercise.

Creating Radial Gradients

1. With the Ellipse tool, hold the Shift key to draw a circle.

2. Fill the circle with a Radial gradient fill, using two of the Crayon colors for the top and bottom drop boxes, and stroke it with 2 pt. Black.

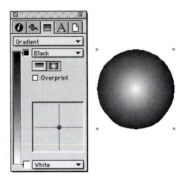

3. Click on the Point of Origin (the dot in the center of the crosshairs) in the **Gradient Inspector**, moving it down and to the left.

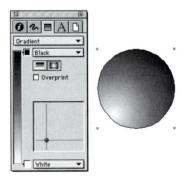

4. The center part of the radial gradient in the circle is moved to the same position. Practive moving the Origin Point in the Inspector and observe how this affects the radial gradient in the circle.

5. **Close** the file without saving.

Complete Project F: Tropical Fish Art

Chapter 10

Anchor Points, Paths, and Segments

Chapter Objective:

To learn and master Freehand's types of anchor points and paths, and the means by which they are modified. In Chapter 10, you will:

- Learn that a segment is the relationship between two points, and what the difference in these relationships means to you.
- Learn about the different kinds of anchor points.
- Understand how the Curve, Corner, and Connector points are used to draw and alter curving segments.
- Learn how to select one or more anchor points in an object.
- Know how to join unconnected anchor points.
- Learn how to select, edit, and modify anchor points and their curves.
- Learn the easiest way to duplicate a path.
- Learn how to modify Direction Handles through the Object Inspector and become comfortable with path modification.
- Learn how to use the Freeform tool to alter anchors or entire paths — even possessing the ability to push and shove against a path to change it.
- Understand how to modify paths and segments by using the Knife tool; learn the difference between the Knife and Freeform tool.

Projects to be Completed:

- Steaming Coffee
- Last Mango Cafe Logo
- Last Mango Business Cards
- Java Jungle
- Coffee Du Jour Ad
- Tropical Fish Art
- **Ball & Mirror**
- Joker's Wild
- Tropical Treasure Logo
- Tropical Treasure Mailer
- Grocery Ad

Anchor Points, Paths, and Segments

It's necessary to know how to draw basic shapes and curves, but the real power of FreeHand's drawing tools is ability to select and modify paths, segments of paths, and points. For example, to get an object "just right" it might be necessary to move one anchor point or adjust its curves. How do you select just one point?

The ability to single out and modify anchor points is the foundation to becoming a proficient user and designer in digital illustration.

Selecting a Single Anchor Point

Selecting a single anchor point is necessary when modifying an object by moving or deleting its points.

- You cannot click directly on the anchor point of an unselected path to select it. The path must first be clicked on to be the selected path, then any of its anchor points can be singled out by clicking on them. If you hold the Shift key, multiple anchor points can be selected.

- You do not have to select a path first if you draw a marquee around the anchor points you wish to select.

- Only hollow anchor points are selected for individual editing.

*Objects made with the Rectangle or Ellipse tools must first be **Ungrouped** before individual anchor points can be selected. Objects made with the Polygon do not need ungrouping.*

 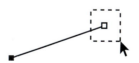 

The path must be selected before clicking individual anchor points

A marquee can select an anchor point without the path being selected

Only hollow anchor points are selected individually for modifications

CHAPTER 10/ANCHOR POINTS, PATHS, AND SEGMENTS

Double-clicking an object will put it in the interactive transform mode, which we haven't discussed yet (the object will be surrounded by a box with handles). If this happens, press the Tab key to exit transform mode.

Adding Points to a Path

Adding anchor points is sometimes necessary depending upon the nature of your design, or the use that works best on many anchor points. You can add more points to any path with the Pen tool.

- The path to receive the added points must first be selected with the Pointer tool; then the Pen tool is clicked on the segment where you want to add the point. This will add an anchor point that can now be moved around or modified.

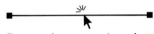 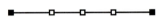

The path to receive the added points must first be selected   **The Pen tool clicked on the selected path adds anchor points where clicked**

Deleting Anchor Points

To delete a single anchor point of an object, select a single anchor point and press the Delete key to remove the point.

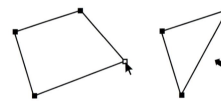

Moving Segments of a Path

You cannot click directly on a segment to move it. Segments are controlled by their anchor points. To move a single segment, the anchor points on either end of the segment must be selected.

If this single segment were to require moving   **The two anchor points on either side of it must be individually selected**   **Then, by dragging on either anchor point, the segment will be isolated for moving**

Connecting Anchor Points

Often, separate anchor points need to be connected to other points to complete a design, or to close a path. This is not always as simple as it sounds because there are several ways to select and connect two points. It's important to get to know these techniques and when to use them:

- Use the Pointer tool to select the two anchor points of two separate paths, then choose **Modify->Join** to connect them. This can only be used for separate paths. It cannot be used to close a single path.

- Use the Pen tool to click on an endpoint of an open path. If want to close the path, click the check box next to the **Closed** option in the Object Inspector. This cannot be done with separate segments. It must be a single, open path.

- Either method can be enhanced by using the Smart Cursors (which can be turned on in **Preferences->General**) to see the status of points that the Pen tool is touching.

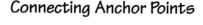

The hollow square means the Pen tool is going to create a new path

The angular "V" shape means that the Pen tool will continue the existing path

The black square means that the point the Pen tool is touching will close the path

It is easier to add anchor points in the Keyline mode when working with thick strokes.

Selecting, Editing, Modifying Anchor Points

1. Open **SF-Intro Freehand->Select & Connect.FH8**.

2. Select **Preferences->General** and verify that **Smart cursors** is clicked. Click on **Object** and select **Option-drag copies paths** (Macintosh) or **Alt-drag copies paths** (Windows). Press **OK**.

3. With the Pointer tool, click on the segment of this single path. Hold the mouse button down until the cursor turns into a cross with arrowheads.

CHAPTER 10/ANCHOR POINTS, PATHS, AND SEGMENTS

Hold the Option (Macintosh) or Alt (Windows) key and the Shift key as you move the path. Drag the selected path to the right a distance of 1 inch. This will duplicate the path.

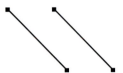

4. With the Pointer tool, marquee the two top anchor points of the paths to select them.

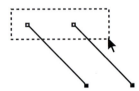

5. Select **Modify->Join**. The two selected points should be connected, yet the wrong points connected.

6. There's a reason for this. When Joining, FreeHand connects the two closest points of the selected paths. In this case, though it wasn't apparent, the bottom anchor point was closer to the top point that it was connected to.

7. Select **Edit->Undo**. Move the right path closer to the original — about 1/2-inch apart.

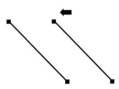

8. Again, marquee the two top anchor points and go to **Modify->Join**.

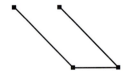

Don't get frustrated. We're showing you what could go wrong to save you hours on the phone with the FreeHand Technical Helpline. Yes, the two top anchors are much closer together, and should, theoretically, connect.

The easiest way to duplicate a path is to hold the Option (Macintosh) or Alt (Windows) key as you drag the object. Make certain that "Option/Alt-drag copies paths" is clicked in File->Preferences->Object.

198 CHAPTER 10/ANCHOR POINTS, PATHS, AND SEGMENTS

The keyboard shortcut for Undo is Command-Z (Macintosh) or Control-Z (Windows).

But they didn't. The reason for this is Path Direction. When first drawn, the bottom points were the endpoints of the paths. You must reverse direction to put emphasis on the top points.

9. Select both paths, then go to **Modify->Alter Path->Reverse Direction**. One last time, marquee the top anchor points and go to **Modify->Join**.

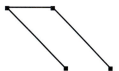

10. Don't bother selecting the bottom points and using Join. It only works on two separate paths. Your path is almost a closed path now. Closing this path actually can be done with three different methods.

11. To use the simplest method, select the path. Select the Object Inspector and click on the **Closed** box, you will see a closing segment appear. The object is now a closed path that can be **Filled**. Select **Edit->Undo**.

12. Select the Pen tool and click its crosshair on one of the bottom anchor points. Now touch (don't click) the crosshair to the other bottom point; a black dot appears on the crosshair.

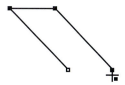

This tells you that this point will close the path when clicked. Click the Pen tool on this point. Notice how the path has become closed with this new segment. Select **Edit->Undo**.

13. The third method is only used in certain cases. With the Pointer tool, select and drag one of the bottom points so that it is directly over the other bottom point. Release the mouse — the path is now closed. Leave the path in this closed state and keep it selected.

The keyboard shortcut for the Join command is Command-J (Macintosh) or Control-J (Windows).

You can easily select one or more objects and/or paths with the marquee, which appears when you click and drag over objects with the Pointer. To completely select an object (such as a group, primitive shape, or path) you must completely surround it with the marquee. You can select specific points on a path by drawing a marquee over the area containing the points you want (note that the entire path will also be selected, but that the points you drew the marquee over will become hollow, which means you can now edit them as you wish).

14. Access the Pen tool and click the crosshair on the middle of the left side segment. Click on this new point with the Pointer tool to select it, then drag the point to the lower left.

15. Use the Pointer tool to select the path, then select the two bottom points (don't marquee). Drag one of the selected points to move the segment.

 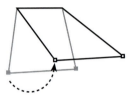

16. Let's imagine that the design now requires the bottom segment to be deleted. How do you delete a segment? Yes, you can delete anchor points, but if you delete the bottom anchor points you will not have much left to work with.

17. What if you toggled off the **Closed** box in the Object Inspector? Yes, this does delete one single segment. Will it be the right segment? Try it. Select the Object Inspector and unclick the **Closed** box.

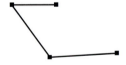

That was not the correct segment. Select **Edit->Undo**.

18. Select the path, then use the Pen tool to create a new anchor point on the bottom segment. Use the Pointer tool to marquee-select just this point.

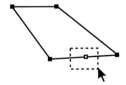

The keyboard shortcut for the Split command is Command-Shift-J (Macintosh) or Control-J (Windows).

19. Select **Modify->Split**. The path will change slightly. Now marquee the same point again with the Pointer tool. Press the Delete key.

20. Now marquee the two left side anchor points, then press the Delete key.

21. You have now created, added, deleted, moved, and modified anchor points.

22. **Close** the document without saving.

Modifying Direction Handles

Once points have been drawn, the type of points can be changed with the Object Inspector.

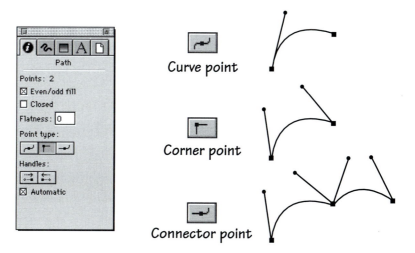

Modifying Curve Anchor Points

1. Create a **New** document. Select **Window->Inspectors->Object** to access the Object Inspector.

2. With the Pen tool, drag an initial curved anchor point. Move the mouse to the right, then, holding the Shift key to constrain, click-drag again to pull out the control handles. Move the mouse to the right and single-click a final endpoint.

3. Select the first anchor point, which, by default, is a Curve point. Move its control handle to see how the curve is affected. In the Object Inspector, click on the middle point type, which is the Corner point. Move the same control handle to see if any changes were made to the curve. Don't be surprised if very little transpires. More will happen as you progress with the points and the Object Inspector.

4. Click on the third point type in the Object Inspector; this is the Connector point. Notice how the segment changed on the path. Now try to move the handle; you will not have much success in maneuvering it. This is because Connector points do exactly what the name implies — connects two segments. This Connector point is at the end of one segment.

5. With this point still selected, access the Pen tool and click down to the left of the Connector point; a new point will appear with a segment between the two points. With the Pointer tool, click on the Connector point and drag the control handle. Be aware that Connector points are not very versatile, but they will alter the curve slightly. Work with its handle to see how far it will go.

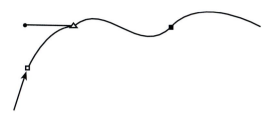

6. With the Pointer tool, select the anchor point to the right of the Connector point. To see its control handles look at the Object Inspector and notice how the point type changed to Curve point.

7. Click on the top handle and drag it downward. Notice how the segments on either side of the point were altered. This is one of the easiest ways to recognize a Curve point, which behaves this way:

8. In the Object Inspector, click on the middle point type — the Corner point. You will not see anything obvious happen to the path, but drag the topmost anchor point and observe how much of the path moves. The Corner point does not control two segments at once. This is one of the ways to fine-tune only portions of a curved path.

9. Now, in the Object Inspector, click on the Connector point icon to change the selected pointto flatten out the curve segment. Drag on the Connector point control handle to see just how much you can alter this type of anchor point.

10. Click on the Curve point icon in the Object Inspector to change the selected point back to its original state. Drag on the control handle to see how the point is back to its malleable state.

11. You have now worked with and observed how anchor points can be changed in the Object Inspector.

12. **Close** the document without saving.

Creating and Managing Anchor Points and Segments

1. From the **File** menu, select **New** to create a new document.

2. Select the Pen tool and click the crosshair once on the page; this will create the beginning point of the path. Move the mouse to the right and slightly upward. Click the second anchor point. Move the mouse to the right and downward, then click the third anchor point.

3. With the Pointer tool, click on the last point (endpoint) made to select it. Selected anchor points are hollow. If the clicked anchor point does not look hollow, click again. When selected, anchor points can be moved or deleted. Move the selected point to the upper right.

4. Select the middle anchor point and move it up slightly to the left.

5. With the Pointer tool, select the path. With the Pen tool, click the crosshair on the middle of the second segment. This will add an anchor point.

6. With the Pointer tool, select this new anchor point and drag it downward.

7. Keep the path selected and use the Pen tool to click-drag a curve direction handle from the right endpoint.

8. Move the Pen tool down and single-click an endpoint.

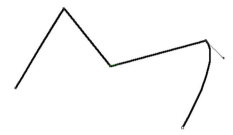

9. Click on the direction handle and pull it to the right to alter the curve of the segment.

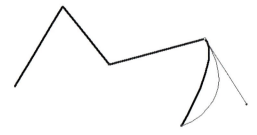

10. Marquee-select the new anchor point created in step 5. Delete this point.

11. Click on the endpoint of the path to see the direction handle of the curving segment. Drag the handle to the right to round the curve more.

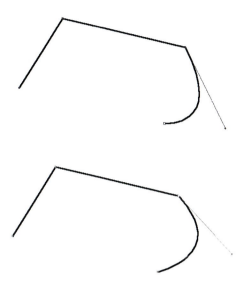

12. Select the Pen tool and click on the endpoint. Now click on the first point you made. This final click has completed the making of a closed path.

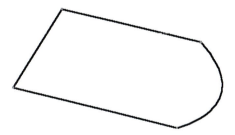

13. **Close** the document without saving.

The Knife Tool

Occasionally, you'll need to make more drastic changes to a path than simply moving a point around. The Knife tool can perform these alterations to a path without disturbing other points or control handles.

You can easily cut through an object with the Knife tool. Select the tool and drag the crosshair through the object. The path is split wherever the Knife tool crosses it, creating two or more separate, open paths.

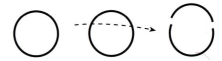

The Freeform Tool

The Freeform tool can easily alter anchors or entire paths. Its most unusual ability lets you push and shove against a path to change it.

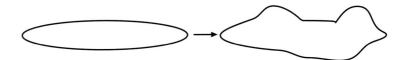

Path Modifying Tools

1. From the **File** menu, select **New** to create a new document. The two path modifying tools are the Knife and Freeform tools.

2. With the Rectangle tool, draw a 1 inch square on the page.

3. Click on the square to select it. With the Knife tool, drag the crosshair in a sweep across the square.

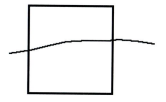

4. You have cut the selected path where the Knife tool touched it. Click on the top part of the square and press the Up Arrow key several times to see the separation. Use **Edit->Undo** to undo the moving and Knife cut to have the uncut square you drew.

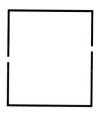

5. Select the square again. Hold the Option (Mactintosh) or Alt (Windows) key as you drag the Knife tool across at an angle. Notice how the Knife cut remains straight, allowing you further control over where it cuts.

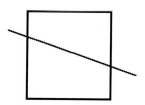

6. With the Pointer tool, select the top part of the square and press the Up Arrow key several times to see the separation. Use **Edit->Undo** to return to the original square.

7. Select the square again. Now drag the Knife tool across the square, but hold both the Shift key and Option (Macintosh) or Alt (Windows) key as you drag. Notice the Knife stroke constrains to 45° increments.

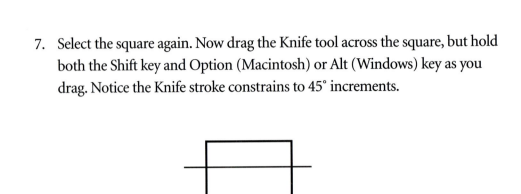

8. Click on the top part of the square and press the Up Arrow key several times to see the separation. Select the paths and delete them.

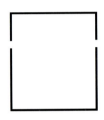

9. The Freeform tool is a new and unique tool that alters a path with two techniques. With the Rectangle tool, draw a simple rectangle.

10. The object does not have to be selected for you to work on. Select the Freeform tool in the Toolbox, then click-drag its hollow arrow directly on the rectangle path. Do this on the top segment near the upper left corner. When you drag, you will see the segment extending in a curved manner.

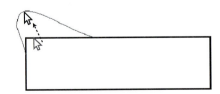

11. Release the mouse. You will see the modified path and its new anchor points.

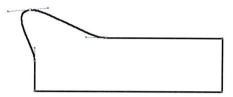

12. Click-drag the Freeform cursor on the bottom segment near the bottom left corner.

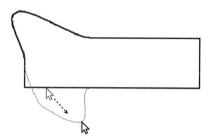

13. Release the mouse. You will see the modified path and its new anchor points.

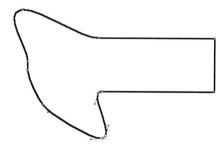

14. If you do not touch the path segments with the Freeform tool when you click-drag, its cursor turns into a circle shape. Select the Freeform tool again and position its cursor inside the rectangle, but do not touch any segment.

Drag upward and you will see the path extending along with the cursor.

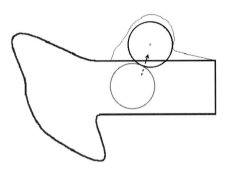

15. Release the mouse. Move the Freeform cursor under the rectangle and click-drag upward.

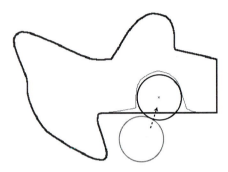

16. Release the mouse. You will now see an entirely different shape than the rectangle you started with.

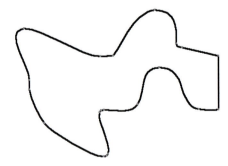

17. You have now seen how the Knife and Freeform tools modify paths.

18. **Close** the document without saving.

Complete Project G: Ball and Mirror

Chapter 11

Transformation Tools

Chapter Objective:

To learn the four transformational techniques with which you can drastically change an object. In Chapter 11, you will:

- Learn about the transformation tools, with which you scale, rotate, skew, and reflect objects.

- Understand the three transformation modes; learn to use the tools in the Transform panel for precise operations.

- Learn how to manually rotate an object with the Rotate tool; how to create a design with the Rotate tool, and to understand the different features of the Rotate panel.

- Learn how to use the Refect tool to mirror a selected object across a specified axis; learn how to set the Reflect axis; understand how to reflect an object from the Transform panel; learn to to use Reflect to create symmetrical designs.

- Learn how to scale objects in the Scale panel.

- Understand how the Skew tool slants or obliques a selected object to create special effects; learn how to skew objects in the Transform panel.

- Learn how to use the Interactive Transformer, and how to make it appear.

Projects to be Completed:

- Steaming Coffee
- Last Mango Cafe Logo
- Last Mango Business Cards
- Java Jungle
- Coffee Du Jour Ad
- Tropical Fish Art
- Ball & Mirror
- Joker's Wild
- Tropical Treasure Logo
- Tropical Treasure Mailer
- Grocery Ad

Transformation Tools

The FreeHand Toolbox includes a set of transformation tools. You can Rotate, Reflect, Scale, and Skew objects with these tools. Transformations can be done three ways: manually with the Toolbox tools, numerically using the Transform panel, or interactively with the Interactive Transformer.

The Three Transformation Modes

When a transformation tool is selected in the toolbox, the cursor changes to a crosshair that can be used to mark the origin of transformation. This is the center of the transformation, often called the origin point, where the transformation occurs. The cursor is dragged on or around the selected object to perform the transformation.

If you double-click on a transformation tool in the Toolbox, the Transform panel with the available options appears. This is a more accurate means of making transformations. Move is not really a transformation, but it's included in the Transform panel so you can precisely move objects.

The Interactive Transformer appears if you double-click on an object with the pointer tool.

Press Command-M (Macintosh) or Control-M (Windows) to open the Transform panel.

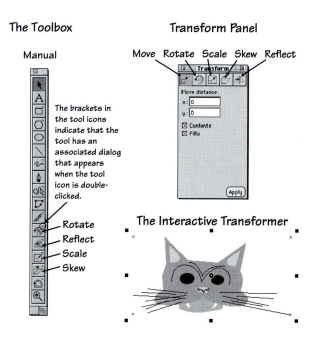

Positive degrees will rotate an object to the left; negative degrees will rotate it to the right.

Rotate

An object can be manually rotated by selecting the artwork, choosing the Rotate tool, and simply rotating the object. Rotation occurs around the point of origin, which is wherever you click the mouse in a simple rotation. Rotation can be accomplished through **Window->Panels->Transform**, or by using the Interactive Transformer, shown later in this section.

Here are the Rotate panel's options:

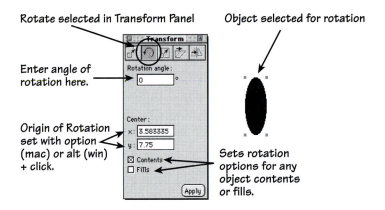

Creating a Design with Rotate

1. Create a **New** document.

2. Use the Ellipse tool to draw an oval like the one shown below. **Edit->Clone** the oval.

3. With the cloned oval selected, click on the Rotate tool. Click the crosshair underneath the oval while holding Option (Macintosh) or Alt (Windows) to set the origin of transformation.

Press Command-= (Macintosh) or Control-= (Windows) to clone an object. Cloning makes a duplicate of the object and places the duplicate exactly on top of the original.

If you move the copy of a duplicated object, then create another duplicate, the copy moves exactly the same distance and/or rotates the same number of degrees as the first duplicate. This is very useful for creating repetitive designs.

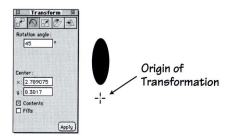

Origin of Transformation

Double-click the Rotate tool to show the **Transform** panel. In the Transform panel, type 45° for the Rotation angle. Click **Apply** (Macintosh) or **Rotate** (Windows). The clone rotates 45° to the left. If you have typed −45°, it would have rotated to the right.

4. Press Command-D (Macintosh) or Control-D (Windows) six times to complete the flower image.

5. Use the Ellipse tool to draw a circle for the center of this flower.

Double-clicking a transformation tool in the Toolbox sets the Origin Point to the exact center of the selected object(s).

CHAPTER 11/TRANSFORMATION TOOLS

6. **Edit->Select->All** the objects and delete them.

7. Keep the document open for the next exercise.

Reflect

The Reflect tool is used to mirror a selected object across a specified axis. You can set the Reflect axis in the dialog box, or set it manually by clicking the tool crosshair on the page while holding the Option (Macintosh) or Alt (Windows) key. Reflect is not available in the Interactive Transformer.

You can also reflect an object just by clicking the tool's crosshair near the selected object. The default reflection is 90°, or about the vertical axis.

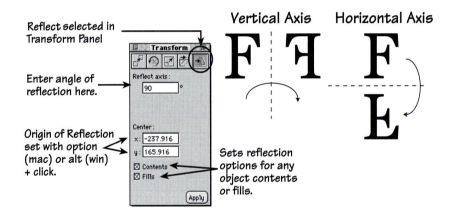

To make a reflection of an object, select the object, then open the Transform panel by double-clicking on the Reflect tool. In the Transform panel, type the Reflect axis into the field. 90° produces a vertical reflection; 180° makes a horizontal reflection, and any other value will reflect the object around an imaginary axis of the specified angle.

The Reflect tool is very useful in generating symmetrical components, to make one side of an illustration look just like a mirror-image of the other side.

Using Reflect to Create Symmetrical Designs

1. Continue working in the open document.

2. Use the Pen tool to create half a champagne glass.

3. **Edit->Clone** the object. Double-click on the Reflect tool to display the Transform panel. Hold the Option/Alt key and click the crosshair on the upper right point of the glass path. Type 90° for the Reflect axis and click Apply (Macintosh) or Reflect (Windows). Both examples show different units, but unless you are setting the center numerically, it's not really an issue, since the end result is the same.

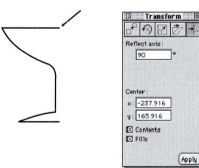 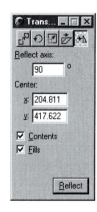

           Macintosh   **Windows**

4. The clone reflects across the vertical axis, originating the transformation from where you clicked the crosshair.

Joining objects is not like grouping them; if two objects are joined, they become one object; if they were grouped, they'd still be two objects after ungrouping.

CHAPTER 11/TRANSFORMATION TOOLS

Remember that selected anchor points turn hollow, which shows that they can be edited, joined, moved, and so forth.

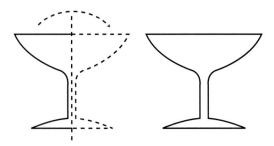

5. Marquee the two center anchor points at the top of the glass. **Modify ->Join** them. Then select the Object Inspector and click Closed, to make it a closed path.

6. Keep the document open for the next exercise.

Scale

The Scale tool allows resizing of selected objects; the scaling can be uniform or not. Uniform scaling means that the object is scaled proportionally and will maintain the same aspects.

Scaling type and objects increases or decreases the thickness of any strokes in the object, and increases or decreases the weight of type. When scaling type, try to avoid horizontal or vertical scaling, which can result in distorted letterforms.

Here's the Scale panel's options:

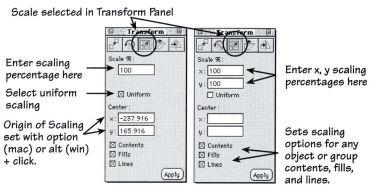

To scale one or more objects, select them, then choose the Scale tool. Hold the Shift key while dragging to scale the object(s) proportionally; otherwise they will be scaled rather non-proportionally. Double-click on the Scale tool to show the Transform panel for scaling.

You can choose **Uniform** and type in the percentage of the desired scale. If you deselect **Uniform**, the **X** and **Y** fields appear so you can use different horizontal and vertical scaling percentages. The default **Center** settings are the actual center of the object, so it will scale in position if you leave these settings alone.

Scaling Objects

1. Continue working in the open document.

2. With the Pointer tool, select the champagne glass.

3. Double-click on the Scale tool in the Toolbox to show the Scaling panel. Select **Uniform**, then type 50 in the **Scale** % box. Click Apply (Macintosh) or Scale (Windows).

CHAPTER 11/TRANSFORMATION TOOLS

4. The champagne glass reduces 50% in size and doesn't change its relative position, since no change in center was applied. Changing the center will scale the object and move the object to the specified coordinates relative to the object's center.

5. Keep the document open for the next exercise.

Skew

The Skew tool slants or obliques a selected object to create, for example, a reflected shadow of an object. Like the other transformational tools, you can use the Skew tool manually or with the Skew panel. Skew is not available in the Interactive Transformer.

You can easily skew an object by selecting the Skew tool and manually experimenting with different mouse moves to skew the object interactively.

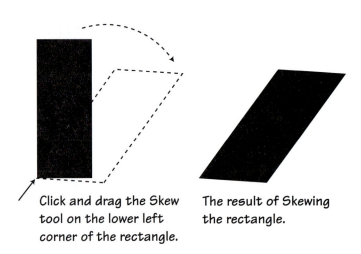

Click and drag the Skew tool on the lower left corner of the rectangle.

The result of Skewing the rectangle.

You can also use the Skew panel to set numeric skew angles and centers.

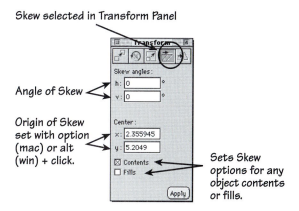

Skew selected in Transform Panel
Angle of Skew
Origin of Skew set with option (mac) or alt (win) + click.
Sets Skew options for any object contents or fills.

Skewing Objects

1. Continue working in the open document.

2. Use the Pointer tool to select the scaled champagne glass.

3. Select the Skew tool. Click the crosshair on the bottom left point of the base of the glass. Drag the tool so that the glass begins to skew.

4. Move the mouse around while dragging to see how it affects the skewing procedure.

5. Click the crosshair on other points of origin and drag to see how the Origin of Transformation affects the skewing procedure.

6. **Close** the document without saving.

The Interactive Transformer

New to FreeHand 8 is the interactive transform tool with which you can move, scale, and rotate (but not reflect or skew) an object. Double-click on any object with the Pointer and you'll see the Interactive Transformer:

You click and drag on the handles to scale the object. Click outside the bounds of the transformer to rotate the item with reference to the center point (the dot in the middle). You can move the center point anywhere within the bounds as a reference point for rotation. Click inside the bounds and you can move the object anywhere on the page. Simply moving the mouse over the various parts of the transformer will change it to the appropriate tool for moving, rotation, or scaling.

Here's what the handles do:

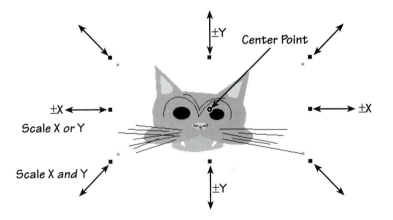

Confusing? Not really. Corner handles scale the image along the X and Y axes (hold the shift key down to scale proportionally). Handles on the top, bottom, and sides scale along either the X or Y axis. Moving the pointer outside, near any handle, changes the cursor to a rotation tool, and you can use any handle to rotate the object. Hold the Shift key to constrain rotation to 45° increments. It doesn't matter which handle you use for rotation; the object rotates only around the center point.

Moving the center point changes the reference for rotation. Here, the center point has been moved to the right, and rotation started from the lower right corner. The cat rotates relative to the center point.

Using the Interactive Transformer

1. Choose **File->New** to create a new document.

2. Draw a star or any other shape you like.

3. Double-click the shape to invoke the interactive transformer.

4. Hold down the shift key, then click and drag on the lower right corner handle to scale the object proportionally.

5. Move the center point anywhere within the bounds of the transformer, then rotate the object any way you like.

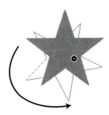

6. You've just seen a much faster way of scaling and rotating an object, instead of using the panels and tools.

Complete Project H: Joker's Wild

Chapter 12

Xtras

Chapter Objective:

To learn about the Xtras included with Freehand, which accomplish a wide range of functions. In Chapter 12, you will learn:

- Learn about FreeHand's additional plug-in functions called Xtras; learn how to use Xtras to enhance standard features with special features.
- Find out what defines Xtras, and where to acquire new ones.
- Learn how to locate Xtras in the Xtras menu and the Xtra Tools panel.
- Understand how to use the 3D rotation, smudge, fisheye lens, and bend Xtras to alter an object.
- Understand how to use the arc, spiral, shadow, chart, and mirror extras to create new objects based on either an existing object or from values that you supply.
- Understand how to use the graphic hose Xtra to "spray" objects across the page.
- Learn how to use the chart Xtra to create simple graphic bar charts.

Projects to be Completed:

- Steaming Coffee
- Last Mango Cafe Logo
- Last Mango Business Cards
- Java Jungle
- Coffee Du Jour Ad
- Tropical Fish Art
- Ball & Mirror
- Joker's Wild
- **Tropical Treasure Logo**
- **Tropical Treasure Mailer**
- Grocery Ad

Xtras

FreeHand has additional plug-in functions called **Xtras**, which enhance the standard features with special features that have been requested in the past by FreeHand users. You can further customize a design to meet your requirements by applying the appropriate **Xtras**.

A number of **Xtras** are standard features in FreeHand. You can purchase specialized plug-ins from Macromedia and other software developers. If you have Adobe Illustrator, you can bring Illustrator filters into the **Xtras** menu and use them in FreeHand.

The Xtras

There are too many Xtras to show how each one affects selected objects, but we will do an overview of some of the more frquently-used Xtras.

Xtras have their own menu in the Menubar.

Press Option-Command-X (Macintosh) or Alt-Control-X (Windows) to show the Xtra Tools panel.

Additional Xtra Plug-ins are found in **Window->Xtras->Xtra Tools**.

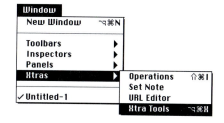

CHAPTER 12/XTRAS

229

Xtra Tools

Xtra Tools are a variety of operations that perform path modifications that would be either difficult or time-consuming to do by hand. Think of Xtra Tools as an extended and enhanced Toolbox. Usually, you just select an Xtra Tool and drag its crosshair cursor over an object, but some have dialog boxes that allow you to modify certain options to suit your particular needs.

The Xtra Tools panel looks like this:

Xtra Tool icons that have little angle brackets in the upper right corners will show behaviour-controlling dialogs.

We won't cover every Xtra in FreeHand; some of them are not very useful or are beyond the scope of this course, but we'll take a look at some of the more fun and useful ones that can really make complex operations much easier.

3D Rotation

The 3D tool skews objects, creating a 3D effect. You can adjust the tool's behaviour by double-clicking on it in the Xtra Tools panel.

Original   3D Rotated

Double-click on the 3-D Rotation icon to display its dialog box. It has two modes: Easy and Expert. We'll describe the options in the Easy mode for this course.

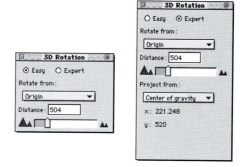

- **Rotate From** — choose the point of origin of the rotation from this pop-menu: *Mouse Click* rotates the object with respect to where you click the mouse. *Center of Selection* rotates from the center of the object. *Center of Gravity* rotates by the apparent visual center of the object. *Origin* rotates from the lower left corner of the object.

- **Distance** — Drag the slider to the left to increase distortion or to the right to minimize distortion.

Arc

The Arc tool draws several types of arcs. The way you drag the tool on the page determines the arc's orientation. Double-click on the Arc tool and experiment with the Arc settings to see the effects you can achieve.

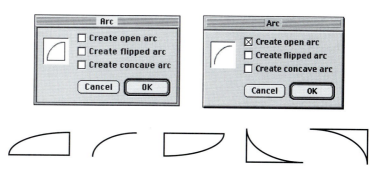

Fisheye Lens

The Fisheye Lens magnifies portions of objects to look like they were viewed through a fisheye camera lens. You can set the curvature to be concave (inward) or convex (outward) in the Fisheye Lens dialog.

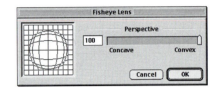

Original

After Convex Fisheye Lens

After Concave Fisheye Lens

Smudge

The Smudge tool creates graduated tones of the selected object. You can specify different fill and stroke colors in the Smudge dialog. Double-click the Smudge tool icon to show the dialog.

Drag color swatches to the Fill and Stroke color wells in the dialog.

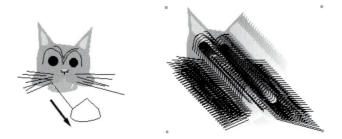

Drag tool to set direction of smudge   After Smudging

Spiral

The Spiral tool draws a spiral much faster and more accurately than trying to draw one with the Pen. Double-click the Spiral tool to display its dialog box.

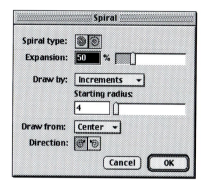

These settings will draw a spiral like this:

Experiment with the settings to draw different spirals. If you hold the shift key while drawing, the origin of the spiral can be constrained to 45° angles. Try expanding the stroke of a spiral and applying some cool fills.

Shadow

The Shadow tool creates a shadowed copy of the original. The Shadow dialog has several options and you can create some interesting effects by experimenting with them.

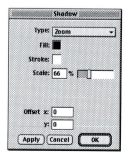

These settings produced this type of shadow; you can also add colors or tints to a shadow in the Shadow dialog.

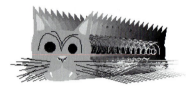

Roughen

Roughen takes the segments and anchor points of a path and breaks them into random anchors, making erratic or rough edges of the object. You can set the amount of roughness in the Roughen dialog box. Moving the slider to the right creates finer gradations; to the left creates coarser gradations.

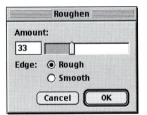

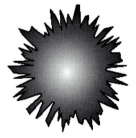

Before Roughen   After Roughen, set to 33

Mirror

Used as an enhanced reflecting tool, Mirror reflects a duplicate across a 90° axis when clicked on or near a selected object. This eliminates the need to duplicate an object and reflect it. You can also set the mirroring across the X, Y, or both axes in the Mirror dialog and you can also rotate the objects while mirroring them. The Mirror dialog has a few settings.

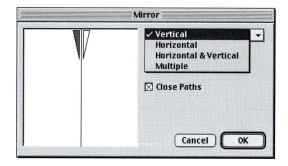

Choosing Multiple lets you also rotate the objects.

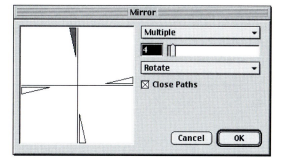

This is the result of multiple mirror with rotate:

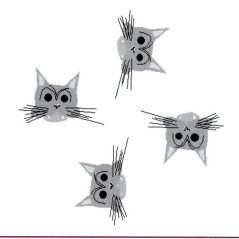

Graphic Hose

The Graphic Hose "shoots" an object with each click, or "sprays" one or more objects if the mouse button is held down. FreeHand comes with a few pre-made hose objects but you can easily add your own, and you can add up to ten FreeHand objects to a hose to create a series of hose "splats." It's easier and more fun to just try it.

Hosing a Page

1. Choose **File->New** to create a new document.

2. Choose **Windows->Xtras->Tools** to show the Xtra Tools panel.

3. Double-click on the Graphic Hose tool to open the control box.

Press Option-Command-X (Macintosh) or Alt-Control-X (Windows) to show the Xtra Tools panel.

4. Choose **Flowers** from the pop-up menu and spray a few on the page.

Choose **Clover** from the pop-up menu and place a few clover leaves on the page.

5. Select and Open **SF->Intro FreeHand->Kitties.FH8**. Choose **Edit->Select** all and group the objects. Scale the cat down to about 20%. Copy the cat. **Close** the document without saving.

6. In the **Graphic Hose** control box, select **New** from the pop-up menu, and name the new hose pattern "Kitties". Click **Paste In** to paste the cat into the hose pattern.

7. Spray a cornucopia of cats on the page.

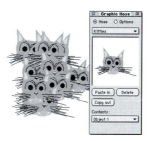

8. Experiment with the Graphic Hose settings. Click the **Options** button to reveal more hose controls. Try hosing other objects and changing the settings in the control options.

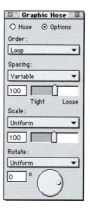

9. **Close** the document without saving.

Chart

The Chart Xtra creates a chart according to numeric data that you supply. **Chart** is selected from **Window->Xtras->Xtra tools**.

To create a chart, click the Chart tool and drag a rectangle on the page. The chart data input dialog box appears and the numeric chart data can be entered on the input line above the data cells. Type your information into the input line and press the Return key to enter the data into a cell. Click a cell to change the data.

When you click **OK**, the chart will appear.

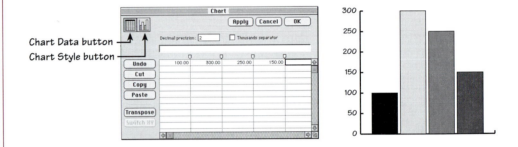

Editing Charts

Select the chart with the pointer and double-click the Chart tool to edit the chart's data or appearance. Click the Chart Style icon to change the chart's style.

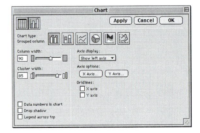

The changes will be applied to the chart when you click **OK**.

Pictograph

Pictograph replaces chart columns with artwork copied to the clipboard. Select **Xtras->Chart->Pictograph** to replace the columns of the selected chart with the objects in the clipboard.

Bend

The Bend Xtra tool bends segments of a path depending upon how you drag the cursor. You can control the amount of bend with the slider in the Bend dialog box.

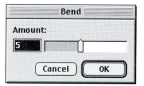

After clicking the Bend tool, you can drag anywhere around or on the selected object. If you pull the cursor down, the curves will round outward; if you pull the cursor up, they go inward.

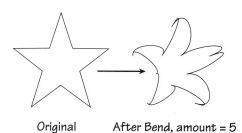

Original   After Bend, amount = 5

Press Option-Command-X (Macintosh) or Alt-Control-X (Windows) to show the Xtra Tools panel.

Experimenting with Xtras

1. Create a **New** document.

2. Draw an object of any shape and select it.

3. Select **Window->Xtras->Xtra tools** and click the Roughen tool. Drag the crosshair cursor on or near your selected object. Watch what happens when you drag the object. Experiment with how the tool affects the object you have drawn. Press Command (Macintosh) or Control (Windows)-Z to **Undo**.

4. With the object selected, open the **Xtra Tools** panel and click on the Fisheye Lens tool. Drag the cursor on top of the object; the tool bends an object to look as if it were seen through a fisheye camera lens. Experiment with dragging this tool on various parts of an object to see the interesting effects that you can create. Delete the object when finished.

5. Click on the Arc tool in the Xtra Tools panels and drag the cursor on the page to draw an arc. Release the mouse when the arc is drawn.

6. Double-click on the Arc tool in the Xtra Tools panel. Click the **Create open arc** option to deselect it.

7. Drag the cursor on the page to draw another arc. The arc is now a closed path.

8. Select this path and click on the 3D Rotation tool in the Xtra Tools panel. Drag the cursor near the object and see how it skews. You could use it to create a 3-dimensional look.

9. With the object selected, click on the Mirror tool in the Xtra Tools panels. Drag the cursor on the image and observe how it will reflect without the Reflect tool. Duplicate it. Select and delete these objects.

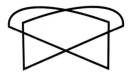

10. Click on the Spiral tool in the Xtra Tools panel. Drag its cursor on the page to draw a spiral.

11. Select the Smudge tool in the Xtra Tools panel. Drag the cursor-hand across the selected spiral. When you let go, you will see the smudge.

13. Click on the Chart tool in the Xtra Tools panel.

14. With the Chart cursor, draw a square about 3 inches across.

15. In the **Chart** input box, type the following information:

    100   300   250   150

16. Press **OK**. FreeHand makes a simple bar chart based on the data entered.

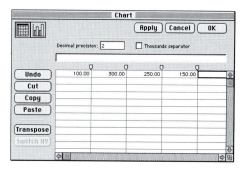 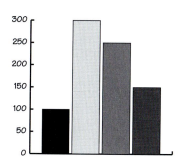

17. **Close** the document without saving.

Complete Project I: Tropical Treasure Logo

Complete Project J: Tropical Treasure Mailer

Notes:

Chapter 13

Importing, Exporting, and Output

Chapter Objective:

To learn how to print documents, and how to export documents for use in other applications. In Chapter 13, you will:

- Know why and when you need to export FreeHand documents.

- Learn how to import, export, and print a document; understand how to exchange information between other applications.

- Understand the two main types of imported graphic files: Vector and Raster images, and the differences between them.

- Learn how a vector image is drawn in certain applications as path-oriented outlines; understand the screen appearance of a vector image.

- Learn how to edit Vector EPS images with tools from within Freehand.

- Understand how a vector image and FeeHand path image will differ in its on screen appearance.

- Learn how to modify raster images in Freehand; study how the Object Inspector can provide information about a specific object.

- Understand how to link and embed imported graphics; how FreeHand copies the source graphic and stores it in the FreeHand document and the advantage that brings to you.

- Understand how to set up the print options.

Projects to be Completed:

- Steaming Coffee
- Last Mango Cafe Logo
- Last Mango Business Cards
- Java Jungle
- Coffee Du Jour Ad
- Tropical Fish Art
- Ball & Mirror
- Joker's Wild
- Tropical Treasure Logo
- Tropical Treasure Mailer
- **Grocery Ad**

Importing, Exporting, and Output

Today's designers don't work in a vacuum. You may be expected to work with other designers and layout artists who may be using completely different applications (such as Adobe Illustrator, Corel Draw, QuarkXPress, Adobe Pagemaker) and computer platforms (Windows or Macintosh). There are established standards for exchanging information (text, images, drawings, completed publications) between these applications and platforms, and FreeHand is designed with these standards and realities in mind.

Getting Information into FreeHand

You can Import a variety of graphic file formats into a FreeHand document, such as artwork from other drawing applications like Adobe Illustrator or CorelDraw, or photographic images from Photoshop or a desktop scanner. Different graphic formats have their advantages, and their drawbacks. Knowing how an image is built, and how it can be modified, is the secret to confidently managing images.

There are two main types of imported graphic files:

- Vector

- Raster (bitmapped)

Vector and Raster images are created in different ways. Artwork drawn in FreeHand, Illustrator, or CorelDraw is created in a Vector-based format, made with points and paths. Raster images are bitmapped, originating from a variety of sources, such as scanning, or from image-editing applications such as Adobe Photoshop.

Vector Images

Vector images are those made in programs such as FreeHand and Adobe Illustrator that draw path-oriented outlines based on mathematical algorithms. You can enlarge or reduce these images infinitely without suffering a loss of quality. Remember the old kids' game of Cat's Cradle? If not, it is played with a long piece of string laced between the fingers to form different patterns.

Replacing the string with a big rubber band lets you pull your hands apart to make the pattern bigger; although the rubber band will become thinner, the curves and lines made with it remain smooth.

Vector images are analogous to the rubber band: you can enlarge them as much as you like (and they won't snap). However, just as the rubber band gets thinner when stretched, vector images will reflect enlargement. Strokes become thinner relative to their placement, type may stretch unexpectedly, patterns may distort. Similarly, when reduced, strokes may become too fat for the size of the art; type may plug up and vanish, images may turn into formless blobs. If you plan on drastically enlarging or reducing artwork, you need to account for these results in your design.

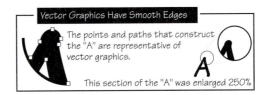

The Screen Appearance of Vector Images

When Vector images are imported, what you see on the screen is a low-resolution raster preview of the image. When printed, though, the image will reproduce as smoothly as your printer can possibly make it.

In this example, the left star is an imported Vector EPS; the right star is a path residing in the document. Notice how the imported image has some jagginess on its exterior. The path is much smoother, because FreeHand displays resident objects as smooth vectors, not low-resolution raster previews.

The two objects look like this in Keyline mode. The imported EPS is on the left; the path is on the right.

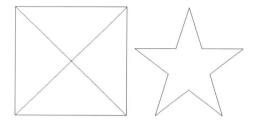

The bounding box with an "X" in it is also a way to identify an imported Vector EPS in most programs. Raster images also have a bounding box, but do not have the "X".

Editing Vector EPS Images

Most Vector EPS images, when imported, can be edited with tools from the Toolbox. This is controlled in the **File->Preferences->Import** option. The feature, **Convert editable EPS when imported**, must be clicked if you want the image to have editable paths. Otherwise, the graphic will be one single image on which you can only perform certain transformations.

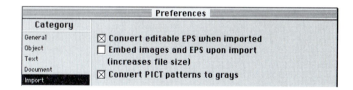

Sometimes, FreeHand can't even import its own EPS files. Always keep the original artwork in the native FreeHand format and use EPS as an export format only, or save your work in the Editable EPS format.

Other programs, such as PageMaker or QuarkXPress have the ability to export their files as EPS, but this does not mean that they can be imported into FreeHand with editable paths. You must use discretion and your knowledge of the elements in the EPS file when you import them into FreeHand for editing.

In this example the left image was imported with **Convert editable EPS when imported** clicked in Preferences; the right image was imported without this option clicked. The left image has paths that you modify, but the right image is a single, uneditable object and only limited FreeHand transformations can be performed on it.

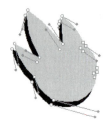 

Exporting Vector EPS Images Imported into FreeHand

You might have an imported Vector EPS image as a part of your design. Then the client calls and wants a TIFF (a raster image format) file of the design to give to a newspaper for advertising. The job is simple enough in FreeHand — You simply Export the design in TIFF format.

But how is this TIFF image going to look? Look at this example. The left image was a path object in the document; the right image is a Vector EPS image imported into the same document. Both images were exported as a TIFF, then printed here. The imported Vector EPS has jagged edges and a faint pattern in it. This is because FreeHand is only exporting the low-resolution raster preview of the EPS, and not the defining vector information.

If you Export a document as a raster (TIFF) file, make sure all the objects are Vector paths. Placed EPS files that were not or could not be converted to editable artwork will render to a raster format in a coarse, low-resolution manner.

FreeHand Paths   Placed Vector EPS

It is not recommended to export imported Vector EPS images as Raster formats. Vector EPS images should always be exported as EPS format.

Raster (bitmapped) Images

Raster graphics are represented as a fine grid of individual dots (pixels). Imagine a chessboard where each red and black square is a pixel. Imagine further that this chessboard is printed on a big balloon. As the balloon is inflated, the squares get bigger. Eventually the squares become distorted and no longer resemble what they looked like when you started.

Raster images behave the same way when enlarged. The pixels (squares) just get bigger and bigger, eventually to the point that the image looks very grainy and rough. Overly-enlarged raster art becomes *pixelated*. Raster images are very useful in the graphic arts to represent photographs or artwork created in a raster-based program like Photoshop. Raster images can be reduced without an apparent loss of quality, but cannot be enlarged much more than 5–10% without becoming pixelated. Consequently, raster images should be scanned or created as close to the finished size needed as possible.

Raster image – no enlargement   Raster image enlarged 300%

Raster Formats

The most common bitmapped format used in the graphic arts industry is TIFF (Tagged Image File Format). Other Raster formats used are JPEG, GIF, BMP, and PICT, but these are specialized for various purposes and aren't suitable for print reproduction. GIF and JPEG formats are widely used for graphics in web pages. If you are creating images for use on a web page for the Internet, you would probably select either JPEG or GIF format. Printed projects require the TIFF format.

The Raster EPS Format

This file format encloses a raster image within an EPS "wrapper." Don't assume that the raster EPS format is going to smooth out jagged pixels when the image is enlarged; being raster in format, it will still become pixelized. If you need to create a raster EPS file to give to a printer, FreeHand is capable of exporting this graphic format.

The Raster EPS file format, when viewed in Keyline mode is identified, just like a Vector EPS, by the "X" in its bounding box.

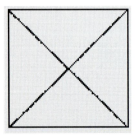

Raster Images in FreeHand

Most raster images are only recognizable when viewing them in Preview mode. But you obviously can't always work in Preview mode, so you should be very careful if you have several raster images in a document along with squares and rectangles. You might get them mixed up.

Here's a quiz question: "Of the three objects shown in Keyline mode, without cheating by looking at the Object Inspector, which one was drawn by the Rectangle tool, the Pen tool, and which one is an imported raster image?"

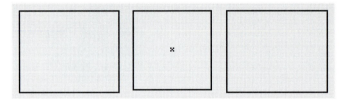

Answer: The only image that can be identified in Keyline mode is the middle object, because it has a center point. This means that it was created using the Rectangle tool. Otherwise, the other two images are indistinguishable in Keyline view. If you were in a hurry and stretched and distorted the wrong image, Undo or Revert is the only alternative.

Modifying Raster Images in FreeHand

The Object Inspector can tell you a lot about a selected object, such as whether it is a path, a FreeHand group, a Grayscale TIFF, an imported EPS, or an RGB TIFF.

If the image is a Grayscale TIFF, Object Inspector lets you make certain modifications. This feature is found at the bottom of the Object Inspector, using the Edit button.

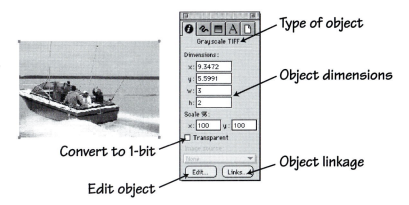

The Object Inspector shows selected objects by their type and format.

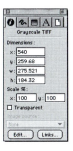

Make backup copies of imported raster images in your document before applying effects. You might apply several mofications, then change your mind.

When you select the Edit option of the Object Inspector, a dialog box displays that allows you to lighten, darken, adjust contrast, and change effects of the image. The four buttons across the top give these changes:

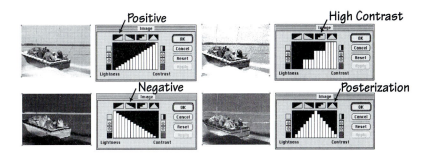

Under these buttons is the light-to-dark palette that shows you what the balance of image is set for. The button to the right of this palette gives you control over adding or subtracting lightness, darkness, or contrast.

Clicking **OK** will apply the modifications you have made to the selected object. Remember, you can always **Undo** these changes.

Linking and Embedding Imported Graphics

An image link is simply the location of the image on your computer's hard disk, so FreeHand can find it if necessary.

When importing graphics, FreeHand automatically creates a link to the image, controlled by the **Edit->Links** option. If you embed a graphic, FreeHand copies the source graphic and stores it in the FreeHand document and does not require the original image for print or display. Everything needed to reproduce the graphic is stored within the document.

Use Command-R (Macintosh) or Control-R (Windows) to access the Import dialog box.

We once heard of a situation where an entire series of bitmapped images had to be recreated from scratch because of a corrupted file. There were no originals; they were all saved in the document that became corrupted.

Always think about the organization of your environment; not just the document itself, the layers and measurements, but also the outside links that are established when working with imported graphics.

If you choose to keep the imported graphic linked and not embedded, you will conserve disk space. Embedding graphics increases the file size of the document. When you import a graphic without embedding, FreeHand generates a low-resolution screen preview (a placeholder) to retain the position of the graphic and must locate the original to print or preview at high-resolution. When a graphic is linked, FreeHand updates the location and data from that link each time the document is opened.

Embedding is often used to transport completed documents. If your graphic files are embedded you don't have to worry about collecting and managing them when you send your job to the service provider. Remember to make your settings for linking and embedding from **Preferences->Import**.

Drawbacks

There are advantages and disadvantages to linking and embedding. FreeHand won't change the name or location of the original imported file. A broken link makes all screen previews of imported images disappear, and the image will not print.

If you embed objects, your document file will grow in size, sometimes spectacularly. Large files require more memory and may make FreeHand run more slowly.

Managing Links

When you link or embed a graphic, FreeHand records the file name, size, disk location, and file type. This information is used whenever you open, export, or print the document; FreeHand checks to see that all links are still present. When opening a document with a linked image, FreeHand searches for the original graphic from where it was initially imported.

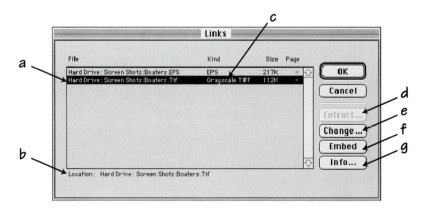

The Links dialog box can be accessed either by selecting **Edit->Links**, or selecting a linked or embedded object and clicking on the Links button in the Object Inspector.

a — Name of the imported file.

b — Location of where the file was imported from.

c — The file format or kind.

d — Extract allows you to save the file out of the document.

e — Change lets you update or change the link to the imported file.

f — Embed will save a copy of the imported file into the document.

g — Info gives original file location, kind, last date modified, and file size.

The stored information on each graphic can be viewed from the Links dialog box. At any time you can select **Edit->Links** to display the Links dialog box to allow you to manage your links, repair broken links, search for missing links, update links, extract embedded objects, embed graphics, and view information about the graphic.

Be careful not to break a link by moving or deleting the source files. If FreeHand cannot locate the original graphic, you will be asked for the location of the file each time you open the FreeHand document.

If you see "????" listed under Size in the Links dialog box, the file's link has been broken. Click Change to select the file and locate it. This can happen if you move the source file to a different folder.

Have the Computer Manage Your Links

If you are using FreeHand on the Macintosh you can have FreeHand reestablish links for you. Sometimes it is acceptable to have one graphics folder; this usually occurs when users create individual folders for categories of files (eg.: a folder for Documents, Applications, Graphics, etc.).

When a single folder contains all the files used for importing, change your **Preferences->Document** to "Search for missing links". This preference searches the specified folder and its subfolders to locate the missing links.

It's easier to keep track of imported art if you save all imported files and the master document in the same folder. This will allow you to easily see all the file names, sizes, and types.

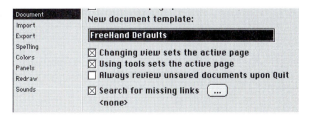

Chapter 13/Importing, Exporting, and Output

Exporting

The need to transfer data between multiple applications and platforms as well as through the hands of many people involved in some aspect of the job requires a common file format. FreeHand can export data in more ways than you'll probably ever use. When you export a FreeHand document, you convert the illustration into a file format that is compatible with other applications on Windows or Macintosh computers. This is usually a vector EPS file, though it could also be a TIFF raster file.

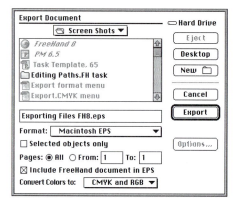

Supported File Formats for Exporting

Selecting the Format pop-up menu of the Export window will display a list of supported export file formats.

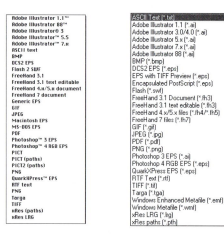

Macintosh   Windows

Importing and Exporting Files

1. From the **File** menu, **Open** the file **SF-Intro Freehand->Exporting Files.FH8**.

If you are trying to export objects that are on the pasteboard, you might wonder why you aren't having any luck. Objects to be exported must be on a document page.

2. The image is made up of vector paths. To convert this to image formats suitable for external use, such as placing the image in other applications, or use on a web page for the internet, it must be exported.

3. Select **File->Export**. This is the window you will see. Select the file format and name the file to be exported. Many of the settings will be covered in the Advanced FreeHand course.

Macintosh   Windows

4. Leave the Format set for Macintosh EPS (if you are using a Macintosh) or EPS with TIFF preview (for Windows users). The suffix .EPS is always added to the name of the file. If you want different names, you can always rename the file above the Format submenu (but remember to preserve the .EPS suffix). Leave the name as it is, locate your folder for saving work, and click Export.

5. The original FreeHand document is unaffected. The exported file is a separate, external file saved to the folder you just specified.

6. Select **File->Preferences->Import** and turn off **Convert editable EPS when imported**, if it's on. Click **OK**.

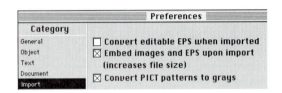

7. Select **File->Import** and choose the file you just saved. The image's preview appears under the Preview title (Macintosh only). Click **Open** to import this file.

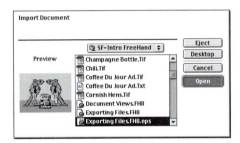 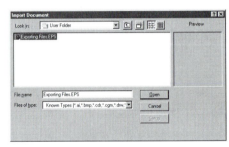

Macintosh   Windows

8. Back in the document, click the cursor to place this graphic on the page. Click on the image and try to ungroup it or select a path. What happened? It was imported as a single EPS image that can't be edited any further, except for scaling or a few other transformations.

   Select **File->Preferences->Import** again and turn **Convert editable EPS when imported** back on. Leave this option on when you want imported images that you can edit, which is usually preferable. Click **OK**.

9. Select the imported image and delete it. Choose **File->Import** and import the same EPS file. Click the cursor on the page to place the image. It is now an editable FreeHand object that you can modify any way you like.

10. Delete the imported file. From **File->Export**, click on the Format submenu to choose GIF. The suffix **.GIF** is appended to the file name.

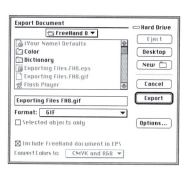
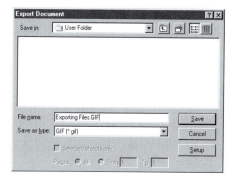

Macintosh   Windows

The **Options** (Macintosh) or **Setup** (Windows) feature is also accessible for raster formats. Click **Options** or **Setup** to display this dialog box. Set the resolution for 72, then click **OK**. Return to the Export window, click **Export**, and save the file in your **Work in Progress** folder.

11. In the document, select **File->Import** and import the new GIF file. Click the cursor on the page to place the image.

12. Click on the placed image, then select **View->Magnification 400%**. This will enlarge the GIF image enough for you to see the pixelization (left image shown). Scroll the page upward to see the original vector image and how smoothly its preview looks (right image shown).

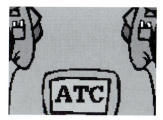
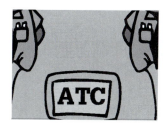

Press Command-5 (Macintosh) or Control-5 (Windows) to switch to a 50% magnifcation.

13. Use the Magnification pop-up menu to go to 50% view.

14. Use the Viewing pop-up menu at the bottom of the screen to go to Keyline view. Notice that the GIF image, viewed in Keyline mode, has no distinguishable characteristics that can help identify it.

15. Delete the GIF image. Use the Rectangle tool to draw a simple square, keeping it selected. Select **File->Export** and, in the Export dialog box, click on the **Selected objects only** option. Set the **Format** for **TIFF**. Click the **Options** (Macintosh) or **Setup** (Windows) button and set the **Resolution** for 300. Click **OK** and Save the file in your **Work in Progress** folder.

16. In the document, select **File->Import** and import the TIFF image you just exported. Click the cursor on the page. Some thin-lined images do not show well on the screen at a small size; if parts of this square are not apparent, select **View->Fit Selection** to fill the screen with the image. Enlarged, you will see that it is intact. The **Selected Objects Only** option will export only those objects that are selected; this is a good method of singling out specific images for exporting.

17. You have now seen a sample of the power and versatility of the Import and Export features of FreeHand. Experiment with file formats and resolution of raster images such as JPEG, GIF, and TIFF.

18. **Close** the document without saving.

Printing

We have shown you how to output FreeHand artwork for use in other applications by Exporting. Printing the document to paper is the other way to output a document; even if you plan to use the art in another application, it's a good idea to print it out for proofing purposes.

Printing Documents

Choosing **File->Print** displays the Print dialog box.

Macintosh users: What you see here may vary depending upon which version of the Laserwriter printer driver you have installed. If your print dialog looks like this, click and hold on the "general" menu, and choose "Freehand 8."

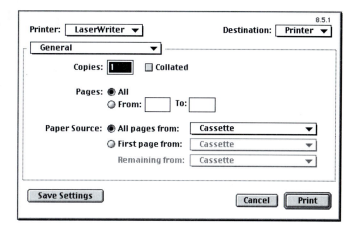

CHAPTER 13/IMPORTING, EXPORTING, AND OUTPUT

Print dialog boxes should look similar to these:

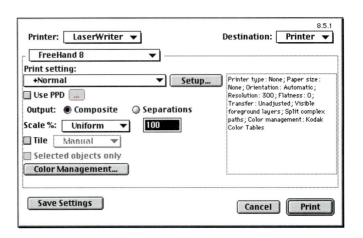

Macintosh

Choosing "Color/Grayscale" will automatically print in color if you have a color printer, and will convert colors to shades of gray if you have a black and white printer.

Windows

If you are using a PostScript printer driver, you will see a dialog box similar to this one. Most of the functions in the Macintosh driver are available in the Windows driver. Most buttons and pop-up menu options in the two Macintosh dialog boxes are in the main Windows print dialog boxes.

Options (Macintosh)/Properties (Windows)

The **Options** or **Properties** button allows you to make settings for a cover page (Macintosh only), as well as determining how your document will print. You can print in either color, if you have a color printer, or in grayscale. In grayscale, colors and photos are converted to shades of gray.

260 Chapter 13/Importing, Exporting, and Output

(Macintosh only): If you want a document to print purely in black and white with no gray tones, select the Black and White option.

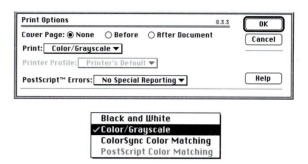

(Windows only): The *Properties* dialog is where you make your printer driver settings. If you select Grayscale, all color will be converted to shades of gray.

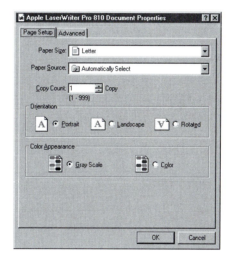

Color Management

Color Management offers color representation on your monitor that will match the printed output as closely as possible. Keep the default set at None.

Scale %

To see how well your design might hold up when reduced and printed, you do not need to scale the art in the document. You can use the **Print** window to set your own percentage of scaling for the printed version. Sometimes you will need to reduce the printed size of the document to fit on your printer's page size; for example, if your document is set up as an 11 inches by 17 inches (tabloid) page but your printer can only use 8½ inches by 11 inches (letter) paper, you would need to reduce it 50% or more.

Printing a Document

1. Select **File->Open** to navigate to the **SF-Intro Freehand** folder and open a FreeHand document of your choice.

2. Select **File->Print**. Make certain that **Composite** is clicked.

3. Click **Options** in the **Print** window, and select **Color/Grayscale**. Click **OK**.

4. In the main **Print** window, click **Print** to send the document to the printer.

5. **Close** the document without saving.

Complete Project K: Grocery Ad

Final Review

Chapters 7 Through 12:

In Chapters 7 through 12, we learned how to arrange and align objects, control curves and anchor points, transform them, learn the use of the Xtras, import artwork, export FreeHand documents and print them. After completing the second part of this book, you should:

- Know how to arrange stacked objects, and the methods by which objects are moved from front to back; how to align objects with respect to other objects or with respect to the document page; how to group and ungroup objects, and know the usefulness of this feature; how to distribute objects over a range of space based on different parameters.

- Understand how the path operations work; how to join two objects to create a third with the path modification tools; how to use the inset path function; how to simplify paths and remove path overlap; how to create a blend of two objects.

- Know how to paint objects; select and create colors; how to apply different painting techniques to fills and strokes; understand what gradients are and how to create and use them.

- Know how to change anchor points and their curve handles to modify a path or segment; understand how to select, add, delete, and connect anchors.

- Understand how to cut and alter path segments with the knife and freeform tools.

- Know the function and effects of FreeHand's transformational tools; how to use the Transform panel to precisely modify objects; how to use the freeform transformer.

- Know the functions of the Xtras discussed and how to create new shapes with them, and how to modify existing shapes; how to use the graphics hose to randomly spray objects across the page; and create a simple bar chart.

- Know how to print a document and adjust the print settings to suit your needs; understand how to export a document for use in another application.

Project A: Steaming Coffee

Setting Up the Template

1. **Open** the student file **Steaming Coffee.TIF** from **SF-Intro FreeHand**.

2. Move the image to the top center of the page. With the image selected, navigate to **Window->Panels->Layers** and click on the Background layer to make it a template.

3. Click on the padlock icon on the Background layer to lock the layer. Click on the Foreground layer to continue.

4. Use the Units pop-up menu to set the measuring for Points. (Line widths should always be measured in points.)

The keyboard shortcut for the Layers panel is Command-6 (Macintosh) or Control-6 (Windows).

5. We will begin by analyzing the steam curves. If you were to draw two circles conforming to the curves, you would see that they meet at point (A). This would certainly be the spot to put a Curve point (B) to create a smooth adjustment. The opposite side (C) would also be a good Curve point spot.

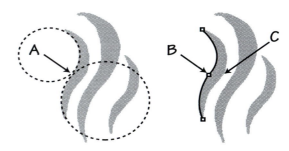

6. Start at the bottom of the first steam curve. Drag a beginning point (a) with the Pen tool, pulling the handle in the direction of the next point. Release the mouse. Move the tool up to acquire a Curve point. Drag a Curve point (b) and release the mouse. Single-click a point at the top of the steam curve to finish(c).

   Select each point and adjust its handles with the Pointer tool to make the path fit the template. Keep the path selected.

When finished drawing a path, press the Tab key to deselect.

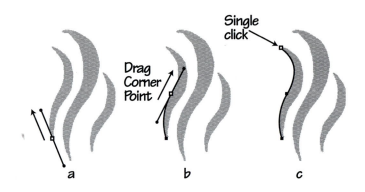

7. Single-click with the Pen tool on the last point that you made and drag a curve handle out of this same point (d). Release the mouse. Now move the mouse down to the midway point, next to the first Curve point. Drag a Curve point, pulling the handle downward (e). Click on the first point you made to complete and close the path (f). Adjust the curves with the Pointer tool to make the path fit the template.

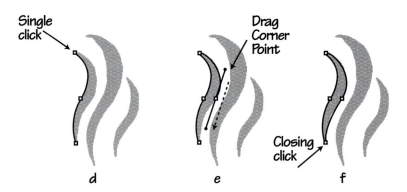

8. The other two steam curves in the template are so similar that you could draw the steams from scratch in the same manner. It would be easier, though, to **Clone** this path two times, moving the clones onto the other steams and making modifications with the Pointer tool to adjust the paths to fit. Do this now, using either method.

9. The three steam curves need to be filled with a 30% Black tint and no stroke. To create the tint, select the Tints panel (**Window->Panels->Tints**). In the Tints panel, click on the pop-up menu to select Black.

Press Command-9 (Macintosh) or Control-9 (Windows) to display the Color List. In the Tints panel the tints will be listed in percentages. Click on the 30% swatch and drag it into the Color List panel.

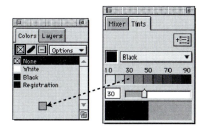

10. Use the Pointer tool to select all three coffee steams. In the Color List, make certain that the Fill icon is clicked. Click on the 30% Black tint name in the list.

The steams will be filled with this. Drag the None swatch up to touch the Stroke icon.

The finished steam curves should look like this:

11. Now draw the coffee cup and saucer. All six paths that make up the cup and saucer are 4 pt. Strokes with no Fill. You could draw the paths and paint them afterward, but when settings are made in the Fill or Stroke Inspectors (with no objects selected), the next paths drawn will reflect these new settings.

12. Set the measurement Units to Points. Make certain that no objects are selected. Select the Fill Inspector and make certain its pop-up menu is set for None. Click on the Stroke Inspector icon, next to Fill. Set the Width for 4. In the Caps section, click the Rounded Caps icon.

13. Select the Pen tool. To draw the top of the cup, you must first drag a beginning point (a). Move the mouse to the bottom of this template object and drag a Curve point (b). Move the mouse to the end of the template piece and single-click (c). Use the Pointer tool to adjust the handles of the points to fit the path to the template.

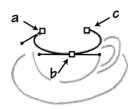

A-4   INTRODUCTION TO FREEHAND 8: STEAMING COFFEE

14. The two small segments making up the cup body require simple dragging and clicking. With the Pen tool, drag a beginning point on the first curve in the template (a). Move the mouse to the end of the template curve and single-click an ending point (b). Press the Tab key to deselect.

    Drag a beginning point on the next curve in the template (c), then move to the end of the curve and single-click (d). Use the Pointer tool to adjust the curving paths to fit the template.

    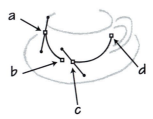

15. Moving on to the saucer, with the Pen tool, drag a beginning point on the curve in the template (a). Move to the bottom of the template curve and drag a Curve point (b). Move up to the end of the template saucer piece and single-click (c). Use the Pointer tool to adjust these curves to fit the template.

    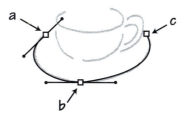

16. For the coffee cup handle, use the Pen tool to drag a beginning point at the start of the larger handle in the template (a). Move slightly to the right and single-click a point (b). Single-click on this point again and drag a curve handle. Go to the end of the curve in the template and single-click a final point (c). Press the Tab key to deselect everything. Repeat the same drawing process for the smaller handle curve in the template. Deselect all paths. Use the Pointer tool to adjust the curves to fit the template.

    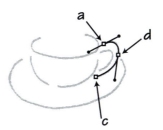

17. The Steaming Coffee design is now finished. You've now used FreeHand's Pen tool to draw various curves as well as having applied different painting techniques. The artwork should look like this:

18. Select **File->Save As** to save the document in your **Work in Progress** folder in the **FreeHand Document** format. Name it "Steaming Coffee". **Close** the document.

Project B: Last Mango Cafe Logo

Creating Curves with the Pen Tool

1. Select **File->Open** to open the graphic file **Last Mango Logo.TIF** from the **SF-Intro FreeHand** folder. A converted FreeHand document opens with the image in the document. Move the image to the top center of the page.

2. Select the image, then access the **Layers** panel (**Window->Panels->Layers**). Click on the Background layer to assign the image. Click on the padlock icon next to the Background layer to lock the layer. You now have a template from which to work. Press Tab to deselect all, then click on the Foreground layer to continue.

3. For alignment assistance, drag a vertical guide to show the center of the umbrella, running down its handle. Drag a horizontal guide to mark the bottom of the umbrella hood.

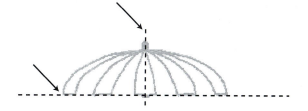

4. With the Pen tool, draw the paths of the umbrella's hood. You will find shortcuts here to save time drawing all five paths individually. Start by drawing the first piece of the umbrella hood.

5. Drag the first point, creating a curve handle (a). Move the cursor to the top of the umbrella and single-click (b). Click on this second point and drag a curve handle downward. Release the mouse. Move down to the bottom of this piece and single-click on the template, even with the guide. To close the path, click on the first point you started with.

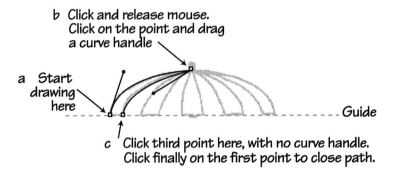

You could also try using the Mirror tool, found in the Xtra Tools panel. This duplicates the selected object, Reflecting it 90° across a vertical axis.

6. You have just created a closed path with curve handles. Rather than clicking and dragging again four more times, **Edit->Clone** the path and drag the duplicate to the right, holding the Shift key to constrain the move (a). Position it on the second umbrella piece in the template. Use the Pointer tool to adjust its curve handles to fit the template. To give you adequate room to click on curve handles, select the first umbrella path you drew and navigate to **View->Hide Selection**. Now click on the first anchor point of the duplicate to see its curve handle. Adjust all the anchor points and curves of this path to fit the template (b).

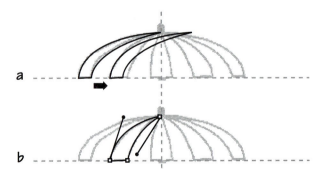

Press Command- = (Macintosh) or Control/Shift-C (Windows) to clone a selected object.

7. When you are finished, you will need to create the middle path that bridges the centerline guide. **Clone** the path you just edited and move the duplicate on top of the middle of the template. Adjust the curve points of this duplicate path to fit the template.

8. Select **View->Show All** to bring the first umbrella piece back to view. The last step to creating the umbrella paths is to reflect/duplicate the first two paths by using the Mirror tool. The Mirror tool automatically duplicates and reflects selected objects across a 90° vertical axis when clicked.

   Select the first two umbrella paths. Navigate to **Window->Xtras->Xtra Tools** and select the Mirror tool. Click its cursor directly on the vertical centerline guide you created. The two new paths will appear on the other side of the centerline guide.

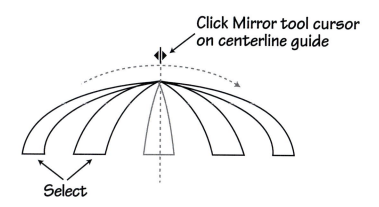

9. Select the five umbrella paths with the Pointer tool.

10. **Fill** the umbrella paths with Black and **Stroke** with None.

Modifying Paths

11. Draw a circle with the Ellipse tool to match the curvature at the bottom of the umbrella handle in the template.

12. Select the circle with the Pointer tool and **Modify->Ungroup** it.

The keyboard shortcut for Ungroup is Command-U (Macintosh) or Control-U (Windows).

Hold down the Command (Macintosh) or Control (Windows) key to temporarily select the Pointer tool, no matter which tool you are using.

13. Cut the left/right anchor points with the Knife tool. Delete the top half.

14. Select the remaining half of the circle with the Pointer tool, then click on the right anchor point with the Pen tool. Follow the template as a guide. Click again at the top of the umbrella, holding down the Shift key as you click to constrain a straight line.

15. Paint the umbrella handle as: **Fill** = None, **Stroke** = 6 pt. Black. Set the end caps to rounded.

16. Send the handle to the back (**Modify->Arrange->Send to Back**).

Setting Type to Fit

17. Select the Text tool and click the cursor on the template. Type the words:

Last Mango

18. Highlight the text and navigate to the **Text Inspector**. Apply these settings: **Font** = ATC Mango, **Size** =33 pt.

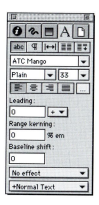

19. Create another text block and type the word:

    Cafe

    Highlight the text and apply these settings: **Font** = ATC Mango, **Size** = 25 pt.

20. Reposition the text on the template. Use kerning to adjust the letters to fit the letters in the template.

21. The logo is now complete. Select all the objects in the design and **Modify ->Group** them. Select **Save As** to save the document in your **Work in Progress** folder. Save as **FreeHand Document** format, naming the file "Last Mango Cafe Logo". **Close** the document.

The keyboard shortcut for Send To Back is Command-B (Macintosh) or Control-B (Windows).

Notes:

Project C: Last Mango Cafe Business Cards

Creating the Last Mango Business Card

1. Select **File->Open** to open the graphic file **Last Mango Card.TIF** from the **SF-Intro FreeHand** folder. A converted document will open with the TIFF image in the lower left portion of the page.

2. Move the image to the top center of the page. Open the Layers panel and assign the image to the Background layer.

3. Click on the lock icon next to the Background layer to lock the layer. Click on the Foreground layer to continue.

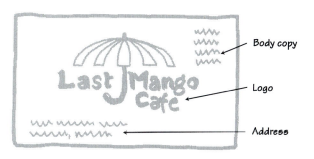

4. Set the Units for Inches. Use the Rectangle tool to trace the template border depicting the size of the card. Select the Object Inspector and fine-tune the dimensions by entering W = 3.5 inches, H = 2 inches.

5. **Fill** the border with None, **Stroke** with 1 pt. Black.

6. **Open** the FreeHand document **Last Mango Cafe Logo** that you created earlier and saved in your **Work in Progress** folder. Click on the design to select it, then **Edit->Copy** the group.

7. **Close** the **Last Mango Cafe Logo** file without saving.

8. **Paste** the group into the working document.

9. Move the logo into position and scale it to better fit the template.

10. Select the Text tool. Click on the page and type the address:

    1334 Bayshore Circle
    Freeport, Bahamas

11. Press Tab to deselect. Click again with the Text tool and type the words:

    Beer
    Wine
    Food
    Fun

12. Hold down the Shift key and select both text blocks with the Pointer tool. Select the **Text Inspector.** Make and apply these settings: **Font** = ATC Daquiri, **Size** = 10 pt., **Leading** = 10 pt. (Fixed "=").

13. Position the address and the four words into place on the template.

    The completed business card should look like this:

Setting the Card "Four-up"

14. Use **Edit->Select->All** to select all elements in the art and **Modify->Group** them. **Clone** the group. Select the Transform panel and select the Move option. Since the card is 3.5-inches wide, enter 3.5-inches for the "x" distance. Click **Apply**. This will move the clone to the right, lining up the two.

15. When the left side of the duplicate border matches the right side border of the original, the move is complete. You should have two business cards butted up against each other.

16. Select the two groups and **Clone** them. In the **Transform->Move** panel, enter 2 inches for Y. Click **Apply** (Macintosh) or **Move** (Windows).

Most commercial printers prefer printing business cards "four up," or duplicated and arranged so that they can print and cut four cards at once. If you deliver your job to the printer already set up this way you will avoid extra charges for you or your client.

17. Choose **Edit->Select All** and move the four cards to the center of the page.

18. You will want to show the trim marks for the printer to use when cutting the cards. Mark this with guides. Turn the Page Rulers on and drag guides to match the business card borders. Then, to mark a 1/2 inch distance away from the borders, drag guides to the outside of the cards to show this. The result should look like this:

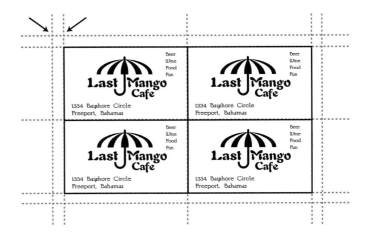

19. With the Line tool, draw a rule that is ½ inch long. Drag a duplicate of this line to the right side (a.). Position the two lines so they are ½ inch away from the border (b.).

    Fill both lines with None, and **Stroke** with Registration, 1 pt.

    Select both lines and drag duplicates downward to mark the horizontal centerline by matching the guide (c.). When the first duplicate is made, press Command-D (Macintosh) or Control-D (Windows) to repeat the duplication.

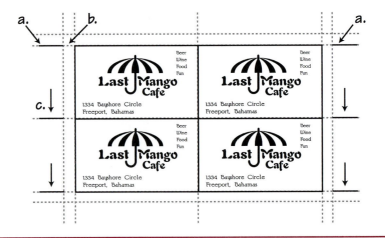

20. Use the Line tool to draw two vertical rules (a.) to mark the ½″ distance and the vertical trim cut. Drag-duplicate these rules to the right to match the middle guide. When this is done, press Command-D (Macintosh) or Control-D (Windows) to repeat this duplication. You have now created trim marks for the printer.

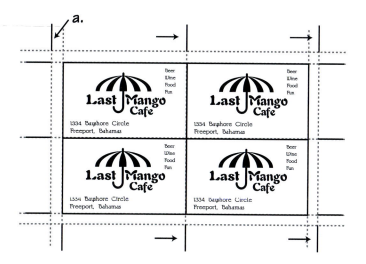

21. Toggle **View->Guides->Show** to turn the guides off. Holding Option (Macintosh) or Alt (Windows) along with the Shift key, click on the four business card borders and change the Stroke to None. Your design should look like the below picture with four business cards (Four Up) butted up to each other so that the printer can cut out four cards in a minimal amount of time.

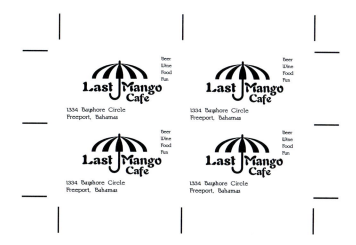

22. The business card mechanical is now complete. Select **Save As** to save the file in your **Work in Progress** folder. Save in **FreeHand Document** format, naming it "Last Mango Cafe Business Cards". **Close** the document.

Notes:

Project D: Java Jungle Logo

Modifying Paths

1. Select **File->New** to create a new document in FreeHand.

2. Select the Units pop-up menu at the bottom of the screen to set the units of measurement to Inches.

3. With the Ellipse tool, draw an ellipse approximately 3 inches x 0.5 inches.

4. With the Pointer tool, choose the ellipse and open the **Object Inspector**. Fine-tune the width to 3 inches and the height to 0.4 inches. Press Return (Macintosh) or Enter (Windows) to apply.

The keyboard shortcut for Ungroup is Command-6 (Macintosh) or Control-6 (Windows).

5. Select the ellipse, then go to **Modify->Ungroup** and ungroup the selection to view its anchor points. Now choose the **Knife** tool and click on the left and right anchor points. The Object Inspector will now list this as two objects. Press the Tab key to deselect.

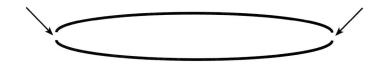

The keyboard shortcut for the Transform panel is Command-M (Macintosh) or Control-M (Windows).

6. Select the bottom curved path. Select the **Transform->Move** panel to reposition the entire path downward: X = 0, Y = –2.985 inches. Click **Apply** (Macintosh) or **Move** (Windows).

Remember that you set the Units for Inches at the beginning of this exercise. Make certain that it is still set to Inches before entering your dialog box numbers.

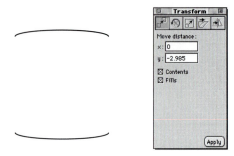

7. Marquee-select the center anchor point of the bottom path. **Open** the **Window->Panels->Transform** panel and select the **Move** option.

8. Enter x = 0, y = –0.259 inches as the amount and click **Apply** to move the anchor point down.

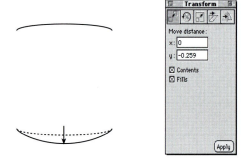

9. Marquee-select the two right endpoints. Press Command-J (Macintosh) or Control -J (Windows) to **Join** them (a). With the path still selected, navigate to the **Object Inspector** and click **Closed** (b).

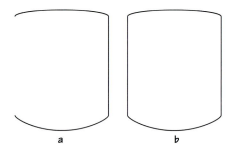

10. Set the Units for Points. **Fill** the cup with White and **Stroke** it with a 1 pt. Black stroke.

11. Set the Units for Inches. Draw another ellipse of width = 2.875 inches and height = 0.4 inches.

12. **Fill** the ellipse with Black and **Stroke** it with None. Reposition it at the top of the cup to represent the interior.

 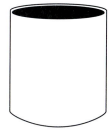

13. Draw another ellipse to create the cup handle. In the Object Inspector, use these measurements for the handle: width = 1.75 inches and height = 2.25 inches. Click **Apply**. Paint the ellipse: **Fill** = White, **Stroke** = 1 pt. Black.

14. **Edit->Clone** this ellipse. Double-click the Scale tool in the Toolbox. In the **Transform** dialog box, enter 80 for the Scale %. Make certain that **Uniform** is selected. Click **Apply** (Macintosh) or **Scale** (Windows).

15. Position the smaller ellipse so that its right side almost touches the right side of the larger ellipse.

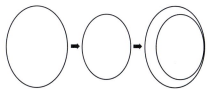

16. Select both ellipses and **Modify->Group** them. Reposition the two ellipses to create the look of the coffee cup handle. Send the handle to the back (**Modify->Arrange->Send to Back**).

17. Select all the objects in this design and **Modify->Group** them.

The keyboard shortcut for Group is Command-G (Macintosh) or Control-G (Windows).

Setting Type to Fit Layout

18. Select the grouped cup and **Modify->Lock** it. Use the Text tool to create a text block on the cup. Type these words on two lines:

    Java

    Jungle

19. Highlight the words, then access the **Text Inspector**.

20. Make and apply these settings: **Font** = ATC Nassau, **Size** = 70 pt., **Leading** = 65 pt. (Fixed "="), **Alignment** = Center. Click on the Horizontal scale icon in the Text Inspector. Set the **Horizontal scale** = 85%. Press Return (Macintosh) or Enter (Windows) to apply these settings.

The keyboard shortcut for the Text Inspector is Command-T (Macintosh) or Control-T (Windows).

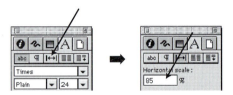

21. Use the Pointer tool to position the text block so that it centers the cup. Leave the letters Black.

22. Select the text block with the Pointer tool. Navigate to **Text->Convert To Paths** to turn the text to outlines.

23. The converted text will automatically be grouped. To ungroup the text outlines to individual letters, select the text group with the Pointer tool and navigate to **Modify->Ungroup**. "Java" and "Jungle" will now be two separate word groups. Select each and **Modify->Ungroup** again.

24. The letters need to fit the curvature of the cup, so you will need to make a guide to follow. Select the cup body path and drag a duplicate to the right, holding the Option (Macintosh) or Alt (Windows) key.

Holding the Option (Macintosh) or Alt (Windows) key while dragging an object will duplicate it.

25. Use the Knife tool to cut the duplicate's bottom segment away from the rest of the path (a). Delete the upper portion, leaving just the bottom segment (b).

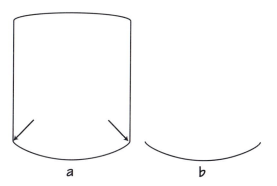

26. Move the segment under the word "Jungle" so that it touches the letters from the "J" to the "e".

27. Selecting with the Pointer tool, and moving one letter at a time with the Down Arrow key, move the letters of "Jungle" down to conform to the curvature of the guiding path. Use your own visual judgment for fine-tuning the letters to look balanced and evenly spaced.

28. With the Pointer tool, move the guiding path up under "Java". Select each letter and use the Down Arrow key to move the letters to fit the curving line.

29. When finished, select the curving path guide and delete it.

30. Select all the letters, holding the Shift key, and **Modify->Group** them. With this group selected, move it up to be better centered in the cup space.

31. The logo is now complete. Click on the cup and **Modify->Unlock** it.

32. Select **Save As** the file in **FreeHand Document** format to your **Work in Progress** folder. Name the file "Java Jungle Logo".

33. **Close** the document.

Project E: Coffee Du Jour Ad

Setting the Layout

1. Choose **File->Open** to open the graphic file **Coffee Du Jour Ad.TIF** from **SF-Intro FreeHand** folder. A new converted FreeHand document will be created with the image in the document. Move the image to the top center of the page.

2. Select the image and access the **Layers** panel (**Window->Panels->Layers**). Click on the Background layer to assign the image.

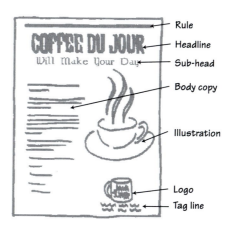

3. Click on the padlock icon next to the Background layer to lock it. You now have a template to work from. Press the Tab key to deselect all, then click on the Foreground layer to continue.

4. Double-click on the Foreground layer and rename it "Steaming Coffee". Press Return (Macintosh) or Enter (Windows) to apply the name.

5. **Open Steaming Coffee** from your **Work in Progress** folder. Select the grouped artwork.

6. Select **Edit->Copy** to copy the group to the clipboard. **Close** the **Steaming Coffee** document without saving.

7. Select **Edit->Paste** to paste the illustration into the working document. Position the art piece to match the template layout. Since it is assigned to the Steaming Coffee layer, click the padlock icon of this layer to lock the layer.

8. In the Layers panel, use the Options pop-up menu to create four new layers. Rename them: Headline, Body Text, Logo, and Border. Rearrange the sequence in the layer list so that it is in this order:

    Headline

    Steaming Coffee

    Body Text

    Logo

    Border

9. **Open Java Jungle Logo** from your **Work in Progress** folder. Select the grouped artwork and **Edit->Copy** it. **Close** the document without saving.

10. Click on the Logo layer in the Layers panel. Paste the **Java Jungle Logo** group into the working document, positioning it to match the template layout. Scale the pasted logo 30%. Click the padllock icon of this layer to lock the layer. Press the Tab key to deselect all.

11. Click on the Headline layer in the Layers panel. Select the Text tool and click it once near the headline at the top of the ad. Type the words:

    COFFEE DU JOUR

    Highlight this text and open the **Text Inspector**.

12. Make the **Font** = ATC Tequila, **Size** = 72 pt. Press Return (Macintosh) or Enter (Windows) to apply the settings. Position the type to match the template. Use kerning to tighten or expand the letter spacing to fit the template headline.

13. Deselect the headline text block. Select the Text tool, then click under the headline type. In the new text block, type the words:

    Will Make Your Day

    Highlight this phrase with the Text tool. In the **Text Inspector**, make these settings: **Font** = ATC Daquiri, **Size** = 30. Apply this to the text.

14. Position the type block to match the template. Press the Tab key.

15. Click on the Body Text layer in the Layers panel. For the body text, navigate to **File->Import->SF-Intro FreeHand** and choose **Coffee Du Jour Ad.TXT.** Click **Open** in the **Import** window.

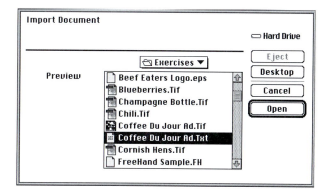

16. With the Import tool, draw a text block where you want to position the body to match the template's body text image. When you release the mouse button, the text will appear in the created text block.

17. Select the Text tool. Click in the text block and choose **Edit->Select->All**.

18. With the text highlighted, navigate to the **Text Inspector** and make the **Font** = ATC Colada, **Size** = 10 pt., **Leading** = 13 pt. (Fixed "="). Apply these settings and deselect the text block.

19. Unlock the Logo layer, then click on the Logo layer in the Layers panel. Select the Text tool and click on the bottom right corner. Type the words:

    Coffee That Will

    Make You Growl

20. With the text highlighted, make the **Font** = ATC Coconuts, **Size** =14 pt., **Leading** = 14 pt. (Fixed "="), **Alignment** = Centered. Position this text below the Java Jungle Logo in the lower right corner. Deselect the text block.

21. Click on the Border layer in the Layers panel. Use the Line tool to draw a line across the top of the ad. Constrain the line by holding down the Shift key as you draw.

22. Using the **Stroke Inspector**, set the line **Width** for 10 pt. Position the line to fit the template.

23. Use the Rectangle tool to draw a border around the ad that matches the template. Paint it: **Fill** = None, **Stroke** = 1 pt. Black.

24. Select **Edit->Select->All**, then **Modify->Unlock** to unlock all locked objects. Unlock the Steaming Coffee Layer.

    The completed ad should look similar to this:

    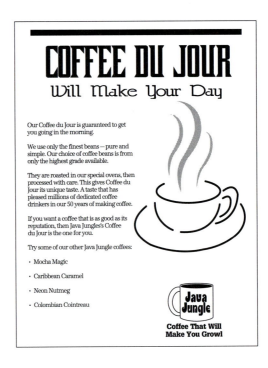

25. Select **Save As** to save the file in your **Work in Progress** folder. Save in **FreeHand Document** format, naming the file "Coffee Du Jour Ad". **Close** the file.

Project: Tropical Fish

Creating Shapes with the Pen Tool

1. Select **File->Open->SF-Intro Freehand->Tropical Fish.TIF**.

2. Move the image to the top-center of the page.

3. **Open** the **Layers** panel (**Window->Panels->Layers**). With the image selected, click on the Background layer.

4. Click on the padlock icon next to Background to lock the layer, to avoid accidentally moving the template while you are drawing.

5. Double-click on the Foreground layer in the **Layers** panel and rename it "Polygon". Press Return (Macintosh) or Enter (Windows) to apply the name. Click on this layer to make it active. Any objects you make will be assigned to this layer until another layer is chosen.

6. Click on the four corners of the four-sided polygon in the template with the Pen tool.

Fill the polygon with Black, **Stroke** = None. Click the check mark of the Polygon layer to Hide the layer and this object.

7. Zoom in on the set of waves at the top of the template with the Magnification tool by clicking on that portion of the image with the tool.

8. Create a new layer. In the **Layers** panel and name it "Waves". Click on it to make it the active layer.

9. Select **Keyline** view. Select the Pen tool and drag the left side of the top wave to create a beginning curve anchor point.

10. Move the mouse to the right and click-drag down a handle to create another curve.

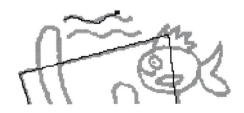

The keyboard shortcut for Duplicate is Command-D (Macintosh) or Control-D (Windows).

11. Move the mouse to the right then click-drag to draw the next curve point. Click the tool on the end of the template wave to complete the path. Press the Tab key to deselect everything.

12. Use the Pointer tool to adjust and refine the curves to fit the template.

13. Create three more waves by choosing **Edit->Duplicate** to duplicate the wave three times, then position them to match the template.

Applying Colors

14. Select Preview mode.

15. In the **Color List**, select **Options** and select the Pantone Uncoated library.

16. Type 3155 in the **PANTONE** field. FreeHand will locate the color for you.

17. With 3155 CVU selected, hold down the Shift (Macintosh) or Control (Windows) key, then scroll and select color number 312 CVU. Click **OK** to add them to your **Color List**.

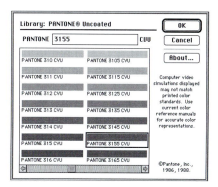

18. In the Layers panel, click the check mark of the Polygon layer to Show the polygon you previously drew.

19. To **Fill** the polygon, select the **Color List**. Make certain that the **Fill** icon is clicked. Select the color swatch to the left of Pantone 312 CVU and drag it to touch and color the polygon.

20. Click the check mark again on the Polygon layer to hide it.

21. Select all four waves. In the **Color List**, make certain that the Stroke icon is selected. Click on Pantone 3155 CVU in the list; this is another way of applying color to an object.

22. Select the **Stroke Inspector.** Enter 5 for the **Width** of the waves. Press Return (Macintosh) or Enter (Windows) to apply.

23. Click on the check mark of the Waves layer to hide the waves.

Working with Shapes

24. Create a new layer in the Layer panel. Double-click on the new layer.

25. Type in "Fish" for the name and press Return (Macintosh) or Enter (Windows) to apply.

26. Keep the Fish layer active and continue drawing.

27. Draw a circle with the Ellipse tool that matches the circle of the fish's eye.

28. In the **Options** pop-up menu of the **Color List**, scroll to Pantone Uncoated. Select **Pantone Process Yellow C** and click **OK**.

29. **Fill** the circle with **Pantone Process Yellow C** and **Stroke** = None.

30. Draw an ellipse that matches the side fin. **Fill** it with Pantone 3155 CVU and **Stroke** = None.

31. Draw an ellipse that matches the fish body. **Fill** it with Pantone 312 and **Stroke** = None. Send it to back (**Modify->Arrange->Send to Back**).

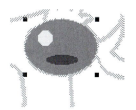

32. With the Freehand tool, draw the top and tail fins, making certain that these objects are closed by using the **Object Inspector.**

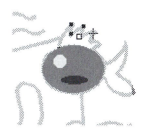

33. **Fill** the fins with Pantone 3155 CVU and **Stroke** = None. Select both fins and **Modify->Arrange->Send to Back**.

34. Double-click on the Freehand tool and select the **Variable stroke** option. Set the **Width** to **Min.** = 4 pt., **Max.** = 4 pt., then click **OK**.

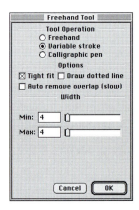

35. Zoom in on the fish with the Magnification tool. Draw the mouth of the fish with the Freehand tool. Click the tool one time for the pupil.

36. **Fill** the mouth and pupil with Pantone 3155 CVU and **Stroke** with None. Fine-tune the fish to fit the template. Click on the check mark of the Fish layer to Hide it.

Creating Shapes with the FreeHand Tool

37. Create a new layer and rename it "Coral". Press Return (Macintosh) or Enter (Windows) to apply the name. Leave this layer active.

38. Double-click on the Freehand tool, select the **Variable Stroke** option and set the **Min./Max.** widths to 20 pt., then click **OK**.

39. Trace the coral piece in the template with four different strokes. Select the four coral paths, then navigate to **Modify->Combine->Union** to make this a single, combined path.

40. Open the **Window->Panels->Color List**, and under the **Options** pop-up menu, choose Pantone Uncoated and select Pantone 1535 CVU. Click **OK**. **Fill** the coral with Pantone 1535 CVU and **Stroke** = None.

41. Double-click the Freehand Drawing tool in the Toolbox. Set the Variable Stroke option to **Min./Max.** = 5 pt. Click on the dots of the template coral to add texture to its surface. Select all the dots, **Group** them, and paint the group: **Fill** = Pantone 3155 CVU, **Stroke** = None.

42. Press Tab to deselect all objects. Click the check mark of the Coral layer to Hide it.

43. Create a new layer and rename it "Ocean Floor". Keep this layer active.

44. Double-click on the Freehand tool and reset the **Variable stroke** to **Min./Max.** width to 10 pt.

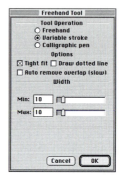

45. Draw a rounded curve above the the starfish.

46. Change the Variable Stroke option in the Freehand tool to 3 min/max. Draw some sand grains under the curve that match the template.

47. Open the **Window->Panels->Color List** and, under the **Options** pop-up menu, choose Pantone Uncoated and select Pantone Yellow CVU. Click **OK**. Select all the sand grains and **Fill** them with Pantone Yellow.

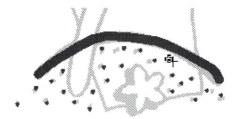

48. **Fill** the curve with Pantone 3155 CVU and **Stroke** = None.

49. With the Polygon tool, create a star approximately the same angle as the starfish in the template. Select **Window->Xtras->Xtra Tools** to use the Bend tool to round the points of the starfish until it resembles the template.

50. Select the starfish and choose **Edit->Copy**. Select **Edit->Paste Behind**, which will paste the copy behind the starfish. Press the Left Arrow key four times and the Down Arrow key four times. Paint the starfish with **Fill** = Pantone 3155 CVU, **Stroke** = None. Paint the copy with: **Fill** = Black, **Stroke** = None.

Select the starfish and its shadow. Move them into place on the template.

51. All the objects in the design have now been created. In the **Layers** panel, select the Options pop-up menu and select **All on** to show all the layers that have been hidden.

52. The layers now need final sequencing to complete the design's look. Select the **Layers** panel and move the layers up and down the list so they are in this sequence:

    Fish layer
    Waves layer
    Coral layer
    Polygon layer
    Ocean Floor

Selecting all the objects after you've finished a project is a good way to tell if you have any stray anchors or paths left over. If you see any, delete them.

53. When all the layers are in sequence, the design should look like this:

54. The design is complete. Select all the objects in this design and **Modify ->Group** them.

55. Use **Save As** to save the file in your **Work in Progress** folder. Save the file in **FreeHand Document** format, naming it "Tropical Fish".

56. **Close** the document.

Project G: Ball & Mirror

Creating the Ball & Mirror Design

1. Select **File->New** to create a new document.

2. Select **File->Import** to navigate to the **SF-Intro FreeHand** folder and import the graphic **Ball & Mirror.TIF**.

3. Center the image in the top half of the page.

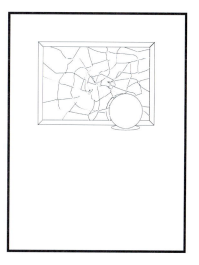

4. To create a template, access the Layers panel from **Window->Panels**. Select the imported graphic and click on the Background layer in the **Layers** panel.

   Click on the padlock icon on the Background layer to Lock the template.

   Click on the Foreground layer to continue.

PROJECT G: BALL AND MIRROR

Creating the Frame

Objects drawn with the Rectangle tool must be ungrouped to make the anchor points accessible. The rectangles in this project must be ungrouped in order for the Divide operation to have anchor points to work with.

5. Double-click on the Foreground layer and rename it "Frame". Press the Return (Macintosh) or Enter (Windows) key to apply.

6. Double-click on the Rectangle tool and make certain its Corner radius is set at 0. With the Rectangle tool, draw a rectangle 5.5 inches x 3.75 inches. Inside this rectangle, draw another rectangle 5.1 inches x 3.35 inches. Select both rectangles. Select the **Align** panel (**Window->Panels->Align**) to center the two rectangles. Select **Align center** in both the vertical and horizontal pop-up menus, and then click **Align** (Macintosh) or **Apply** (Windows).

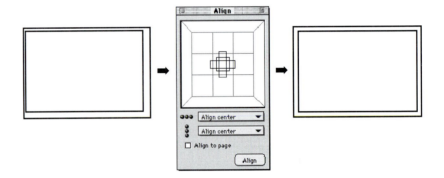

7. **Ungroup** the two rectangles and select the Line tool. Holding the Shift key to constrain the angles, draw a 45° line at each corner. Position each line so that it touches the corner anchor points of both rectangles, extending outside and inside the rectangles as shown below:

When positioning the 45° lines to the corners, it will help if you use **View->Snap To Point** toggled on. The lines will now snap to the anchor points of the rectangles.

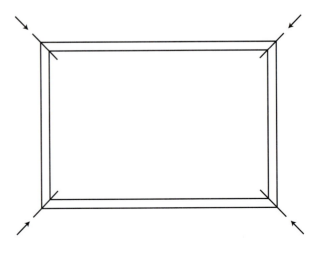

8. It is very easy to be slightly off. After the lines are drawn, zoom in on each corner with the Magnification tool and navigate to Keyline mode to see the paths better for precise fine-tuning with the Pointer tool. The line must touch the corner anchor points of both rectangles.

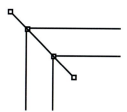

9. Select **File->Preferences->Object**. Make certain that **Path operations consume original paths** is not selected.

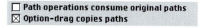

10. Select **Edit->Select->All**, then navigate to **Xtras->Path Operations ->Divide**. The operation will create four separate objects that butt up to each other at the corners where the lines were drawn.

   We've moved the four objects slightly in this example to show how they look and fit.

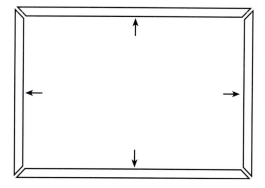

   Shift-select all four of these new pieces and navigate to **View->Hide Selection**. This will leave the original two rectangles on screen. Click on the larger one and delete it; click on the remaining rectangle and **Edit ->Cut** it.

11. Select **View->Show All** to bring the four frame piece back into view. You will need to paint them with a multi-color gradient that you will now build. Select the Fill Inspector and, in its pop-up menu, select Gradient. Select all four frame pieces.

12. Select the **Color List** (**Window->Panels**). With its **Options->Import** function, navigate to the **Work in Progress** folder and access the **ATC Custom Colors.BCF** library. Hold the Shift key and select Maroon, Pink, Navy, Blue, and Gray. Click **OK**.

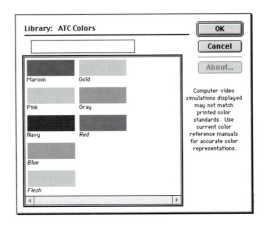

13. In the **Fill Inspector->Gradient** panel, click on the top gradient drop box and drag it down halfway along the color ramp; this will create a new drop box for a third color. Use the method of clicking on a drop box, then clicking the appropriate color name in the Color List. Click the name, not the swatch. Color the three drop boxes in the Gradient panel as:

    Top drop box = Navy.

    Middle drop box = Blue.

    Bottom drop box = Navy.

    Stroke all frame pieces with 1 pt. Black.

14. Select only the left and right frame pieces. In the gradient panel, set the Angle for 0 (zero). This will make the gradient colors flow from side to side. Press Return (Macintosh) or Enter (Windows) to apply.

15. The frame is complete and painted. Select all four frame pieces and **Modify->Group**. Select **Edit->Paste In Front** to paste the rectangle that you copied earlier to the exact location on the page from where it was cut. Keep the pasted rectangle selected.

Creating the Mirror

16. Create a new layer, naming it "Mirror". By creating the new layer, you have assigned the selected rectangle to this layer. Move the layer below the Frame layer.

17. You will now create the mirror surface, which is a gradient.

18. Select **Fill Inspector->Gradient** and create a gradient that alternates between the colors Blue and White, accessed in the Color List. To build the gradient, drag the top drop box down to make a new color drop box. Repeat this until you have five new drop boxes between the top and bottom drop boxes.

19. Select the top drop box and click the Blue color name in the Color List. The next drop box is White. Alternate from Blue to White with the color drop boxes until you finish with a Blue bottom drop box. Change the angle of the gradient to 315 degrees.

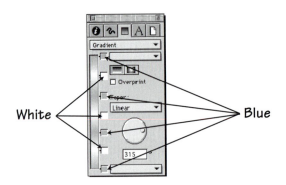

20. Press the Tab key to deselect all. The rectangle filled with this gradient will resemble a mirror.

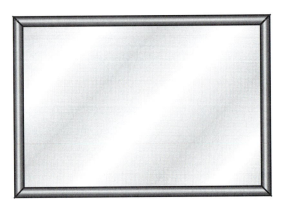

The Mirror Cracks

21. Click the Hide check mark on the Mirror layer for a better view of the template to draw the mirror cracks. Create a new layer and name it "Cracks". Drag the Cracks layer down until it is under the Frame layer. Click on the Cracks layer to make it active.

22. Select the Freehand tool and draw the cracks of the mirror to match the cracks in the template. Hold the Shift key and select all the cracks, then **Modify ->Group** them. Color this group with: **Fill** = None, **Stroke** = 1 pt. Navy.

23. Use **Edit->Clone** on the cracks group and offset the clone by pressing the Left Arrow key three times. Color the cloned cracks with: **Fill** = None, **Stroke** = 1 pt. White. Deselect all.

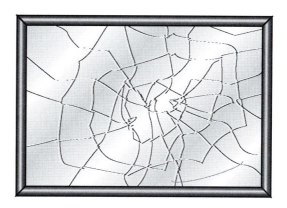

The Ball

24. Create a new layer and name it "Ball". Keep it selected as the active layer.

25. With the Ellipse tool, draw a circle 1.6 inches in diameter. Set a **Stroke** of None and **Fill** the circle with a Radial gradient built from:

> Top drop box = Maroon
> Bottom drop box = Pink

Adjust the radial so the highlight is in the upper left area to give the ball a round appearance.

26. Select the Ellipse tool and draw an ellipse 1.6 inches wide x 0.25 inches tall. Navigate to **Modify->Ungroup** to view the ellipse's anchor points.

27. With the Knife tool, cut both side anchor points. Delete the top half. Paint the remainder: **Fill** = None, **Stroke** = 2 pt. Gray. Move this path on top of the rubber ball and rotate the path 15°. Fine-tune the position to create the look of a ridge on the ball's surface.

28. To create the reflection in the mirror, click on the ball and **Edit-> Clone** it.

29. In the Layers panel, click on the Cracks layer to assign the cloned ball to this layer. Select **Modify->Arrange->Send to Back** to send the shadow behind the cracks. Press the Left Arrow key six times to see it better. Paint the shadow: **Fill** = Gray, **Stroke** = None.

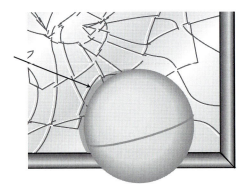

30. Deselect the shadow. Click on the Ball layer to create the shadow underneath the ball. With the Ellipse tool, draw another ellipse 1.6 inches x 0.25 inches. Paint it: **Fill** = White, **Stroke** = None. **Clone** the ellipse and **Scale** the clone 50%. Paint it: **Fill** = Gray, **Stroke** = None.

31. Select both ellipses, and navigate to **Modify->Combine->Blend**.

   Select **Modify->Arrange->Send To Back** so that it will be behind the ball.

32. Position the shadow under the rubber ball. Fine-tune all objects for more accurate positioning in the design.

33. The design is now finished. It should look like this:

   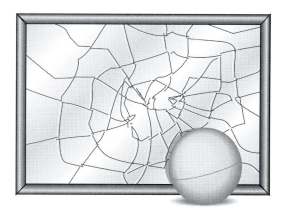

34. Select **Save As** to save the document in your **Work in Progress** folder. Save in the **FreeHand Document** format, naming it "Ball & Mirror".

35. **Close** the document.

Notes:

Project H: Joker's Wild

Creating the Joker's Wild Design

1. Choose **File->Open** and open **Joker.TIF** from the **SF-Intro Freehand** folder. Turn the **Page Rulers** on.

Center the graphic in the top half of the page. Access the **Layers** panel from **Window->Panels**. Select the imported graphic and click on the Background layer. This will gray the graphic so it will not conflict with your drawing. Now click on the padlock icon on the Background layer to Lock the template. Click on the Foreground layer to continue.

2. Drag a vertical ruler guide to mark the line running down the center of the Joker. Select **File->Preferences->Object**, and click on **Path operations consume orginal paths**, if it is not checked.

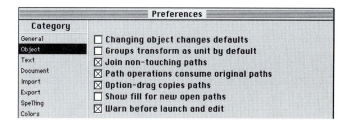

PROJECT H: JOKER'S WILD   PAGE H-1

You will now begin the project by working on the Joker. The whole design technique of achieving a Joker with two opposing sides colored differently, is to first create half the Joker. The center guide acts as an axis to Reflect across 90 degrees. You will be using the new Mirror tool, which, when clicked, automatically reflects a duplicate of the selected object across a 90-degree vertical axis.

3. To make your colors paint the Joker, select the Color List and use its **Options->Import** to navigate to the **SF-Intro Freehand folder** and import **ATC Custom Color.BCF.** In the following window, hold the Shift key and select all the colors. Click **OK**. These colors will now be available in the Color List.

The Joker's Head

4. Select the Pen tool and on the left side of the centerline guide, begin drawing half the crown shape. End the last point of the path on the centerline guide. Select this path and navigate to the **Object Inspector.** Click on **Closed** to make it a closed path. Paint the half-crown: **Fill** = Navy, **Stroke** = 1 pt. Black.

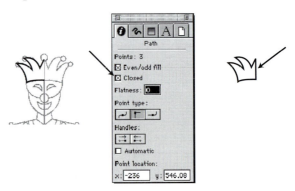

5. To Reflect the half-crown object, select **Window->Xtras->Xtra Tools**. Select the Mirror tool, and click its cursor on the centerline guide at the right side of the object.

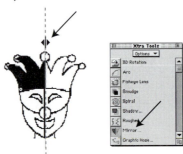

6. The half-crown will reflect, butting up against the original.

7. Use the Ellipse tool to draw circles for the first two crown tops.

8. Click on the two crown halves and select **View->Hide Selection**. This will eliminate any possible interference as you create the top circle.

9. With the Ellipse tool, draw a circle to match the top crown circle in the template. Select **Modify->Ungroup** to select anchor points. Marquee-select the top/bottom anchor points of the circle. Select **Modify->Split** to split the path. Click on the left side of the circle and select the Object Inspector to click **Closed**. Do this for the right side of the circle. You have now created two half-circle closed paths.

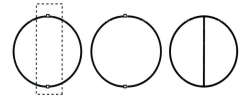

10. Select the first two whole circles that were drawn. Access the Mirror tool and click its cursor on the centerline guide to reflect duplicates. Select all the circles and half-circles on either side of the centerline. Paint them: **Fill** = Gold, **Stroke** = 1 pt. Black. Select **View->Show All** to bring back the crown.

11. For the Joker's nose select the two half-circles at the top of the crown and hold down the Option/Alt key while dragging to duplicate them down to the Joker's nose in the template. **Scale** the two halves 125%. Fine-tune to fit the halves on the nose.

12. Select Keyline mode to get a clear view of the template. With the Pen tool, draw the left half of the cheek and jaw shapes separately as closed paths. Draw the jaw first, then the cheek. Select the two objects.

13. Select Preview mode. Paint the jaw and cheek a flesh tone: **Fill** = Flesh, **Stroke** = 1 pt. Black. Access the Mirror tool and click its cursor on the centerline guide. Select all the jaw/cheek paths and navigate to **Modify ->Arrange->Send to Back**.

14. Select Keyline mode to view the Joker's eyes and mouth in the template. Use the Pen tool to draw the left eye and half-mouth as closed paths. Use the Mirror tool to reflect the eye and mouth across the centerline.

15. Select Preview mode. Select the eyes and paint them: **Fill** = Navy, **Stroke** = 1 pt. Black. Select the mouth pieces and paint them: **Fill** = White, **Stroke** = 1 pt. Black.

The Joker's Upper Body

16. The angled row of circles are created and repeated by using the **Edit ->Duplicate** command. Select Keyline view to get a clear view of the objects. Use the Ellipse tool to draw the top button on the Joker's left side. Paint the circle: **Fill** = Gold, **Stroke** = 1pt. Black.

17. Holding the Option (Macintosh) or Alt (Windows) key, drag the circle to match the second button. Press Command-D (Macintosh) or Control-D (Windows) nine times to repeat this duplication. The bottom button on the template remains to be made. We will get to this soon.

18. Shift-select the buttons you created and use the Left Arrow key to nudge them slightly away from the centerline. With the buttons selected, navigate to the Mirror tool and click its cursor on the centerline guide to reflect/duplicate.

19. For the bottom center button, drag-duplicate the two circle-halves at the top of the crown and make this the bottom button. Access the Transform panel, and Scale the two halves 65%. Return to Preview mode.

    Select all the chest buttons, including the two halves, and **Modify->Group** them. Select **View->Hide Selection** to hide them from view while you work on the chest pieces.

20. The upper chest area is achieved by drawing straight lines with the Pen tool. Starting with the collar, draw the four pieces on the left side of the center guide. Press the Tab key to deselect after drawing each piece. Make certain that they are all closed paths.

    Remember to hold the Shift key when drawing vertical or horizontal lines, to constrain straight lines. You'll need to do this when drawing the lines that run up and down the middle centerline.

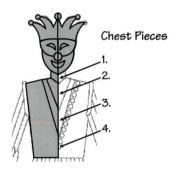

Chest Pieces

When drawn, select each piece and paint:

1. **Fill** = Flesh, **Stroke** = 1 pt. Black.

2. **Fill** = Red, **Stroke** = 1 pt. Black.

3. **Fill** = Gold, **Stroke** = 1 pt. Black.

4. **Fill** = Blue, **Stroke** = 1 pt. Black.

21. You have now created the four chest pieces. Select them, then use the Mirror tool to reflect/duplicate them across the centerline guide. Select **Modify->Arrange->Send To Back**. Select **View->Hide Selection** to hide the chest pieces.

22. The shoulder pads are drawn with the Pen tool as closed paths. Draw the left side first, then use the Mirror tool to reflect/duplicate it across the centerline. Paint the shoulder pads: **Fill** = Gold, **Stroke** = 1 pt. Black.

23. To create the arm, select the Rectangle tool. Draw a vertical rectangle $\frac{1}{16}$ inch x $\frac{3}{4}$ inch (a.)

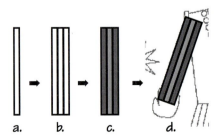

Drag-duplicate a copy that butts against the original. Select **Edit->Duplicate** to repeat this action. You will now have three rectangles next to each other (b.). Paint the first and last rectangle: **Fill** = Red, **Stroke** = 1 pt. Black. Paint the middle rectangle: **Fill** = Navy, **Stroke** = 1 pt. Black (c.).

Select the three rectangles and **Modify->Group** them. Double-click the Rotate tool in the Toolbox. Set the Rotate angle for −19.284° and click **Apply** (Macintosh) or **Rotate** (Windows). Move the rotated group into position on the template.

24. Access the Mirror tool and use it to reflect/duplicate the sleeve across the centerline guide.

Hands, Feet, and Arms

25. The Joker's hands and feet are created using the Freehand drawing tool. Draw the hand/foot on the left side of the center guide. Make certain that each is a closed path.

Paint the hands: **Fill** = Flesh, **Stroke** = 1 pt. Black. Paint the feet: **Fill** = Gold, **Stroke** = 1 pt. Black.

After they are painted, use the Mirror tool to reflect/duplicate them across the centerline. Send them to the back, then **View->Hide Selection**.

The Joker's Pants

26. To begin making the Joker's pants, use the Pen tool to draw the enclosing pant leg outline.

27. Following the template, trace the first line with the Pen tool (a.). Select this line and drag-duplicate it to match the second line in the template. Hold the Shift key to contrain the movement. Press Command-D (Macintosh) or Control-D (Windows) four times to repeat the duplication (b.). Select the top anchor points of the first two lines (c.) and **Modify->Join** them. In the Object Inspector, click on **Closed** to make it a closed path. Do this same joining and closing to the remaining line paths (c.).

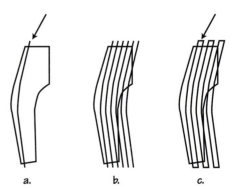

Paint the enclosing pant leg path: **Fill** = Red, **Stroke** = 1 pt. Black. Paint the three joined paths: **Fill**= Blue, **Stroke** = 1 pt. Black.

28. Select the three joined paths, then select **Edit->Cut** (a.). Click on the enclosing pant leg path and select **Edit->Paste Inside** (b.). Use the Mirror tool to reflect/duplicate this pant leg object across the centerline. Select both the original and the reflected pant leg, and navigate to **Modify ->Arrange-Send To Back**.

a.   b.

29. The Joker is now finished, though many parts are hidden. Select **View ->Show All** to bring all the hidden Joker parts back into view. If any parts are overlooked and are obscuring other objects, use **Bring to Front** or **Send to Back** from the **Object->Arrange** menu to fine-tune the positions.

30. With the Pointer tool, marquee-select only the left side paths. Be careful. If you accidentally select a right side path, start over. With the left side paths selected, navigate to **Modify->Group**. Now select **View->Hide Selection** to hide the left side from view. This will allow you to freely marquee-select the right side paths and **Group** them.

The Joker's Right Side

31. Keep the right side grouped object selected. Navigate to **Xtras->Colors ->Color Control** and click the **HLS** option. Make the setting: **H** = 191, **L** = 22, **S** = 60 and click **OK**. The reason for this color adjustment is to perform an across-the-board changing of color tones without having to spend a great deal of time with the Color Mixer, mixing and adjusting colors.

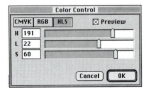

32. Select **View->Show All** to bring the left side back into view. The Joker should look like this:

33. Access the Layers panel (**Window->Panels->Layers**). Double-click on the Foreground layer and rename it "Joker" by pressing Return (Macintosh) or Enter (Windows). Use its Options pop-up menu to create two more layers, renaming them "Stars" and "Card".

    Arrange the layers in the list in this sequence:

    Joker
    Stars
    Card

34. Shift-select both the Joker left and right sides, and click on the Joker layer to assign them here. Click on the check mark of the Joker layer to Hide the two objects. You will now go on to the juggling stars.

The Joker's Stars

35. Click on the Stars layer in the Layers panel to continue. Double-click the Polygon tool to display its dialog box. Enter these settings: **Number of Sides** = 10, **Shape** = Star. Set the acute/obtuse slider slightly toward acute. Click **OK**.

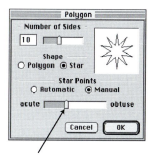

36. Place the Polygon tool cursor in the middle of the top star in the template. Hold the Option (Macintosh) or Alt (Windows) key and drag the star to fit the template. Holding this key makes the star begin drawing from the center. This expedites the drawing and fitting process.

37. **Clone** the star and select the Rotate tool. Holding the Option (Macintosh) or Alt (Windows) key, single-click on the center of the Joker's nose to set the Origin Point. In the Rotate panel, enter 45 for the Rotation angle and click **Apply**. The clone will rotate 45° to the left.

38. Press Command-D (Macintosh) or Control-D (Windows) six times. The stars will continue to duplicate around the clicked Origin Point.

39. Delete the bottom star on the Joker's belly and fine-tune the stars with the Pointer tool to make them better fit the template stars. Remember that templates are usually rough sketches that you use for a guide, so do not try to fit the stars exactly, star point to star point, on the template.

40. Before painting the stars you will need to access the **Color List** panel. Use the **Options** pop-up menu to access the **Crayon** library of colors. Use your own artistic style to pick seven different colors, holding the Shift (Macintosh) or Control (Windows) key as you select them.

Fill each of the seven stars with a different color of your choice. Apply a 1 pt. **Stroke** with a different color, other than the fill.

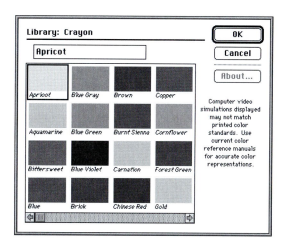

When all the stars are painted, click the check mark on the Stars layer to Hide the layer objects.

The Card and the Shadow Tool

41. Click on the Card layer to continue. To create the card shape and shadow, first double-click on the Rectangle tool. In the dialog box that appears, enter a **Corner Radius** of 20 pts., then click **OK**. Draw a rectangle that matches the card shape in the template. Paint the card: **Fill** = Black, **Stroke** = 1 pt. Black (a.) In the Xtra Tools panel, select the Shadow tool. Drag its cursor on the black card (b.). You will see the shadow's outline as you drag. When offset as a shadow, release the mouse (c.). The Shadow tool groups the two. Hold the Option (Macintosh) or Alt (Windows) key to select just the card. Paint its Fill with White (d.).

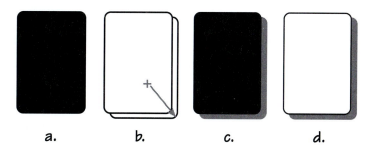

a. b. c. d.

PROJECT H: JOKER'S WILD PAGE H-13

42. In the Layers panel, click the check marks of the hidden layers to bring back the Joker and the Stars. Use the Pointer tool to position the card and shadow to frame these objects.

The Card Letter "J"

43. Continue working on the Card layer. For the letter "J", select the Text tool, then click the cursor in the upper left corner of the card. Type the capital letter "J". Highlight the letter and select the **Text Inspector** panel. Apply these settings: **Font** = ATC Tequila, **Size** = 66 pt.

44. Selecting the text block with the Pointer tool, position the "J" to fit the template. Select **Text->Convert to Outlines** to turn the text letter into a path outline.

45. **Edit->Clone** the outline. Double-click on the Rotate tool. In the **Transform** panel, type 180 for Rotation angle, and click **Apply**. Leave the letter outlines painted Black.

46. Move the rotated letter to fit the lower "J" of the card template. The finished Joker card should like this:

47. Select **Save As** to save the file in your **Work in Progress** folder. Save in **FreeHand Document** format, naming it "Joker's Wild". **Close** the document.

Notes:

Project I: Tropical Treasure Logo

Creating Rules with the Pen Tool

1. Select **File->Open** to open **Tropical Treasure.TIF** from the **SF-Intro Freehand** folder.

2. Move the image to the center of the page and keep it selected.

3. **Open Window->Panels->Layers** and click on the Background layer.

4. Click the padlock icon on the Background layer to lock it to avoid accidentally moving the template while drawing. Press Tab to deselect all, then click on the Foreground layer to continue.

5. Turn on **Page Rulers** and **Guides** in the **View** menu. From the left side ruler, drag out vertical guides to mark the left and right sides of the logo template.

Press Command-Option (Macintosh) -M or Control-Alt - M (Windows) to show the Page Rulers.

6. You will begin with the thick/thin rules at the top of the logo. With the Pen tool, click on the left end of the thick rule against the vertical guide. Holding the Shift key, go to the far right side of this template rule and click.

The keyboard shortcut for Clone is Command-"=" (Macintosh) or Control-Shift-C (Windows).

7. Press the Tab key to deselect everything.

8. Select this segment with the Pointer tool, then **Edit->Clone** it. Press the Down Arrow key several times to move the duplicate segment downward, matching the position of the thin rule underneath the thick rule on the template.

9. Select the upper segment. In the **Stroke Inspector** panel, enter 6 pt. for the **Width**. Select the lower segment and apply 2 pt. for the **Width**.

10. Select both segments, then choose **Edit->Clone.** Move the clones down to almost match the bottom two rules of the template.

11. With the clones still selected, double-click on the Reflect tool. In the Transform panel, enter 180° for the Reflect axis, then click **Apply** (Macintosh) or **Reflect** (Windows).

12. The cloned rules will Reflect. Use the Arrow keys to fine-tune the rules to better fit the template.

The keyboard shortcut for Select All is Command-A (Macintosh) or Control-A (Windows).

13. Select all the rules with **Edit->Select->All**.

14. Open the **Color List**. In the **Options** pop-up menu, select **Pantone Uncoated**. Type in the number 3155 and click **OK**. The color will be added to the **Color List**. Paint the rules: **Fill** = None, **Stroke** = Pantone 3155 CVU.

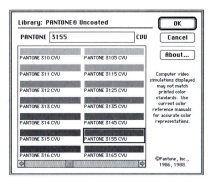

15. You have now created and colored the rules of the logo. We will now draw and color the treasure chest.

Drawing Shapes with the Rectangle Tool

16. Select the Rectangle tool and trace the template to create the treasure chest. There should be four rectangles: the trunk bottom, the trunk top, the plate, and the keyhole.

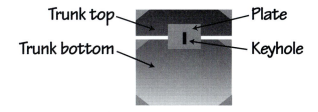

17. Select the **Color List**. In the **Options** pop-up menu, select the **Crayon** Library. Choose the colors Blue, Brown, Gold, and Salmon by holding the Shift key (Macintosh) or Control key (Windows). Click **OK**.

18. Select the two large rectangles (trunk top and bottom) and navigate to the **Fill Inspector**. Select Gradient from its pop-up menu.

PROJECT I: TROPICAL TREASURE LOGO

19. Create a linear gradient of Brown (top drop box) and Salmon (bottom drop box.) **Fill** the selected trunk top and bottom with this gradient. **Stroke** them with None.

20. **Fill** the plate with Gold and **Stroke** = None. **Fill** the keyhole with Black and **Stroke** = None.

The Brass Corners

21. Creating the brass corners of the trunk top and bottom is accomplished by drawing a square to fit the corner on which you are working. Objects drawn with the Rectangle tool must be **Ungrouped** to make their anchor points accessible.

22. Draw a square to fit the upper left corner of the trunk top. Select **Modify** ->**Ungroup** to see the anchor points of this new square.

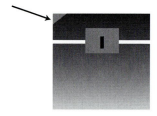

23. Select the bottom right anchor point (a) to create a triangle that fits the corner. Delete the selected anchor point (b).

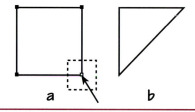

24. Select the triangle with the Pointer tool and drag a duplicate down to the trunk box corner while holding the Option (Macintosh) or Alt (Windows) key.

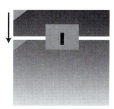

25. With duplicate selected, **Edit->Clone** the triangle. Double-click the Reflect tool in the Toolbox and enter 180° for the Reflect axis. Click Apply (Macintosh) or Enter (Windows). Drag the reflected duplicate down to fit the bottom left corner of the trunk.

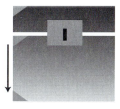

26. Drag a vertical guide to the center of the trunk's keyhole. With the Pointer tool, select the three corners. Select **Window->Xtras->Xtra Tools**. Select the Mirror tool and click its cursor on the vertical guide. This will automatically duplicate/reflect the corners to the right side.

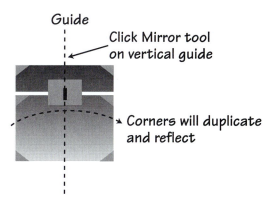

27. Use the Pointer tool or the arrow keys to fine-tune the corners to fit their places. Select all size corner pieces and paint them: **Fill** = Gold and **Stroke** = None.

Drawing Shapes with the Ellipse Tool

28. Using the Ellipse tool, trace the coins at the bottom of the chest. With the Pointer tool, select all the coins. Select the **Color List** and click on the Fill icon. Click on Gold to paint the coins. Drag None to the Stroke icon.

29. Select **Modify->Group** to group the selected coins. Select **Edit->Clone**.

30. With the duplicate group selected, apply a **Basic Fill** in the Fill Inspector of Black, **Stroke** = None.

31. Send this duplicate group to the back (**Modify->Arrange->Send to Back**) and press the down and right Arrow keys a few times for a shadow effect.

32. The chest and coins are now created. Marquee-select all these objects and **Modify->Group** them. You will now work on the type.

Turning Type into Outlines

33. With the Text tool, click the cursor once on the page and type:

   TROPICAL TREASURE

   Highlight the text with the Text tool and make the **Font** = ATC Tequila and **Size** = 72 pt.

34. Click this text block with the Pointer tool to see the box handles. Drag the right middle handle to the right side guide; drag the left middle handle to the left side guide. This will space the letters evenly across the width of the text block.

35. Click the text cursor between the two words and press the Spacebar once or twice, depending upon how far the letters moved.

36. If the TROPICAL letters do not fit the template well enough, highlight the word and use kerning to fine-tune them. To kern, hold the Option (Macintosh) or Control-Alt (Windows) key as you press either the Left or Right Arrow keys. The Left Arrow key will close up the spacing of the letters. The Right Arrow key will widen the spacing between the letters. Do this now.

37. Once the letters are kerned, click on the text block with the Pointer tool. In the **Text** menu, choose the **Convert To Paths** option. The type will automatically be **Grouped**. Paint it with: **Fill** = Blue, **Stroke** = None.

38. With this group selected, choose **Edit->Clone**, then **Modify->Arrange ->Send To Back**. This will be the first clone.

39. Press the Right Arrow key five times and the Down Arrow key five times to make a shadow effect. Paint this duplicate: **Fill** = Black, **Stroke** = None.

TROPICAL   TREASURE

40. With this duplicate still selected, choose **Edit->Clone**. Clones go to the front when created. Your clone will be in front of the original group.

41. To move this new clone, select **Modify->Arrange->Move Backward**. It will now be behind the original and in front of the first clone. Paint this new clone: **Fill** = White, **Stroke** = None.

42. Press the Up Arrow key two times, then the Left Arrow key two times.

43. Your letters should look like this:

TROPICAL   TREASURE

44. With the Text tool, click the cursor under the bottom rule lines in the logo.

Press Command-Shift (Macintosh)-P or Control-Shift -P (Windows) to convert selected text to paths.

45. Type the words:

    Gifts From Under The Sea

46. Highlight the text, then go to the Text Inspector and apply these settings: **Font** = ATC Daquiri, **Size** = 36 pt., **Horizontal scale** = 120%. Be certain to use kerning to make the letters fit the template. Select the text block with the Pointer tool and choose **Text->Convert to Paths**.

47. Color the text with: **Fill** = Pantone 3155 CVU, and **Stroke** = 1 pt. Pantone 3155 CVU.

    ## Gifts From Under The Sea

48. Move "Gifts From Under The Sea" in position on the template. After moving the elements you have drawn onto the template, and after fine-tuning their positions, the logo should look like this:

49. The logo is now complete. Select all the objects in the design and **Modify ->Group** them.

50. Select **Save As** to save your file in the **Work in Progress** folder. Save in the **FreeHand Document** format, naming it "Tropical Treasure Logo".

51. **Close** the document.

Project J: Tropical Treasure Mailer

Setting the Layout

1. Select **File->Open** to open the graphic file **Tropical Mailer.TIF** from the **SF-Intro FreeHand** folder.

2. Move the image to the top center of the page, then open the **Layers** panel. With the image selected, click on the Background layer to make the image a template.

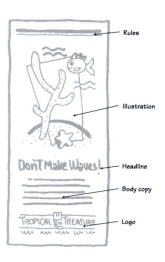

3. Click on the padlock icon next to Background to lock the layer. Press Tab to deselect all, then click on the Foreground layer to continue.

4. Open the **Tropical Treasure Logo** file that you created and saved earlier.

5. Click on the design to select it, then **Edit->Copy** the group.

6. **Close** the Tropical Treasure Logo file without saving.

7. **Edit->Paste** the logo in the working document. Position it on the template.

8. With the pasted logo selected, double-click on the Scale tool in the Toolbox. The **Transform** panel will appear with Scale selected.

The keyboard shortcut for the Transform panel is Command-M (Macintosh) or Control-M (Windows).

The keyboard shortcut for Clone is Command- "=" (Macintosh) or Control-Shift-C (Windows).

The keyboard shortcut for Send To Back is Command-B (Macintosh) or Control-B (Windows).

9. Enter 35 for the Scale % (Uniform). Click **Apply**. Position the logo to match the template.

10. Create a text block with the Text tool, then type the words:

    Don't Make Waves!

11. Highlight the text. In the **Text Inspector**, make these settings: **Font** = ATC Sea Breeze, **Size** = 36 pt., **Horizontal scale** = 50%, **Alignment** = Centered.

12. Select **Text->Convert To Paths**, turning the text into outlines. Use the Pointer tool to position this group to match the template.

13. Open the **Window->Panels->Color List**.

14. Use the **Color List->Options** pop-up menu to go to the **Crayon** library and select Salmon. Click **OK**. Salmon will appear in the Color List. Paint the outlines with: **Fill** = Salmon, **Stroke** = None.

15. With the Pointer tool, click on this outline group and **Edit->Clone** it.

16. Send the duplicate to the back (**Modify->Arrange->Send to Back**). Press the Right Arrow key two times, and the Down Arrow key two times to make an offset shadow.

17. Go to Color List->Options->Pantone Uncoated and select 312 for the color list. Select the clone and **Fill** with Pantone Uncoated 312 CVU, no stroke.

    Don't Make Waves!

18. With the Text tool, draw an Area-text block for the body copy. Type this text:

    Dive down to Tropical Treasures. Find exquisite gifts and goodies made from purely natural materials from the sea. See our coral, sea shells, sand dollars, and more!

19. Highlight the text and apply these settings: **Font** = ATC Colada, **Size** = 10 pt., Leading = 12 pt. (Fixed "="). Fine-tune the block so that it will fit the text in the template.

20. Select **File->Open** to open the **Tropical Fish** file you created and saved earlier.

21. Click on the design to select it, then **Edit->Copy** the group.

22. **Close** the file without saving.

23. **Edit->Paste** the logo into the working document. Scale the logo 65%, and position it on the template.

24. Using the Line tool, hold the Shift key and draw a rule at the top of the mailer. Set the **Width** to 10 pt. in the **Stroke Inspector**.

25. **Edit->Clone** this rule. Set the **Width** to 3 pt. in the **Stroke Inspector** and press the Down Arrow key several times, enough to position it slightly under the original. Color both lines: **Fill** − None, **Stroke** = Pantone 312.

26. Using the template as a guide, draw a border around the mailer with the Rectangle tool. Paint the rectangle: **Fill** = None, **Stroke** = 1.5 pt. Black. The finished mailing piece should look like this:

27. Select **Save As** to save the file in your Work in Progress folder. Save in **FreeHand Document** format, naming it "Tropical Mailer". **Close** the document.

Notes:

Project K: Grocery Ad

Creating a Full Page Ad Layout

1. Select **File->New** to create a new document.

2. To prepare the layout, you will begin by setting guides and measurements. Select the Units pop-up menu at the bottom of the document window and set measurements for Inches.

3. Turn on the **View->Page Rulers**.

4. Click on the horizontal ruler and drag down a guide to the 5.5 inch mark.

5. Click on the vertical ruler and drag a guide to the 4.25 inch mark; this will show the center of the page for laying out the ad.

6. Select the Rectangle tool and draw a large rectangle on the page.

7. Select the **Object Inspector** and set the rectangle's **Dimensions** to **W** = 7.5 inches and **H** = 10 inches.

8. Select **Keyline** mode and move the rectangle so that its center point matches where the guides mark the center of the page.

9. Once the rectangle is centered, open the **Layers** panel and click on the Guides layer to convert the rectangle to a guide marking the margins.

10. Click on the padlock icon to lock the Guides layer.

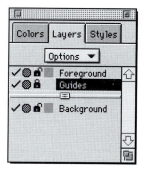

11. The first element to put into the ad is the background for the masthead.

12. Draw a 7.5 inch x 2 inch rectangle at the top of the page. You can use the guides to help you draw this or you can use the **Object Inspector.** Return to Preview viewing mode.

13. Open the **Color List** and set the **Stroke** to None. In **Color List->Options->Crayon**, select the color Navy and click **OK**.

14. You will now use the **Fill Inspector->Gradient** to create a multi-color gradient. Select the **rectangle** and, from **Color List**, drag Navy to the two color swatch boxes, top and bottom. From **Color List**, drag White to the middle of the color ramp. Set the angle for 180. This will create a Dual Gradient as shown in the color ramp.

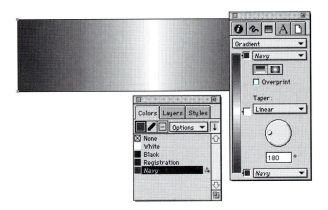

15. In Preview mode the selected rectangle will be **Filled** with this gradient:

The next element to incorporate into this design is the Honeydo Market logo. This has been created previously and you will **Import** it.

16. From **File->Import** select the **Honeydo Market Logo.EPS** in the **SF-Intro FreeHand** folder. Press **Open**. Position the Import tool cursor in the upper corner of the rectangle and click. With the Pointer tool, position the logo in the center of the rectangle.

Press Command-R (Macintosh) or Control-R (Windows) to show the File ->Import dialog.

17. Select the Text tool and, under the Honeydo Market logo, type this text:

    Prices effective Thursday thru Saturday

    Credit Cards Accepted — Quantity Rights Reserved

18. Highlight the text and open the **Text Inspector**. Apply these settings: **Font** = ATC Plantation, **Size** =14 pt., **Alignment** = Center.

19. Highlight only the second line of text and set the **Size** to 12 pt. Center the text container under the logo.

20. Use **Color List->Options->Crayon** to put Yellow into the list. Highlight the text you just typed and **Fill** with Yellow.

Creating The Gourmet Meats Section

21. Select the **Rectangle** tool and draw a rectangle 7.5 inch x 4 inch. Position it below the top masthead that you just created.

22. Open the **Color Mixer**. In the **Color List**, drag the Yellow swatch over to the **Color Mixer**. Click on the **Tint** tab and adjust the tint percentage of Yellow to 20%, which will appear in bottom right sample swatch. From this sample swatch, drag this tint back to the **Color List.** The name 20% Yellow will appear.

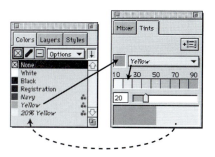

23. With the rectangle selected, paint it: **Fill** = 20% Yellow, **Stroke** = None.

24. Select **File->Import** and locate the file **Beef Eaters Logo.EPS** in the **SF-Intro FreeHand** folder. Click **Open** to import it.

25. Position the logo in the upper left corner of the 20% Yellow rectangle, approximately ¼ inch from the edges.

26. Select **File->Import** to navigate to the **SF-Intro FreeHand** folder to import the three photographs: **Roast Beef.TIF**, **Cornish Hens.TIF**, and **Turkey.TIF**. Position the Cornish Hens and the Turkey images underneath the Beef Eaters logo.

Select the Roast Beef image and double-click on the Scale tool. Enter 150 for the Scale %. Press **Apply** (Macintosh) or **Scale** (Windows). Position the image in the empty area of the Yellow rectangle to the right of the smaller imported images.

27. Draw rectangles the same size as the Cornish Hens and Turkey photos. Paint the rectangles: **Fill** = Black, **Stroke** = None. Place each rectangle on top of its respective photo.

28. With the rectangles selected, press the Right Arrow key two times, then the Down Arrow key two times. **Edit->Cut** the rectangles. Select the Cornish Hens and Turkey photos. Select **Edit->Paste Behind**; this will make the rectangles appear as offset shadows.

29. Draw a rectangle the same size as the **Roast Beef.TIF**. Paint it: **Fill** = Black, **Stroke** = None. Position the rectangle on top of the Roast Beef photo.

30. Press the Right Arrow key two times and the Down Arrow two times. **Edit->Cut** the rectangles. Select Roast Beef photo. Select **Edit->Paste Behind**.

31. Off to the right, away from the page, do the following: Select the Text tool and click to create a text block, then type:

    Gourmet
    Meats

32. Highlight the text, then make and apply these settings in the Text Inspector: **Font** = ATC Sea Breeze, **Size** = 24 pt., **Leading** = 28 (Fixed "="), **Alignment** = Centered.

33. Draw a rectangle that is slightly larger than the text container.

34. Paint the rectangle: **Fill** = Navy, **Stroke** = None.

35. Select the rectangle, then navigate to **Modify->Arrange->Send to Back**. Highlight the GOURMET MEATS text. Paint it: **Fill** = White, **Stroke** = None.

36. Center the text in the middle of the rectangle. **Modify->Group** them both. Position this group to the right of the Beef Eaters logo.

37. Select **File->Import** and import the text file **Grocery Text_1.TXT.** from the **SF-Intro FreeHand** folder.

38. Drag the **Import** cursor to draw a text block under the Gourmet Meats.

39. Highlight the text. In the **Text Inspector**, apply these settings: **Font** = ATC Sands, **Size** = 13 pt., **Leading** = 21 pt (Fixed =). Set a **Decimal Tab** at 1.5 inches. In the Color List, set **Fill** = Black.

40. Position this text block to fine-tune its placement under Gourmet Meats and away from the two small photos.

41. Select the Text tool and click and type the words:

    ROAST BEEF SPECIAL

    Highlight the text and apply these settings: **Font** = ATC Plantation, **Size** = 24 pt., **Leading** = 28 pt. (Fixed =).

42. With the Text tool, create a new text container and enter "$5.49 lb."

43. Highlight the text and apply: **Font** = ATC Plantation.

    Highlight the individual items and apply these settings:

    - $ — Size = 26 pt., Baseline shift = 14 pt.

    - 5 — Size = 48 pt., Baseline shift = 0 pt.

    - .49 lb. — Size = 26 pt., Baseline shift = 14 pt.

    $$\$5.49\text{ lb.}$$

44. Move ROAST BEEF SPECIAL and $5.49 lb. into position under the top of the Roast Beef photo.

45. The Grocery Ad should look similar to this:

Creating The Produce Section

46. With Units set to Inches, access the Rectangle tool and draw a 3.5 inch x 3.5 inch square. Paint it: **Fill** = None, **Stroke** = 1.5 pt. Black.

47. Draw a rectangle of 3.5 inch x 0.5 inch and **Fill** it with a multi-color gradient with 100% Navy in the top/bottom drop boxes. Drag a 30% Navy tint to the middle of the color ramp. Set the gradient angle for 180. Make the **Stroke** = None.

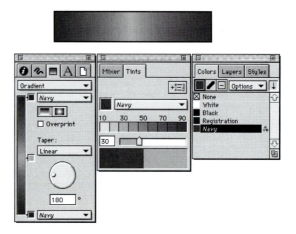

Position this rectangle at the top of the 3.5 inch x 3.5 inch square. Send the rectangle to back (**Modify->Arrange->Send To Back**).

48. With the Text tool, click a type block and type the word:

PRODUCE

In the Text Inspector, apply these settings: **Font** = ATC Sea Breeze, **Size** = 26 pt. Paint the text: **Fill** = White, **Stroke** = None.

49. Highlight the text and, in the **Text Inspector**, choose **Shadow Effect** from the **Effects** option.

50. Position the text in the center of the new rectangle.

51. **Import** the three images: **Salad.TIF**, **Blueberries.TIF**, and **Oranges.TIF**. Position the three images across the top, beneath the Produce header.

52. On top of each photo, draw a rectangle the same size as the photo.

53. Select the three rectangles and paint them: **Fill** = Black, **Stroke** = None.

54. Select all three rectangles and **Edit->Cut** them. Select the three photos and navigate to **Edit->Paste Behind**. Press the Right Arrow key twice and the Down Arrow key twice.

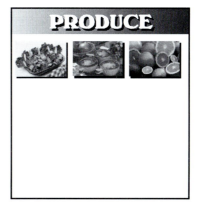

55. From **File->Import** select the **SF-Intro FreeHand** folder and import the file **Grocery Text_2.TXT**. With the **Import** cursor, draw a text block in the empty portion of the square.

56. Open the **Text Inspector** and select the Column-and-Row icon. Set 2 columns with spacing of 0.165 inches between them.

57. In the **Text Inspector** make these settings: **Font** = ATC Sands, **Size** = 12 pt., **Leading** = 16 pts. ("="), **Decimal Tab** at 1-1/8 inches.

58. Fine-tune the text to fit the square evenly. The finished section should like this:

59. Marquee-select this Produce section and **Modify->Group**. Move the group into a place on the ad under the Gourmet Meats section.

Creating Grocery Ad Coupons

60. To begin making the two coupons, draw a rectangle 3.5 inches x 1.75 inches.

61. **Fill** the coupon with None. Set the **Stroke** to dashed lines, with a **Width** of 2 pts.

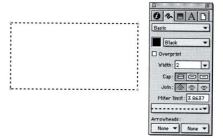

62. Select the Rectangle tool and draw a rectangle 2 inches x 0.3125 inches. **Fill** it with Black, **Stroke** = None. Move this rectangle to the upper center of the dashed border.

63. With the Text tool, click and type the word:

    COUPON

64. Highlight the text and apply these settings: **Font** = ATC Plantation, **Size** = 18 pt. In the **Fill Inspector**, set the **Fill** = White. Position this text centered in the black rectangle of the coupon.

Your coupon should look like this:

65. Select all the elements of this coupon, then **Modify->Group** them.

66. Move the group into position in the ad layout at the top of the remaining empty space.

67. Select **Edit->Clone** to clone the group and move (holding the Shift key to constrain) the clone down to fill the empty space under the original coupon.

68. With the Text tool, click and type this text:

    $199

69. Highlight this text and make these settings: **Font** = ATC Plantation, **Size** = 50 pt., **Baseline shift** = 20 pt.

70. Highlight just the 1 in the $199 and change to: **Size** = 80 pt., **Baseline shift** = 0.

71. Create another text block and type:

    48 oz. Various flavors
    Regularly $2.57

    Apply these settings: **Font** = ATC Sands, **Size** = 13 pt., **Leading** = 15 pt. (Fixed "="), **Alignment** = Centered.

72. Create another text block and type:

    Ocean
    Spray
    Juice

73. Apply these settings: **Font** = ATC Plantation, **Size** = 30 pt., **Leading** = 32 (Fixed"="), **Alignment** = Centered. Move the three text blocks into place on the top coupon. The coupon should look like this:

74. With the Text tool, create a text block and type:

    99¢

    Apply to 99¢: **Font** = ATC Plantation, **Size** = 80 pt., Baseline shift = 0 pt.

    Change just the ¢ in the 99¢ to: **Size** = 50 pt., Baseline shift = 20 pt.

75. Create a new text block and type:

    Regularly $1.99

    Make these settings to this text: **Font** = ATC Sands, **Size** = 13 pt., **Leading** = 15 pt. (Fixed "=").

76. Create a new text block and type:

    Vlasic
    Olives

    Make these settings to this text: **Font** = ATC Plantation, **Size** = 30 pt., **Leading** = 32 (Fixed "="), **Alignment** = Centered.

77. Create a new text block and type:

    Spanish 5 3/4 oz.
    or Ripe 5 3/4 oz.

    Make these settings: **Font** = ATC Sands, **Size** = 13 pt., **Leading** = 15 pt. ("="), **Alignment** = Centered.

The "¢" symbol is made by typing the "$" key, holding the Option (Macintosh) or Alt (Windows) key.

78. Move the text blocks into position on the second coupon.

79. You have now finished the ad. It should look like this:

80. Select **Save As** to save the file in your **Work in Progress** folder. Save in **FreeHand Document** format, naming the file "Full Page Grocery Ad".

81. **Close** the document.

Glossary

4/1
A job printed using four colors of ink on one side of the sheet, and one color of ink on the other.

4/4
A job printed with four colors of ink on both sides of the sheet. A full four-color project. See *process colors, subtractive color*.

Acetate
A plastic material used to block or expose specific portions of a layout through "windows" cut from the material by a stripper. The resultant "masks" are used to generate film separations for generating printing plates.

Achromatic
By definition, having no color; therefore, completely black or white or some shade of gray.

Acrobat
This program by Adobe Systems, Inc. converts any document from any Macintosh or Windows application to PDF format, which retains the page layout, graphics, color, and typography of the original document. It is widely used for distributing documents online because it is independent of computer hardware. The only software needed is a copy of Acrobat Reader, which can be downloaded free.

Adaptive Palette
A sampling of colors taken directly from an image, and used in a special compression process usually used to prepare images for the world wide web.

Additive Color Process
The additive color process is the process of mixing red, green, and blue light to achieve a wide range of colors, as on a color television screen. See *Subtractive Color*.

Adjacent Color
The eye will respond to a strong adjacent color in such a way as to affect the perception of the particular color in question. That is, a color having different adjacent colors may look different than it does in isolation. Also referred to as metamerism.

Adobe Systems Incorporated
A major software developer responsible for the creation of the PostScript page description language (see *PostScript*), used in almost all graphic arts environments. PostScript resides in a printer or Raster Image Processor (see *Raster Image Processor*) and is used to convert graphics from the screen to high-resolution output. Adobe also develops the highly popular Photoshop, Illustrator, PageMaker, and Premiere graphics and video applications, in addition to a range of others.

Airbrush
A tool driven by compressed air that applies a very fine spray of color to artwork to produce various effects. Its effects are simulated in digital illustration and imaging programs.

Algorithm
A specific sequence of mathematical steps to process data. A portion of a computer program that calculates a specific result.

Alley
The white space, or margin, between columns on a page.

Alpha Channel
An 8-bit channel of data that provides additional graphic information, such as colors or masking. Alpha channels are found in some illustration or graphics programs, and are used in video production.

ANSI
The American National Standards Institute. ANSI establishes and publishes industry standards in many fields including data transmission and graphics.

Anti-aliasing
A graphics software feature that eliminates or softens the jaggedness of low-resolution curved edges.

Apple Computer, Inc.
A computer manufacturer based in Cupertino, California. Apple was responsible for the development of the Macintosh computer and the first Postscript-equipped laser printer, which ushered in the "desktop publishing" revolution.

Archival storage
The process of storing data in a totally secure and safe manner. Archiving differs from backup in that it's meant to be used to restore entire systems or networks, rather than providing quick and easy access to specific files or folders.

Art
Illustrations and photographs in general; that is, all matter other than text that appears in a mechanical.

Artifact
By definition, something that is artificial, or not meant to be there. An artifact can be a blemish or dust spot on a piece of film, or unsightly pixels in a digital image.

Ascender
Parts of a lower-case letter that exceed the height of the letter "x". The letters b, d, f, h, k, l, and t have ascenders.

ASCII
The American Standard Code for Information Interchange, which defines each character, symbol, or special code as a number from 0 to 255 (8 bits in binary). An ASCII text file can be read by any computer, and is the basic mode of data transmission on the Internet.

ATM (Adobe Type Manager)
A utility program which causes fonts to appear smooth on screen at any point size. It's also used to manage font libraries.

Author's Alterations (A/As)
Changes made to the copy by the author after typesetting, and thus chargeable to the author.

Backing Up
The process of making copies of current work or work-in-progress as a safety measure against file corruption, drive or system failure, or accidental deletion. Backing up work-in-progress differs from creating an archive (see *Archiving*) for long-term storage or system restoration.

Backslant
A name for characters that slant the opposite way from italic characters.

Banding
A visible stair-stepping of shades in a gradient.

Banner
A large headline or title extending across the full page width, or across a double-page spread.

Baseline
The implied reference line on which the bases of capital letters sit.

Bézier Curves
Curves that are defined mathematically (vectors), in contrast to those drawn as a collection of dots or pixels (raster). The advantage of these curves is that they can be scaled without the "jaggies" inherent in enlarging bitmapped fonts or graphics.

Binding
In general, the various methods used to secure signatures or leaves in a book. Examples include saddle-stitching (the use of staples in a folded spine), and perfect-bound (multiple sets of folded pages sewn or glued into a flat spine).

Bit (Binary Digit)
The smallest unit of information in a computer, representing one of two conditions, ON or OFF; HIGH or LOW, etc. Eight bits comprise one byte. One byte can represent any text character.

Bitmap
A rectangular array of dots that, taken together, form an image. Bitmap file formats include: .BMP, .DIB, .GIF, .PCX and .TIFF (see *Raster Graphics*).

Bitmapped
An image formed by a grid of dots or pixels whose curved edges have discrete steps because of the approximation of the curve by a finite number of pixels.

Black
The absence of color; an ink that absorbs all wavelengths of light.

Blanket
The blanket, a fabric coated with natural or synthetic rubber wrapped around the cylinder of an offset press, transfers the inked image from the plate to the paper.

Bleed
Page data that extends beyond the trim marks on a page. Illustrations that spread to the edge of the paper without margins are referred to as "bled off."

Blind Emboss
A raised impression in paper made by a die, but without being inked. It is visible only by its relief characteristic.

Blow up
An enlargement, usually of a graphic element such as a photograph.

Body Copy
The text portion of the copy on a page, as distinguished from headlines.

Boldface
A heavier, blacker version of a typeface.

Bond
A sized (coated) writing paper used for business or personal stationery that normally has significant rag (cotton) content.

Border
A continuous line that extends around text; or a rectangular, oval, or irregularly-shaped visual in an ad.

Bounding Box
The imaginary rectangle that encloses all sides of a graphic, necessary for a page layout specification.

Brightness
1. A measure of the amount of light reflected from a surface. 2. A paper property, defined as the percentage reflection of 457-nanometer (nm) radiation. 3. The intensity of a light source. 4. The overall percentage of lightness in an image.

Bug
See *Logo*

Bullet
A marker preceding text, usually a solid dot, used to add emphasis; generally indicates that the text is part of a list.

Burn
1. To expose an image onto a plate. 2. To make copies of ROM chips or CD-ROMs. 3. To darken a specific portion of an image through photographic exposure.

Byte
A unit of measure equal to eight bits (decimal 256) of digital information, sufficient to represent one text character. It is the standard unit measure of file size. (See also *Megabyte*, *Kilobyte*, and *Gigabyte*).

Calibration Bars
A strip of reference blocks of color or tonal values used to check the registration, quality, density, and ink coverage during a print run.

Calibration
Making adjustments to a color monitor and other hardware and software to make the monitor represent as closely as possible the colors of the final printed piece.

Callout
A descriptive label referenced to a visual element, such as several words connected to the element by an arrow.

Camera Ready
A completely finished mechanical, ready to be photographed to produce a negative from which a printing plate will be made.

Cap Line
The theoretical line to which the tops of capital letters are aligned.

Caps and Small Caps
A style of typesetting in which capital letters are used in the normal way, while the type that would normally be in lower case has been changed to capital letters of a smaller point size. A true small-caps typeface does not contain any lower-case letters.

Caps
An abbreviation for capital letters.

Caption
The line or lines of text that identify a picture or illustration, usually placed beneath it or otherwise in close proximity.

CD-ROM
A device used to store approximately 600MB of data. Files are permanently stored on the device and can be copied to a disk but not altered directly. ROM stands for Read-Only Memory. Equipment is now available on the consumer market for copying computer files to blank CD-ROMs.

Character Count
The number of characters (letters, figures, signs or spaces) in a selected block of copy. Once used to calculate the amount of text that would fit on a given line or region when physically setting type.

Choke
See *Trapping*

Chooser
A part of the Macintosh operating system that permits selection of a printer or other peripheral device. Chooser is also used to access resources on a network.

Chroma
The degree of saturation of a surface color in the Munsell color space model.

Chromaticity Diagram
A graphical representation of two of the three dimensions of color. Intended for plotting light sources rather than surface colors. Often called the CIE diagram.

Cicero/Didot Point
The cicero is a unit of horizontal distance slightly larger than the pica, used widely in continental Europe. A cicero equals 0.178 inches, or 12 Didot points.

CIE (Commission Internationale de l'Eclairage)
An international group that developed a universal set of color definition standards in 1931.

CIE Diagram
See *Chromaticity Diagram*

Clip Art
Collections of predrawn and digitized images stored on disk that can be pasted into word processing and DTP documents.

Clipboard
The portion of computer memory that holds data that has been cut or copied. The next item cut or copied replaces the data already in the clipboard.

Cloning
Duplication of pixels from one part of an image to another.

CMS
See *Color Management System*

CMYK (Cyan, Magenta, Yellow, Black)
The process colors (subtractive primaries) used in color printing. The letter K stands for "Key," although it is commonly used to refer to the Black ink that is added to the three colors when necessary. When printing black text as part of a four-color process, only the black ink is used. A normal four-color separation will have a plate for each of the four colors. When combined on the printed piece, the half-tone dots of each color give the impression of the desired color to the eye.

Coated
Printing papers having a surface coating (of clay or other material) to provide a smoother, more even finish with greater opacity.

Cold type
Type produced by photographic or digital methods, as opposed to the use of molten metal as in the old Linotype machine.

Collate
To gather separate sections or leaves of a publication together in the correct order for binding.

Color Balance
The combination of yellow, magenta, and cyan needed to produce a neutral gray. Determined through a gray balance analysis.

Color Bars
See *Color Control Strip*

Color Cast
The modification of a hue by the addition of a trace of another hue, such as yellowish green, pinkish blue, etc. Normally, an unwanted effect that can be corrected.

Color Chart
A printed chart of various combinations of CMYK colors used as an aid for the selection of "legal" colors during the design phase of a project.

Color Control Strip
A printed strip of various reference colors used to control printing quality. This strip is normally placed outside the "trim" area of a project, as a guide and visual aid for the pressman.

Color Conversion - Copyright

Color Conversion
Changing the color "mode" of an image. Converting an image from RGB to CMYK for purposes of preparing the image for conventional printing.

Color Correction
The process of removing casts or unwanted tints in a scanned image, in an effort to improve the appearance of the scan or to correct obvious deficiencies, such as green skies or yellowish skin tones.

Color Gamut
The range of colors that can be formed by all possible combinations of the colorants of a given reproduction system (printing press) on a given type of paper.

Color Key
An overlay color proof of acetate sheets, one for each of the four primary printing inks. The method was developed by 3M Corporation and remains a copyrighted term.

Color Management System
A process or utility that attempts to manage color of input and output devices in such a way that the monitor will match the output of any CMS-managed printer.

Color Model
A system for describing color, such as RGB, HLS, CIELAB, or CMYK.

Color Picker
A function within a graphics application that assists in selecting a color.

Color Proof
A printed or simulated printed image of the color separations intended to produce a close visual simulation of the final reproduction for approval purposes.

Color Scanner
See *Scanner*

Color Separation
The process of splitting an image or PostScript into cyan, magenta, yellow, and black components for offset printing.

Color Sequence
The color order of printing the cyan, magenta, yellow, and black inks on a printing press. Sometimes called rotation or color rotation.

Color Space
Because a color must be represented by three basic characteristics depending on the color model, the color space is a three-dimensional coordinate system in which any color can be represented as a point.

Color Temperature
The temperature, in degrees Kelvin, to which a blackbody would have to be heated to produce a certain color radiation. (A "blackbody" is an ideal body or surface that completely absorbs or radiates energy.) The graphic arts viewing standard is 5,000 K. The degree symbol is not used in the Kelvin scale. The higher the color temperature, the bluer the light.

Color Transparency
A positive color photographic image on a clear film base that must be viewed by transmitted light. It is preferred for original photographic art because it has higher resolution than a color print. Transparency sizes range from 35mm color slides up to 8x10in. (203x254mm).

Colorimeter
An optical measuring instrument designed to measure and quantify color. They are often used to match digital image values to those of cloth and other physical samples.

Column rule
A thin vertical rule used to separate columns of type.

Comp
Comprehensive artwork used to present the general color and layout of a page.

Compose
To set copy into type, or lay out a page.

Compression
A digital technique used to reduce the size of a file by analyzing occurrences of similar data. Compressed files occupy less physical space, and their use improves digital transmission speeds. Compression can sometimes result in a loss of image quality and/or resolution.

Condensed Type
A typeface in which the width of the letters has been reduced. Condensed type can be a specific font, or the result of applying a percentage of normal width by a formatting command.

Continuous Tone
An image such as an original photograph in which the subject has continuous shades of color or gray tones through the use of an emulsion process. Continuous tone images must be screened to create halftone images in order to be printed.

Contrast
The relationship between the dark and light areas of an image.

Copy
Any material furnished for reproduction such as text or illustrations. As a verb, the computer command to copy data to the clipboard in preparation for pasting it to another location.

Copyfitting
Fitting a certain body of text to a given area by changing the font size, leading, justification, or some other parameter.

Copyright
Ownership of a work by the originator, such as an author, publisher, artist, or photographer. The right of copyright permits the originator of material to prevent its use without express permission or acknowledgement of the originator. Copyright may be sold, transferred, or given up contractually.

CorelDraw - Disk Operating System

CorelDraw
A popular drawing program originally designed for the Windows environment, but now available as a Macintosh program. Corel is known to create files that can cause printing and/or output problems in many environments.

Creep
An unwanted movement of the blanket of an offset printing press that causes registration problems.

Cromalin
A single-sheet color proofing system introduced by DuPont in 1971 and still quite popular in the industry. It uses a series of overlaid colorants and varnish to simulate the results of a press run.

Crop Marks
Printed lines used for final trimming of a printed page.

Cropping
The elimination of parts of a photograph or other original that are not required to be printed.

Dash
A short horizontal rule of varying lengths used to indicate a pause or clause in a sentence; see *En-dash* and *Em-dash*.

DCS (Desktop Color Separation)
An EPS file format that creates one file for each of the four primary printing inks, and a fifth file that contains a thumbnail of the image. DCS files are used for building pages with layout programs; when the file is output, the small placement image is discarded, and the four high-resolution files are automatically substituted. This reduces the need to move large, high-resolution files around a network.

Default
A specification for a mode of computer operation that operates if no other is selected. For example, the default font size might be 12 point, or a default color for an object might be white with a black border.

Densitometer
An electronic instrument used to measure optical density. Reflective (for paper) and transmissive (for film) versions are available.

Density
The ability of a material to absorb light. In film, it refers to the opacity of a specific area of the image. A maximum density of 4.0 refers to solid black. Improper density in film images can result in washed-out or overly-dark reproduction.

Descender
The part of a lower-case letter that extends below the baseline (lower edge of the x-height) of the letter. The letters y, p, g, and j contain descenders.

Desktop
1. The area on a monitor on which the icons appear, before an application is launched. 2. A reference to the size of computer equipment (system unit, monitor, printer) that can fit on a normal desk; thus, desktop publishing.

Desktop Publishing (DTP)
Use of a personal computer, software applications, and a high-quality printer to produce fully composed printed documents. DTP is, in reality, an incorrect term these days. In the early days of Macintosh and PostScript technology, the term Desktop Publishing inferred that the materials produced from these systems was somehow inferior (as opposed to *professional* publishing). Now, the overwhelming majority of all printed materials – regardless of the quality – are produced on these systems, up to and including nationally famous magazines, catalogs, posters, and newspapers.

Dialog Box
A window in a computer application that – in most cases – presents an opportunity for the user to enter information relative to the process that they're executing. A dialog box might ask, for example, how many copies of a document you want to print, or what size a circle should be, or what color. Dialog boxes are an integral part of today's graphic user interfaces – both on the Macintosh and on Windows-based systems.

Digital Camera
A camera which produces images directly into an electronic file format for transfer to a computer.

Digital
The use of a series of discrete electronic pulses to represent data. In digital imaging systems, 256 steps (8 bits, or 1 byte) are normally used to characterize the gray scale or the properties of one color. For text, see *ASCII*.

Digital Proofs
Digital proofs are representations of what a specific mechanical will look like when output and reproduced on a specific type of printing press. The difference with a digital proof is that it is created without the use of conventional film processes and output directly from computer files.

Dingbat
A font character that displays a picture instead of a letter, number or punctuation mark. There are entire font families of pictographic dingbats; the most commonly used dingbat font is *Zapf Dingbats*. There are dingbats for everything from the little airplanes used to represent airports on a map, to telephones, swashes, fish, stars, balloons – just about anything.

Direct-to-plate
Producing printing plates directly from computer output without going through the film process.

Disk
A computer data storage device, either "floppy," "hard," or a high-capacity removable disk, that stores data magnetically.

Disk Operating System (DOS)
Software for computer systems that supervises and controls the running of programs. The operating system is loaded into memory from disk by a small program which permanently resides in the firmware within the computer. The major operating systems in use today are Windows95 and WindowsNT from Microsoft, the Macintosh OS from Apple

Dithering – Emulsion

Computer, and a wide range of UNIX systems, such as those from Silicon Graphics, SUN Microsystems, and other vendors.

Dithering
A technique used in images wherein a color is represented using dots of two different colors displayed or printed very close together. Dithering is often used to compress digital images, in special screening algorithms (see *Stochastic Screening*) and to produce higher quality output on low-end color printers.

Document
The general term for a computer file containing text and/or graphics.

Dongle
A security device that usually plugs into your keyboard or printer port, that allows copy-protected software to run on your system. Such protected software will only run on systems with the dongle present. This prevents a single copy of software from running on any but one machine at a time.

Dot Gain
The growth of a halftone dot that occurs whenever ink soaks into paper. This growth can vary from being very small (on a high-speed press with fast-drying ink and very non-porous paper) to quite dramatic, as is the case in newspaper printing, where a dot can expand 30% from its size on the film to the size at which it dries. Failure to compensate for this gain in the generation of digital images can result in very poor results on press. Generally speaking, the finer the screen (and therefore, the smaller the dot) the more noticeable dot gain will be.

Double-page Spread
A design that spans the two pages visible to the reader at any open spot in a magazine, periodical, or book.

Double-Click
Two clicks of a mouse button in rapid succession that are interpreted as the command to open an application, file, or folder.

Downloadable Fonts
Typefaces that can be stored on disk and then downloaded to the printer when required for printing.

DPI (Dots Per Inch)
The measurement of resolution for page printers, photo-typesetting machines and graphics screens. Currently graphics screens use resolutions of 60 to 100 dpi, standard desktop laser printers work at 600 dpi, and imagesetters operate at more than 1,500 dpi.

Dragging
The process of moving an object on the screen by clicking on it with the mouse, moving the cursor to another location, then releasing the button.

Drop Cap
A large initial cap, usually set down into the block or body of normal text. Excellent examples of ornate drop caps (called illuminated initials) can often be seen in manuscripts illustrated by hand in the Middle Ages.

Drop Shadow
A duplicate of a graphic element or type placed behind and slightly offset from it, giving the effect of a shadow.

Drum Scanner
A color scanner on which the original is wrapped around a rotary scanning drum. See *Scanner*.

DTP
See *Desktop Publishing*

Duotone
The separation of a black-and-white photograph into black and a second color having different tonal values and screen angles. Duotones are used to enhance photographic reproduction in two-, three-, or sometimes four-color work. Often the second, third, and fourth colors are not standard CMYK inks.

Dye
A soluble coloring material, normally used as the colorant in color photographs.

Dye Transfer
A photographic color print using special coated papers to produce a full color image. Can serve as an inexpensive proof.

Electrostatic
The method by which dry toner is transferred to paper in a copier or laser printer, and liquid toners are bonded to paper on some large-format color plotters.

Element
The smallest unit of a graphic, or a component of a page layout or design. Any object, text block, or graphic might be referred to as an element of the design.

Elliptical Dot Screen
A halftone screen having an elliptical dot structure.

Em Dash
A dash – often used in place of parentheses or commas to break a sentence – that is usually equal to the point size. For example, in 10 point type, an em dash would be 10 points wide. Formerly the width of a capital M in a particular font; this definition is still used by some type foundries.

Em Space
A space usually equal to the current point size; in 10 point type, an em space should be 10 points wide. Formerly the width of a capital M in a given font; this definition is still used by some type foundries. Hot lead typesetters often used this space as the standard distance for a paragraph indent.

Embedding
1. Placing control codes in the body of a document. 2. Including a complete copy of a text file or image within a desktop publishing document, with or without a *link* (see *Linking*).

Emulsion
The coating of light-sensitive material (silver halide) on a piece of film.

En Dash
A dash – often used in hyphenated word pairs – that is usually half the width of an em dash.

En Space
A space that is usually equal to half the width of an em space.

EPS (Encapsulated PostScript)
A file format used to transfer PostScript data within compatible applications. An EPS file normally contains a small thumbnail that's used to display the image when it's placed into position within a mechanical or used by another program. EPS files can contain text, vector artwork, and images.

Ethernet
A set of software protocols widely used in network communications.

Excel
A spreadsheet application produced by Microsoft; available separately or as part of Microsoft Office.

Exception dictionary
A file, used within a spell-checking or hyphenation process, that provides exceptions to standard spelling or justification rules.

Expanded Type
Also called extended, a widened version of a typeface design. Type may be extended artificially within a DTP application, or designed as such by the typeface designer. See also *Condensed Type*.

Export
To save a file generated in one application in a format that is readable in another application.

Extension
A modular software program that extends or expands the functions of a larger program. A folder of Extensions is found in the Macintosh System Folder.

Fill
To add a tone or color to the area inside a closed object in a graphic illustration program.

Film
Non-paper output of an imagesetter or phototypesetter.

Filter
In image editing applications, a small program that creates a special effect or performs some other function within an image.

Flat
A group of individual camera-ready pages mounted in the proper order and ready for photographing to produce a signature plate.

Flat Color
Color that lacks contrast or tonal variation.

Flatbed Scanner
A scanner on which the original is mounted on a flat scanning glass. See *Scanner*.

Flexography
A rotary letterpress process printing from rubber or flexible plates and using fast drying inks. Mainly used for packaging.

Floating Accent
A separate accent mark that can be placed under or over another character. Complex accented characters such as in foreign languages are usually available in a font as a single character.

Flop
To make a mirror image of visuals such as photographs or clip art.

Flush Left
Copy aligned along the left margin.

Flush Right
Copy aligned along the right margin.

Folder
1. The digital equivalent of a paper file folder, used to organize files in the Macintosh and Windows operating systems. The icon of a folder looks like a paper file folder. Double-clicking it opens it to reveal the files stored inside. 2. A mechanical device which folds preprinted pages into various formats, such as a tri-fold brochure.

Font
A font is the complete collection of all the characters (numbers, uppercase and lowercase letters and, in some cases, small caps and symbols) of a given typeface in a specific style; for example, Helvetica Bold.

Force Justify
A type alignment command which causes the space between letters and words in a line of type to expand to fit within a line. Often used in headlines, and sometimes used to force the last line of a justified paragraph, which is normally set flush left, to justify.

Four-color Process
See *Process Colors*

FPO
"For Position Only": a low-resolution graphic or simple box to designate the location of a graphic in the final file.

Frame
In desktop publishing, an area or block into which text or graphics can be placed.

FreeHand
A popular vector-based illustration program available from Macromedia.

Full Measure
A line set to the entire line length.

Galley Proof

Proofs, usually of type, taken before the type is made up into pages. Before desktop publishing, galley proofs were hand-assembled into pages.

Gamma Correction

1. Adjusting the contrast of the midtones in an image. 2. Calibrating a monitor so that midtones are correctly displayed on screen.

Gamma

A measure of the contrast, or range of tonal variation, of the midtones in a photographic image

Gamut

See *Color Gamut*

GASP

Acronym for Graphic Arts Service Provider, a firm that provides a range of services somewhere on the continuum from design to fulfillment.

GCR (Gray component replacement)

A technique for adding detail by reducing the amount of cyan, magenta, and yellow in chromatic or colored areas, replacing them with black.

GIF - Graphics Interface File

A CompuServe graphics file format that is used widely for graphic elements in Web pages.

G (Gigabyte)

One billion (1,073,741,824) bytes (2^{30}) or 1,048,576 kilobytes.

Global Preferences

Preference settings which affect all newly created files within an application.

Gradation

A smooth transition between black and white, one color and another, or color and no-color.

Gradient

A fill pattern that goes from dark to light or light to dark, or from one color or shape to another.

Grain

Silver salts clumped together in differing amounts in different types of photographic emulsions. Generally speaking, faster emulsions have larger grain sizes.

Graininess

Visual impression of the irregularly distributed silver grain clumps in a photographic image, or the ink film in a printed image.

Gray Balance

The values for the yellow, magenta, and cyan inks that are needed to produce a neutral gray when printed at a normal density.

Gray Component Replacement

See *GCR*

Gray Scale

An image containing a series of tones stepped from white to black that is used for monitoring tone reproduction.

Grayscale

An image composed in grays ranging from black to white, usually using 256 different shades of gray.

Greeking

1. A software technique by which areas of gray are used to simulate lines of text below a certain point size. 2. Nonsense text use to define a layout before copy is available.

Grid

A division of a page by horizontal and vertical guides into areas into which text or graphics may be placed accurately.

Group

To collect graphic elements together so that an operation may be applied to all of them simultaneously.

GUI

Acronym for Graphical User Interface, the basis of the Macintosh and Windows operating systems.

Guides

Lines created in layout application programs to assist in aligning various design elements.

Gutter

The white space between two facing pages. Sometimes used interchangeably with Alley to describe the space between columns on a page.

Hairline Rule

The thinnest rule that can be printed. A hairline rule on a 1200 dpi imagesetter is 1/1200 of an inch; on a 300 dpi laser printer, the same rule would print at 1/300 of an inch.

Halftone

An image generated for use in printing in which a range of continuous tones is simulated by an array of dots that create the illusion of continuous tone when seen at a distance.

Halftone Tint

An area covered with a uniform halftone dot size to produce an even tone or color. Also called tint or screen tint.

Hanging Indent

Formatting text so that the first line is not indented, and all subsequent lines within the paragraph are indented. Often used with bullets.

Hanging punctuation

Punctuation marks such as quotation marks that are set outside the text block; similar to a hanging indent.

Hard Copy

A tangible permanent image such as an original, a proof, or a printed sheet.

Hard Drive

A rigid disk sealed inside an airtight transport mechanism that is the basic storage mechanism in a computer. Information stored may be accessed more rapidly than on floppy disks and far greater amounts of data may be stored.

Hard Return
A manual line ending (created by pressing the Return or Enter key) that denotes the end of a paragraph.

Header
A fixed body of copy that appears at the top of each page of a section of a book. It may contain variable quantities such as page number, time, date, or file name.

Hide
A command in DTP applications that will render certain elements on the screen invisible, but will not remove them from the file.

High Key
A photographic or printed image in which the main interest area lies in the highlight end of the scale.

High Resolution File
An image file that typically contains four pixels for every dot in the printed reproduction. High-resolution files are often linked to a page layout file, but not actually embedded in it, due to their large size.

Highlights
The lightest areas in a photograph or illustration.

HLS
Color model based on three coordinates: hue, lightness (or luminance), and saturation.

HSV
A color model based on three coordinates: hue, saturation and value (or luminance).

HTML (HyperText Markup Language)
The language, written in plain (ASCII) text using simple tags, that is used to create Web pages, and which Web browsers are designed to read and display. HTML focuses more on the logical structure of a page than its appearance.

Hue
The wavelength of light of a color in its purest state (without adding white or black).

Hyperlink
An HTML tag that directs the computer to a different Anchor or URL (Uniform Resource Locator). The linked data may be on the same page, or on a computer anywhere in the world.

Hyphenation Zone
The space at the end of a line of text in which the hyphenation function will examine the word to determine whether or not it should be hyphenated and wrapped to the next line.

Icon
A small graphic symbol used on the screen to indicate files or folders, activated by clicking with the mouse or pointing device.

Illustrator
A vector editing application owned by Adobe Systems, Inc.

Imagesetter
A raster-based laser device used to output a computer page-layout file or composition at high resolution onto photographic paper or film, from which to make printing plates.

Import
To bring a file generated within one application into another application.

Imposition
The arrangement of pages on a printed sheet, which, when the sheet is finally printed, folded and trimmed, will place the pages in their correct order.

Indent
A typographical technique that lines up the beginnings or ends of lines at a position other than the preset margin.

Indexing
In DTP, marking certain words within a document with hidden codes so that an index may be automatically generated.

Indexed Color Image
An image which uses a limited, predetermined number of colors; often used in Web images. See also *GIF*.

Initial Caps
Text in which the first letter of each word (except articles, etc.) is capitalized.

Inline Graphic
A graphic that is inserted within a body of text, and may be formatted using normal text commands for justification and leading; inline graphics will move with the body of text in which they are placed.

Intensity
Synonym for degree of color saturation.

International Paper Sizes
The International Standards Organization (ISO) system of paper sizes is based on a series of three sizes A, B and C. Series A is used for general printing and stationery, Series B for posters, and Series C for envelopes. Each size has the same proportion of length to width as the others. The nearest ISO paper size to conventional 8-1/2 x 11 paper is A4.

ISO
The International Standards Organization.

Italics
A version of a typeface with letters slanted to the right.

Jaggies
Visible steps in the curved edge of a graphic or text character that results from enlarging a bitmapped image.

JPG or JPEG
A compression algorithm that reduces the file size of bitmapped images, named for the Joint Photographic Experts Group, an industry organization that created the standard; JPEG is a "lossy" compression method, and image quality will be reduced in direct proportion to the amount of compression.

Justification
The alignment of text along a margin or both margins..

Kelvin (K)
Unit of temperature measurement based on Celsius degrees, starting from absolute zero, which is equivalent to -273 Celsius (centigrade); used to indicate the color temperature of a light source.

Kerning
Moving a pair of letters closer together or farther apart, to achieve a better fit or appearance.

Key (Black Plate)
In early four-color printing, the black plate was printed first and the other three colors were aligned (or registered) to it. Thus, the black plate was the "key" to the result.

Kilobyte (K, KB)
1,024 (2^{10}) bytes, the nearest binary equivalent to decimal 1,000 bytes. Abbreviated and referred to as K.

Knockout
A shape or object printed by eliminating (knocking out) all background colors. See *Overprinting*.

L*a*b
The lightness, red-green attribute, and yellow-blue attribute in the CIE Color Space, a three-dimensional color mapping system.

Landscape
Printing from the left to right across the wider side of the page. A landscape orientation treats a page as 11 inches wide and 8.5 inches long.

Laser printer
A high quality image printing system using a laser beam to produce an image on a photosensitive drum. The image is transferred to paper by a conventional xerographic printing process. Current laser printers used for desktop publishing have a resolution of 600 dpi. Imagesetters are also laser printers, but with higher resolution and tight mechanical controls to produce final film separations for commercial printing.

Layer
A function of graphics applications in which elements may be isolated from each other, so that a group of elements may be hidden from view, locked, reordered or otherwise manipulated as a unit, without affecting other elements on the page.

Layout
The arrangement of text and graphics on a page, usually produced in the preliminary design stage.

Leading ("ledding")
Space added between lines of type. Usually measured in points or fractions of points. Named after the strips of lead which used to be inserted between lines of metal type. In specifying type, lines of 12-pt. type separated by a 14-pt. space is abbreviated "12/14," or "twelve over fourteen."

Leaders
A line of periods or other symbols connecting the end of a group of words with another element separated by some space. For example, a table of contents may consist of a series of phrases on separate lines, each associated with a page number. Promotes readability in long lists of tabular text.

Letterspacing
The insertion or addition of white space between the letters of words.

Library
In the computer world, a collection of files having a similar purpose or function.

Ligature
Letters that are joined together as a single unit of type such as oe and fi.

Lightness
The property that distinguishes white from gray or black, and light from dark color tones on a surface.

Line Art
A drawing or piece of black and white artwork, with no screens. Line art can be represented by a graphic file having only one-bit resolution.

Line Screen
The number of lines per inch used when converting a photograph to a halftone. Typical values range from 85 for newspaper work to 150 or higher for high-quality reproduction on smooth or coated paper.

Linen Tester
A magnifying glass designed for checking the dot image of a halftone. See *Loupe*.

Linking
An association through software of a graphic or text file on disk with its location in a document. That location may be represented by a "placeholder" rectangle, or a low-resolution copy of the graphic.

Linotype
A typecasting machine (now obsolete) that injected hot metal into a line of molds to produce lines of type. After printing, the type was melted and used again.

Linotype-Hell
The manufacturer of imagesetters such as the Linotronic that process PostScript data through an external Raster Image Processor (RIP) to produce high resolution film for printing.

Lithography
A mechanical printing process used for centuries based on the principle of the natural aversion of water (in this case, ink) to grease. In modern offset lithography, the image on a photosensitive plate is first transferred to the blanket of a rotating drum, and then to the paper.

Logo
A graphic element normally used as a design to represent a company or product.

Lossy
A data compression method characterized by the loss of some data.

Loupe
A small free-standing magnifier used to see fine detail on a page. See *Linen Tester*.

Lowercase
The uncapitalized letters of the alphabet; so named when type was composed by hand, and the small letters were in the lower part of the type case.

LPI
Lines per inch. See *Line Screen*.

Luminosity
The amount of light, or brightness, in an image. Part of the HLS color model.

LZW
The acronym for the Lempel-Ziv-Welch lossless data- and image-compression algorithm.

M, MB (Megabyte)
One million (1,048,576) bytes (2^{20}) or 1,024 Kilobytes.

Macro
A set of keystrokes that is saved as a named computer file. When accessed, the keystrokes will be performed. Macros are used to perform repetitive tasks.

Manuscript (MS or Mss)
The original written or typewritten work of an author submitted for publication.

Margins
The non-printing areas of page, or the line at which text starts or stops.

Mark up
To prepare copy for a compositor, setting out in detail all the typesetting instructions, or to denote corrections on a printed proof.

Mask
To conform the shape of a photograph or illustration to another shape such as a circle or polygon.

Masking
A digital technique that blocks an area of an image from reproduction by superimposing an opaque object of any shape.

Master Page
A page that holds repeating elements of a layout, such as guides or graphics.

Match Print
A color proofing system used for the final quality check.

Mechanical
A pasted-up page of camera-ready art that is to be photographed to produce a plate for the press.

Mechanical Dot Gain
See *Dot Gain*

Medium
A physical carrier of data such as a CD-ROM, video cassette, or floppy disk, or a carrier of electronic data such as fiber optic cable or electric wires.

Megabyte (MB)
A unit of measure of stored data equaling 1,024 kilobytes, or 1,048,576 bytes (10^{20}).

Megahertz
An analog signal frequency of one million cycles per second, or a data rate of one million bits per second. Used in specifying computer CPU speed.

Menu
A list of choices of functions, or of items such as fonts. In contemporary software design, there is often a fixed menu of basic functions at the top of the page that have pull-down menus associated with each of the fixed choices.

Menu-driven
Programs which allow the user to request functions by choosing from a list of options.

Metafile
A class of graphics that combines the characteristics of raster and vector graphics formats; not recommended for high-quality output.

Metallic Ink
Printing inks which produce an effect of gold, silver, bronze, or metallic colors.

Midtones or Middletones
The tonal range between highlights and shadows.

Mock-up
The rough concept or layout of a publication or design.

Modem
An electronic device for converting digital data into analog audio signals and back again (MOdulator-DEModulator.) Primarily used for transmitting data between computers over analog (audio frequency) telephone lines.

Moiré
An interference pattern caused by the out-of-register overlap of two or more regular patterns such as dots or lines. In process-color printing, screen angles are selected to minimize this pattern.

Monochrome
An image or computer monitor in which all information is represented in black and white, or with a range of grays.

Monospace
A font in which all characters occupy the same amount of horizontal width regardless of the character. See also *Proportional Spacing*.

Montage - Page Layout Software

Montage

A single image formed by assembling or compositing several images.

Mottle

Uneven color or tone.

Mss

See *Manuscript*

Multimedia

The combination of sound, video images, and text to create a "moving" presentation.

Network

Two or more computers that are linked to exchange data or share resources. The Internet is a network of networks.

Neutral

Any color that has no hue, such as white, gray, or black.

Neutral Density

A term that describes images or filters that are gray with no apparent hue.

Noise

Unwanted signals or data that may reduce the quality of the output.

Non-breaking Space

A typographic command that connects two words with a space, but prevents the words from being broken apart if the space occurs within the hypenation zone. See *Hyphenation Zone*.

Nonreproducible Colors

Colors in an original scene or photograph that are impossible to reproduce using process inks. Also called out-of-gamut colors.

Normal Key

A description of an image in which the main interest area is in the middle range of the tone scale or distributed throughout the entire tonal range.

Norton Utilities

A software product that provides programs for maintaining a computer's hardware or software; for example, locating and restoring a file that was accidentally "erased."

Nudge

To move a graphic or text element in small, preset increments, usually with the arrow keys.

Oblique

A slanted character (sometimes backwards, or to the left), often used when referring to italic versions of sans-serif typefaces.

OCR (Optical Character Recognition)

A special kind of scanner software that provides a means of reading printed characters on documents and converting them into digital codes that can be read into a computer as actual editable text rather than pure images.

Offset

In graphics manipulation, to move a copy or clone of an image slightly to the side and/or back; used for a drop-shadow effect.

Offset Lithography

A printing method whereby the image is transferred from a plate onto a rubber-covered cylinder from which the printing takes place (see *Lithography*).

OLE

Object Linking and Embedding, a software technique that permits linking an object in a document to its original file and enabling automatic updating. OLE applications may be OLE containers (able to accept OLE documents) or OLE servers (able to create OLE documents), or both.

Opacity

1. The degree to which paper will show print through it. 2. Settings in certain graphics applications that allow images or text below the object whose opacity has been adjusted, to show through.

OPI

Open Prepress Interface, a software device that is an extension to PostScript that replaces low-resolution placeholder images in a document with their high-resolution sources for printing.

Optical Disks

Video disks that store large amounts of data used primarily for reference works such as dictionaries and encyclopedias.

Orphan

The last line of a paragraph that appears alone at the top of a column or page.

Outline

A typeface in which the letters have outlines only and no fill.

Overlay

A transparent sheet used in the preparation of multicolor mechanical artwork showing the color breakdown.

Overprint Color

A color made by overprinting any two or more of the primary yellow, magenta, and cyan process colors.

Overprinting

Allowing an element to print over the top of underlying elements, rather than knocking them out (see *Knockout*). Often used with black type.

Page Description Language (PDL)

A special form of programming language that describes both text and graphics (object or bit-image) in mathematical form. The main benefit of a PDL is that makes the application software independent of the physical printing device. PostScript is a PDL, for example.

Page Layout Software

Desktop publishing software such as PageMaker or QuarkXpress used to combine various source documents and images into a high quality publication.

Page Proofs
Proofs of the actual pages of a document, usually produced just before printing, for a final quality check.

PageMaker
A popular page-layout application produced by Adobe Systems.

Palette
1. As derived from the term in the traditional art world, a collection of selectable colors. 2. Another name for a dialog box or menu of choices.

Panose
A typeface matching system for font substitution based on a numeric classification of fonts according to visual characteristics.

Pantone Matching System
A system for specifying colors by number for both coated and uncoated paper; used by print services and in color desktop publishing to assure uniform color matching.

Pasteboard
In a page layout program, the desktop area outside of the printing page area, on which elements can be placed for later positioning on any page.

PCX
Bitmap image format produced by paint programs.

PDF (Portable Document Format)
Developed by Adobe Systems, Inc. (and read by Adobe Acrobat Reader), this format has become a de facto standard for document transfer across platforms.

PDL
See *Page Description Language*

Perfect binding
A common method of binding paperback books in which the pages are glued directly to the binding.

Perspective
The effect of distance in an image achieved by aligning the edges of elements with imaginary lines directed toward one to three "vanishing points" on the horizon.

Photoshop
The Adobe Systems image editing program commonly used for color correction and special effects on both the Macintosh and PC platforms.

Pi Fonts
A collection of special characters such as timetable symbols and mathematical signs. Examples are Zapf Dingbats and Symbol. See also *Dingbats*.

Pica
A traditional typographic measurement of 12 points, or approximately 1/6 of an inch. Most DTP applications specify a pica as exactly 1/6 of an inch.

PICT/PICT2
A common format for defining bitmapped images on the Macintosh. The more recent PICT2 format supports 24-bit color.

Pixel
A picture element – the smallest dot or unit on a computer monitor or in a bitmapped image.

Plate
Paper, polyester, or metal sheet used in a printing press to transfer an image onto paper.

PMS
See *Pantone Matching System*

PMT
Photo Mechanical Transfer – positive prints of text or images used for paste-up to mechanicals.

Point
A unit of measurement used to specify type size and rule weight, equal to (approximately, in traditional typesetting) 1/72 inch.

Polygon
A geometric figure consisting of three or more straight lines enclosing an area. The triangle, square, rectangle, and star are all polygons.

Portrait
Printing from left to right across the narrow side of the page. Portrait orientation on a letter-size page uses a standard 8.5-inch width and 11-inch length.

Positive
A true photographic image of the original made on paper or film.

Posterize, Posterization
The deliberate constraint of a gradient or image into visible steps as a special effect; or the unintentional creation of steps in an image due to a high LPI value used with a low printer DPI.

Postprocessing Applications
Applications, such as trapping programs or imposition software, that perform their functions after the image has been printed to a file, rather than in the originating application.

PostScript
A page description language developed by Adobe Systems, Inc. that describes type and/or images and their positional relationships upon the page; the resulting file is processed by a RIP (see *Raster Image Processor*) into a format a laser printer or imagesetter can understand.

PPD
Acronym for PostScript Printer Definition file, the information that ensures that output remains within the capabilities of the selected output device.

PPI
Pixels per inch; used to denote the resolution of an image.

Prepress
All work done between writing and printing, such as typesetting, scanning, layout, and imposition.

Preferences
A set of defaults for an application program that may be modified.

Prepress Proof
A color proof made directly from electronic data or film images.

Primary Colors
Colors that can be used to generate secondary colors. For the additive system (i.e., a computer monitor), these colors are red, green, and blue. For the subtractive system (i.e., the printing process), these colors are yellow, magenta, and cyan.

Printer Command Language
PCL — a language, that has graphics capability, developed by Hewlett Packard for use with its own range of printers.

Printer fonts
The image outlines for type in PostScript that are sent to the printer.

Printer's Spreads
Pages arranged so that, when printed as spreads and assembled, the pages appear in the proper order. For example, the front and back covers are printed on a spread, the inside front and inside back covers are printed on another spread, etc.

Process Colors
The four colors (cyan, magenta, yellow, and black) that are combined to print a wide range of colors. When blended, they can reproduce many, but not all of the colors found in nature. See also *CMYK*.

Profile
A file containing data representing the color reproduction characteristics of a device determined by a calibration of some sort.

Proof
A representation of the printed job that is made from plates (press proof), film, or electronic data (prepress proofs). It is generally used for customer inspection and approval before mass production begins.

Proportional Spacing
A method of spacing whereby each character is spaced to accommodate the varying widths of letters or figures, thus increasing readability. Books and magazines are set proportionally spaced, and most fonts in desktop publishing are proportional. With proportionally spaced fonts, each character is given a horizontal space proportional to its size. For example, a proportionally spaced "m" is wider than an "i."

Pt.
Abbreviation for point.

Pull Quote
A phrase extracted from the copy and used as a graphic to break up a quantity of text visually, and to call attention to an important point.

QuarkXPress
A popular page-layout application.

Queue
A set of files input to the printer, printed in the order received unless otherwise instructed.

QuickDraw
Graphic routines in the Macintosh used for outputting text and images to printers not compatible with PostScript.

Ragged Left
See *Flush Right*

Ragged Right
See *Flush Left*

RAM
Random Access Memory, the "working" memory of a computer that holds files in process. Files in RAM are lost when the computer is turned off, whereas files stored on the hard drive or floppy disks remain available.

Raster
A bitmapped representation of graphic data.

Raster Graphics
A class of graphics created and organized in a rectangular array using bitmaps. Often created by paint software, fax machines, or scanners.

Raster Image Processor (RIP)
That part of an imagesetter that converts the page information from the Page Description Language into the bitmap pattern that is applied to the film or paper output.

Rasterize
Converting mathematical and digital information into a series of dots by an imagesetter for the production of negative or positive film or paper output

Ray Tracing
A software technique for rendering the surface of a reflecting object realistically by tracing the light rays from the source of illumination to the eye of the viewer.

Reader's Spreads
A two-page spread as seen by the reader after printing and collation; thus, the two pages may have been printed in separate locations on the signature.

Reference Marks
Symbols such as the asterisk (*), dagger, double dagger, section mark (§), and paragraph mark (¶) used in text to direct the reader to a footnote.

Reflective Art
Artwork that is opaque, as opposed to transparent, that can be scanned for input to a computer.

Registration - Screen Printing

Registration
Aligning plates on a multicolor printing press so that the images will superimpose properly to produce the required composite output.

Registration Color
A default color selection that can be applied to design elements so that they will print on every separation from a PostScript printer. "Registration" is often used to print identification text that will appear outside the page area on a set of separations.

Registration Marks
Small crosshairs on film used to align the individual layers of film separations.

Resolution
The number of dots or pixels per inch of a monitor or output device.

Retouching
Making selective manual or electronic corrections to images.

Reverse Out
To reproduce an object as white, or paper, within a solid background, such as white letters in a black rectangle.

RGB
Red, Green, Blue, the additive primary colors used to create images on a computer monitor or television screen.

Rich Black
A process color consisting of sold black with one or more layers of cyan, magenta, or yellow.

Right Reading
A positive or negative image that is readable from top to bottom and from left to right.

Right-Click
Clicking the right mouse button on a Windows system, usually to reveal a pop-up menu. A Macintosh mouse has only one button.

RIP
See Raster Image Processor

River
An accidental and undesirable pattern of white space between words in text that appears to flow from one corner to another.

ROM
Read Only Memory, a semiconductor chip in the computer that retains startup information for use the next time the computer is turned on.

Roman Type
The primary serif typeface of a family.

Rosette
The pattern created when color halftone screens are printed at traditional screen angles.

Rotation
Turning an object at some angle to its original axis.

RTF
Rich Text Format, a text format that retains formatting information lost in pure ASCII text.

Rubylith
A two-layer acetate film having a red or amber emulsion on a clear base used in non-computer stripping and separation operations.

Ruler
Rulers displayed at two sides of the working space on a monitor that show measurements in units that can be selected in the set-up process.

Running Head
A line of type at the top of a page that repeats the same information. Also called header.

S/S (Same Size)
An instruction to the printer to reproduce at the same size as the original.

Sans Serif
Sans Serif fonts are fonts that do not have the tiny lines that appear at the top of and bottom of letters.

Saturation
The intensity or purity of a particular color; a color with no saturation is gray.

Scaling
The means within a program to reduce or enlarge the amount of space an image will occupy by multiplying the data by a scale factor. Scaling can be proportional, or in one dimension only.

Scanner
A device that electronically digitizes images point by point through circuits that can correct color, manipulate tones, and enhance detail. Color scanners will usually produce a minimum of 24 bits for each pixel, with 8 bits each for red, green, and blue.

Screen
To create a halftone of a continuous tone image (See *Halftone*).

Screen Angle
The angle at which the rulings of a halftone screen are set when making screened images for halftone process-color printing. The equivalent effect can be obtained electronically through selection of the desired angle from a menu.

Screen Frequency
The number of lines per inch in a halftone screen, which may vary from 85 to 300.

Screen Printing
A technique for printing on practically any surface using a fine mesh (originally of silk) on which the image has been placed photographically. Preparation of art for screen printing requires consideration of the resolution of the screen printing process.

Screen Shot – Spot Color

Screen Shot
A printed output or saved file that represents data from a computer monitor.

Screen Tint
A halftone screen pattern of all the same dot size that creates an even tone at some percentage of solid color.

Script
A typeface designed to imitate handwriting.

SCSI
Small Computer Systems Interface, a standard software protocol for connecting peripheral devices to a computer for fast data transfer.

Selection
The act of placing the cursor on an object and clicking the mouse button to make the object active.

Self-Cover
A cover for a document in which the cover is of the same paper stock as the rest of the piece.

Serif
A line or curve projecting from the end of a letter form. Typefaces designed with such projections are called serif faces.

Service Bureau
A business that specializes in producing film for printing on a high-resolution imagesetter.

Set Solid
Type set with no extra spacing between the lines; for example, 12-pt. type with 12-pt. leading, or 12/12.

SGML
Standard Generalized Markup Language, a set of semantics and syntax that describes the structure of a document (the nature, content, or function of the data) as opposed to visual appearance. HTML is a subset of SGML (see *HTML*).

Sharpness
The subjective impression of the density difference between two tones at their boundary, interpreted as fineness of detail.

Sheet Fed
A printing press that prints single sheets of paper rather than from a continuous roll.

Shortcut
1. A quick method for accessing a menu item or command, usually through a series of keystrokes. 2. The icon that can be created in Windows95 to open an application without having to penetrate layers of various folders. The equivalent in the Macintosh is the "alias."

Show
The opposite of "Hide," a toggle command. For example, the tabs and paragraph marks in a text document can either be shown or hidden by clicking on an icon in the toolbar.

Sidebar
Supplementary text positioned at the side of a page.

Signature
A group of pages ganged together on a large, single sheet for printing, usually comprising an individual section of a publication.

Silhouette
To remove part of the background of a photograph or illustration, leaving only the desired portion.

Skew
A transformation command that slants an object at an angle to the side from its initial fixed base.

Small caps
A type style in which lowercase letters are replaced by uppercase letters set in a smaller point size.

Smart Quotes
The curly quotation marks used by typographers, as opposed to the straight marks on the typewriter. Use of smart quotes is usually a setup option in a word processing program or page layout application.

Snap-to (guides or rulers)
An optional feature in page layout programs that drives objects to line up with guides or margins if they are within a pixel range that can be set. This eliminates the need for very precise, manual placement of an object with the mouse.

Soft Font
See *Downloadable Font*

Soft or Discretionary Hyphen
A hyphen that is coded for display and printing only when formatting of the text puts the hyphenated word at the end of a line.

Soft Return
A return command that ends a line but does not apply a paragraph mark that would end the continuity of the style for that paragraph.

Spectrophotometer
An instrument for measuring the relative intensity of radiation reflected or transmitted by a sample over the spectrum.

Specular Highlight
The lightest highlight area that does not carry any detail, such as reflections from glass or polished metal. Normally, these areas are reproduced as unprinted white paper.

Spine
The binding edge at the back of a book that contains title information and joins the front and back covers.

Spot Color
A color not created by CMYK separations, usually specified by a Pantone swatch number. A spot color is printed by mixing given proportions of various inks in accordance with the percentages given by the Pantone number.

Spread

Two facing pages that can be worked on as a unit, and will be viewed side by side in the final publication.

Stacking Order

The order of the elements on a page, wherein the topmost item will obscure the items beneath it.

Standard Viewing Conditions

A prescribed set of conditions under which the viewing of originals and reproductions are to take place, defining both the geometry of the illumination and the spectral power distribution of the light source.

Standing Cap

A large capital letter sharing baseline with the adjoining text but rising above it. See *Drop Cap*.

Standoff

The distance between a graphic and the text that wraps around it. See *Wrap*.

Stat

Photostat copy.

Stet

Used in proof correction work to cancel a previous correction. From the Latin; "let it stand."

Stipple

Black and white line art where shading is accomplished by the placement of pinpoint dots.

Stochastic Screening

A method of creating halftones in which the size of the dots remains constant but their density is varied; also known as frequency-modulated (or FM) screening.

Stripping

The preparation and assembling of film prior to platemaking.

Stroke, Stroking

Manipulating the width or color of a line.

Stuffit

A file compression utility used in the Macintosh environment.

Style

A set of formatting instructions for font, paragraphing, tabs, and other properties of text.

Style Sheet

A file containing all of the tags and instructions for formatting all parts of a document; style sheets create consistency between similar documents.

Subhead

A second-level heading used to organize body text by topic.

Subscript

Small-size characters set below the normal letters or figures, usually to convey technical information.

Substitution

Using an existing font to simulate one that is not available to the printer.

Substrate

The paper or any other generally flat material upon which an image is printed.

Subtractive Color

Color which is observed when light strikes pigments or dyes, which absorb certain wavelengths of light; the light that is reflected back is perceived as a color. See *CMYK* and *Process Color*.

Superscript

Small characters set above the normal letters or figures, such as numbers referring to footnotes.

Swash Letters

Letters with extra flourishes usually used in logos, headlines, or as initial caps.

Swatch

A sample of a set of papers, inks, etc. that may be provided in physical form, or appear as a menu in a word processing or illustration application program.

Syntax

The rules that govern the structure of statements in a computer language, or in a language in general.

System Folder

The location of the operating system files on a Macintosh.

Tabloid

A paper size 11 inches wide and 17 inches long.

Tabular

Text set in columns or tables.

Tagged Image File Format (TIFF)

A common format used for scanned or computer-generated bitmapped images.

Tags

The various formats in a style sheet that indicate paragraph settings, margins and columns, page layouts, hyphenation and justification, widow and orphan control and other parameters.

Template

A document file containing layout and styles by which a series of documents can maintain the same look and feel.

Text Attribute

A characteristic applied directly to a letter or letters in text, such as bold, italic, or underline.

Text Block

A set of characters that may be manipulated as a group.

Text File

A file containing text in ASCII format that does not contain style formatting.

Text Type - Unsharp Masking

Text Type
Typefaces used for the main text of written material. Generally no larger than 14 point in size, and variable with the type of publication.

Text wrap
See *Wrap*

Text
The characters and words that form the main body of a publication.

Texture
1. A property of the surface of the substrate, such as the smoothness of paper. 2. Graphically, variation in tonal values to form image detail. 3. A class of fills in a graphics application that give various appearances, such as bricks, grass, etc.

Thin Space
A fixed space, equal to half an en space or the width of a period in most fonts.

Thumbnails
1. The preliminary sketches of a design. 2. Small images used to indicate the content of a computer file.

Tick Mark
A small mark at right angles to the axis of a graph that indicates the location of a certain measurement; such as tick marks indicating the numbers 1, 2, 3, etc.

TIFF
See *Tagged Image File Format*

Tight
A characteristic of text in which the characters are set very close together.

Tile
1. A type of repeating fill pattern. 2. Reproduce a number of pages of a document on one sheet. 3. Printing a large document overlapping on several smaller sheets of paper.

Tint
1. A halftone area that contains dots of uniform size; that is, no modeling or texture. 2. The mixture of a color with white.

Tip In
The separate insertion of a single page into a book either during or after binding by pasting one edge.

Toggle
A command that switches between either of two states at each application. Switching between Hide and Show is a toggle.

Tone
Any variation in lightness or saturation while hue remains constant.

Toolbox
An on-screen mouse-operated palette that allows the user to choose from a selection of tools available in computer application programs.

Tracking
Adjusting the spacing of letters in a line of text to achieve proper justification or general appearance.

Transfer Curve
A curve depicting the adjustment to be made to a particular printing plate when an image is printed.

Transparency
A full color photographically produced image on transparent film.

Trapping
Compensating for potential gaps between two adjoining colors because of misregistration.

Trim
After printing, mechanically cutting the publication to the correct final dimensions. The trim size is normally indicated by marks on the printing plate outside the page area.

TrueType
An outline font format used in both Macintosh and Windows systems that can be used both on the screen and on a printer.

Type 1 Fonts
PostScript fonts based on Bézier curves encrypted for compactness that are compatible with Adobe Type Manager.

Type Family
A set of typefaces created from the same basic design but in different weights, such as bold, light, italic, book, and heavy.

Typesetting
The arrangement of individual characters of text into words, sentences, and paragraphs.

Typo
An abbreviation for typographical error. A keystroke error in the typeset copy.

Typography
The design and planning of printed matter using type.

U&lc
An abbreviation for UPPER and lower case. Also the name of a popular design publication.

UCR (undercolor removal)
A technique for reducing the amount of magenta, cyan, and yellow inks in neutral or shadow areas and replacing them with black.

Undertone
Color of ink printed in a thin film.

Unsharp Masking
A digital technique (based on a traditional photographic technique) performed after scanning that locates the edge between sections of differing lightness and alters the values of the adjoining pixels to exaggerate the difference across the edge, thereby increasing edge contrast.

Uppercase
The capital letters of a typeface as opposed to the lowercase, or small, letters. So called because when type was hand composited, the capital letters resided in the upper part of the type case.

Utility
Software that performs ancillary tasks such as counting words, defragmenting a hard drive, or restoring a deleted file.

Varnish Plate
The plate on a printing press that applies varnish after the other colors have been applied.

Varnishing
A finishing process whereby a transparent varnish is applied over the printed sheet to produce a glossy or protective coating, either on the entire sheet or on selected areas.

Vector Graphics
Graphics defined using coordinate points, and mathematically drawn lines and curves, which may be freely scaled and rotated without image degradation. Two commonly used vector drawing programs are Illustrator and FreeHand.

A class of graphics created using mathematically described geometric shapes that overcomes the limitations of bitmapped graphics.

Velox
Strictly, a Kodak chloride printing paper, but used to describe a high-quality black & white print of a halftone or line drawing.

Vertical Justification
The ability to automatically adjust the interline spacing (leading) to make columns and pages end at the same point on a page.

Vignette
An illustration in which the background gradually fades into the paper; that is, without a definite edge or border.

Visible Spectrum
The wavelengths of light between about 380 nm (violet) and 700 nm (red) that are visible to the human eye.

Watermark
An impression incorporated in paper during manufacturing showing the name of the paper and/or the company logo. A "watermark" can be applied digitally to printed output as a very light screened image.

Web Press
An offset printing press that prints from a roll of paper rather than single sheets.

Weight
1. The thickness of the strokes of a typeface. The weight of a typeface is usually denoted in the name of the font; for example, light, book, or ultra (thin, medium, and thick strokes, respectively). 2. The thickness of a line or rule.

White Space
Areas on the page which contain no images or type. Proper use of white space is critical to a well-balanced design.

White Light
Light containing all wavelengths of the visible spectrum.

Widow
First line of a paragraph that appears alone at the bottom of a column or page.

Window Shade
A type of text block used in certain applications, such as PageMaker. Windowshades have handles at the top and bottom which will reveal or conceal text.

Wizard
A utility attached to an application or operating system that aids you in setting up a piece of hardware, software, or document.

Word Break
The division of a word at the end of a line in accordance with hyphenation principles.

Word Processor
A desktop publishing application program designed for creating and formatting text, but not for page layout.

Word Space
The space inserted between words in a desktop publishing application. The optimal value is built into the typeface, and may usually be modified within an application.

Wrap
Type set on the page so that it wraps around the shape of another element.

WYSIWYG (pronounced "wizzywig")
An acronym for "What You See Is What You Get," meaning that what you see on your computer screen bears a strong resemblance to what the job will look like when it is printed.

X-height
The height of the letter "x" in a given typeface, which represents the basic size of the bodies of all of the lowercase letters (excluding ascenders and descenders).

Xerography
A photocopying/printing process in which the image is formed using the electrostatic charge principle. Toner replaces ink and can be dry or liquid. Once formed, the image is sealed by heat.

Zero Point
The mathematical "origin" of the coordinates of the two-dimensional page. The zero point may be moved to any location on the page, and the ruler dimensions change accordingly.

Zip
1. To compress a file on a Windows-based system using a popular compression utility. 2. A removable disk made by Iomega (a Zip disk) or the device that reads and writes such disks (a Zip drive).

Index

SYMBOLS

3d rotation 230

A

adding
  guides 119
  layers 107
align panel 138, 145
aligning 47, 145
  objects 137, 147
alignment 92
all on/off
  using layers 107
anchor points 75, 195
  connecting 197
  joining 198
  modifying 197
  selecting a single point 195
arc 231
area text 87
arranging
  objects 137
artwork 67
axis 138
  of reflection 218

B

background layer 106, 107
baseline shift 91
basic
  fill inspector 178
bend 239
bézier 77
bitmapped images
  importing 248
blends 162
blocks
  of text 101
bounding box 73
bring to front 139

C

cap
  line endings 162
Cartesian coordinate 68
center 215
character 89
charts
  creating 238
circle
  drawing a perfect 64
click-hold method 72
clone 219

closed path 82
color
  highlight 106
  list 47, 99, 182
  list options 186
  mixer 47, 183
  tints 47, 187
  creating new 185
columns & rows 89
combining paths 168
connector point 68, 77, 202
convert to paths 97
converting paths 118
copy fitting 89
corner
  points 68, 77
  creating rounded 64
crayons library 99
crop 169
cursors 39
  smart 197
curve 75
  basics 77
  points 68, 77
custom
  fill inspector 178
  views 49
customize
  toolbars 37

D

delete
  guides 119
direction handles 201
distance 231
distribute 145, 147
distributing
  objects 137
divide 170
document inspector 48
drawing 63
  lines 75, 76
drop shadow 99
duplicate
  layers 107

E

edit
  guides 119
ellipse tool 63, 64
embedded images 251
  drawbacks 252
EPS 247, 248
  editing 247
  exporting 248

expand stroke 160
export
   file formats 245

F

fast keyline 50
fast preview 50
fill
   paths and objects 178
   types 160
fill inspector 48, 69, 177, 178
filling text with a color 97
fisheye lens 232
flush left 92
foreground layer 106, 107
freeform tool 208
FreeHand
   objects 177
   toolbox 215
   xtras 157
   tool 36

G

gradient 51, 160, 189
   creating 192
   fill inspector 178
graphic hose 236
greeked
   views 52
grids 105, 116
   editing 127
   showing and hiding 127
grouping 138, 142
   nesting 143
guides 105, 116
   adding and deleting 119
   creating from an object 121
   dialog 118
   layer 106, 107
   snap to settings 128

H

halftones 47
handles
   direction of 201
hide
   grids 127
   layers 105
hightlight color 106
hollow anchor points 195
horizontal
   reflection 218
   scale 89
hose
   graphic 236

I

importing
   graphics 245
   text 100
info toolbar 36, 42
inset path 165
inspectors 35, 48, 49
   fill 69
   object 69
interactive transformer 215, 224
intersect 168

J

join 161, 168, 198
   objects 162

K

kerning 91
keyline 50, 106
   mode 161
   view 50
knife tool 208

L

layers 47, 105, 107
   adding and removing 107
   highlight 106
   managing multiple 107
   rearranging 111
leading 90
lens
   fill inspector 178
   fisheye 232
line drawing tools 75
linear
   gradients 189
lines
   drawing 76
linking 102
   to external files 251
links
   managing 252
locking
   layers 106
   objects 141

M

magnification tool 53
main toolbar 36, 37
manual
   kerning 91
marquee 70
   drawing a view region 53
menus 35, 49

mirror 218
modes
   object transformation 215
   preview 67
   viewing 49
modifying your artwork 35
move 138
movement methods 74
multiple objects
   selecting 70

N

nesting 143
new
   layer 107
   window 49

O

object inspector 48, 69, 70, 164, 202
objects
   arranging 137, 138
   moving from one layer to another 113
   transformation of 215
operations panel 158
options
   for layers 106
options pop-up
   layers 106
outlines 97
   text 99
overflow
   text 102
overlap
   removing 159

P

page range
   when creating guides 119
page rulers 63, 116, 118
   zero point 116
painting 177
pair kerning 91
panels 35, 47, 49, 105
Pantone 187
paragraph 89
path 75
   adding points 196
   information 70
   inset 165
   operations 157
   outlines 99
path modifying tools 208
path-altering operations 159
paths 97, 195
   applying color to 182

pattern
   fill inspector 179
pen tool 77, 196, 219
pictograph 238
placing text 35
point size 90
point text 87
pointer tool 39, 69, 70, 87
points 68, 77
polygon
   tool 36
polygon tool 63, 65
pop-up menus 145
   for changing views 50
position of guides 119
PostScript
   fill inspector 179
predefined colors 183
preferences
   objects and paths 159
preview mode 50, 69, 145
preview/keyline
   layers 106
primitive shapes 63
print separator 106
printing 245, 259
priority of layers 110
punch 169

Q

quick-move method 73

R

radial 160
   gradients 189
ragged right 92
readability 91
rectangle 36
rectangle tool 63, 64
redraw 51
reflect 215, 218
reflect axis 218
reflection horizontal and vertical 218
release guides 119
remove layers 107
remove overlap 159
removing layers 107
reshaping and sizing objects 35
rotate 215, 216, 231
rotation 3 dimensional 230
roughen 234
rounded corners 64
rows 89
ruler 116
   text 87

S

scale 89, 215, 220, 221
segments 195
selecting objects 88
send to back 139
settings typographic 42, 95
shadow tool 233
shape drawing tools 65
show/hide grides 127
simplify objects 159
sizing an object 221
skew 215, 223
smart cursors 197
snapping to a guide 128
space between characters 91
spiral 233
square 64
stacking order 138
status bar 36
straight lines 82
stroke
   expanding 160
stroke inspector 48, 177, 180
stroking text with color 97
styles 47
submenus 49
symmetrical designs 219

T

tabbed windows 47
text
   blocks 87, 101
   creating outlines from 97
   editing 87
   formatting 93
   importing 100
   linking boxes of 102
   overflow from linked boxes 102
   special effects with 92
text inspector 48, 88, 91
text tool 87
text toolbar 36, 42
texture 160
textured
   fill inspector 179
TIFF 248
tiled
   fill inspector 179
tints 187
tips
   accessing 37
   customizing the 37

toolbars 35, 36, 49
   customizing 43
toolbox 35, 38, 63
   freehand 215
   managing the 38
   options 36
tracking 91
transform panel 36, 215
transformation tools 215
transparency 170
triangle symbol 36
type outlines 97
typographers 92
typographic settings 42, 90
typography 87

U

ungroup 138, 142, 143
uniform 166
uniform scaling 220
union 169
units of measurement 116
unlock
   layers 106
   objects 141

V

vector images
   importing 245
vertical align 146
vertical reflection 218
viewing modes 49
views
   custom 54
   editing 56
   greeking images 52
   magnifaction tool 53

W

width settings
   for expanding strokes 162
window
   creating a new 58
   new 49
working environment 35

X

Xtras 157, 229
   creating and managing 157

Z

zero point 116
   setting 130

Notes:

Notes:

Notes:

Notes:

Notes:

Notes:

Notes:

Notes: